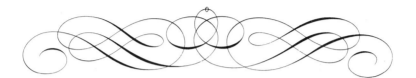

ORCHESOGRAPHY

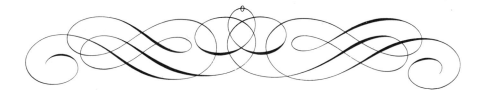

ORCHESOGRAPHY

THOINOT ARBEAU

Translated by
MARY STEWART EVANS

With a new Introduction and Notes by
JULIA SUTTON

And a new Labanotation section by
MIREILLE BACKER
and
JULIA SUTTON

DOVER PUBLICATIONS, INC.
NEW YORK

Published in Canada by General Publishing Company, Ltd., 30 Lesmill Road, Don Mills, Toronto,
Ontario.
Published in the United Kingdom by Constable
and Company, Ltd., 10 Orange Street, London WC 2.

This Dover edition, first published in 1967, is an
unabridged and corrected republication of the English translation of *Orchésographie* by Mary Stewart
Evans first published by Kamin Dance Publishers in
1948. To the present edition has been added the
following material, specially prepared for it: Editor's
Introduction to the Dover Edition and Editor's
Notes, 1966 (with additional Bibliography), prepared by Julia Sutton; and a Labanotation section,
prepared by Mireille Backer and Julia Sutton, and
approved by the Dance Notation Bureau, Inc.

International Standard Book Number: 0-486-21745-0
Library of Congress Catalog Card Number: 65-26021

Manufactured in the United States of America
Dover Publications, Inc.
180 Varick Street
New York, N.Y. 10014

CONTENTS

EDITOR'S INTRODUCTION TO THE DOVER EDITION

THOINOT ARBEAU's *Orchésographie* is one of our most valuable and delightful sources on sixteenth-century dances, dance music, and social mores. The present volume is one of a line of translations and reprints extending back to 1878, all attesting to the importance of the book for present-day studies. A short history of the printed editions of the *Orchésographie*, and a brief explanation of the corrections and additions introduced in this reprint, follow.

The manuscript does not appear to be extant. The book was first published in 1589 by Jehan des Preyz at Langres; a second printing, also by des Preyz, appeared in 1596. With the exception of the title pages, both printings are identical. In 1878 Albert Czerwinski translated into German the portion of the text that is on the dance. In 1888 Laure Fonta published a so-called "reprint" of the *Orchésographie*, with an introductory commentary. In 1925 Cyril W. Beaumont published an English translation, with the music transcribed into modern notation and the steps correlated to the notes by means of a special numbering system; this translation was reprinted in 1965 by Dance Horizons, without alterations. (In 1946 a Spanish translation of the Beaumont was published by Teresa Vriburn de Lavalle Cobo.) In 1948 an independent translation of Arbeau into English was brought out by Lady Mary Stewart Evans, with the musical examples reproduced photographically from the Fonta "reprint." It is this last translation which is being reprinted here.

A simple reprint, however, would not adequately serve the interests of the public today. So much new light has been shed on the music and dances since Beaumont and Evans wrote their commentaries that further annotations incorporating this material have seemed essential. In addition the editor has indicated questionable passages in the text, made pertinent corrections in the translation and notes, and supplied additional information on Arbeau's numerous humanistic references. A complete study of musical concordances has not been undertaken, but some are noted in the appropriate places. All commentaries are signaled in the text with superscript alphabetical letters, and are placed in a special section at the end of the text, beginning on p. 207. In the commentaries the editor has chosen to use the currently accepted names for the dances. Since Lady Evans used sixteenth-century English terms, some discrepancies between the names in the commentaries and those in the text will be noticed.

A comparison of the first publication with the Fonta version reveals that the latter is not a photographic reprint, but a copy. The text is accurate, but the music, which Lady Evans photographed, contains many copyist's errors (e.g., clefs and key signatures are misplaced, there are wrong notes, rests are omitted). These errors have been corrected in the present edition.

Besides introducing numerous minor errors in copying, the Fonta version unfortunately was also unfaithful to the original in the tabulations of the dances. In the original the steps are aligned with the musical notes quite precisely, so that one can easily see their correlations. Fonta maintains the basic arrangement on the page (music running vertically down the left side of each page, and step instructions printed horizontally next to the music), but the instructions are arbitrarily distributed over the page so that step and note correlations disappear. Evans follows the same procedure as Fonta, simply modernizing the spellings. Beaumont is equally arbitrary in his musical transcriptions and step correlations, offering no explanations when these differ from the original. Thus the reader without access to the original has had to guess at the correlations up to now, or to take the interpretations of Beaumont and others (such as Mabel Dolmetsch or Melusine Wood) who have included some of Arbeau's dances in their books. In the present edition all tabulations have been completely revised so that the steps are aligned with the notes as they were at first.

Step and note correlations may be clear in the original, but the descriptions of the steps themselves are not always models of clarity. There is no question that Arbeau frequently gives only the skeleton, or perhaps the first variation, of a dance. He also takes many details for granted, such as arm motions or miming gestures. Many readings of the text are necessary in order to reproduce the dances even in their rudimentary form. A realization in dance notation of the basic steps as well as the most important or most representative dances has been added to this volume to provide practical examples for performers and to assist them in the re-creation of those dances that were not notated. The Labanotation, worked out by Mireille Backer with the editor's assistance, appears in the Appendix, together with the appropriate music transcribed into modern notation. This supplement to the text is the result of careful study which included actual performance of the dances.

It is hoped that this edition of the *Orchésographie* will be both a helpful reference tool and a reliable source book for those who wish to bring these charming and vigorous dances to life.

JULIA SUTTON

New York City
June, 1966

PREFACE TO THE FIRST EDITION

THOINOT ARBEAU, Canon of Langres, was born at Dijon in 1519.[a] He belongs to that honourable line of scholarly churchmen in the Roman tradition who combine spiritual with worldly wisdom to the advantage of both. His family was an old and distinguished one in the region, and the name by which he is best known is an anagram of Jehan Tabourot, his baptismal and family names.

The Orchesography, first published in Langres in 1589, is the most detailed and authentic record of fifteenth and sixteenth century dances that has come down to us.[b] It deals with what we should call today the ballroom dances of the period, considered by both Arbeau and his pupil, Capriol, to be an essential part of the education of every well-bred young man. But the reader will be frequently reminded, if only by the variety and agility of the steps described, that up to the last quarter of the seventeenth century there was no clear cut distinction between ballroom and theatrical dancing, either socially or in the matter of technical skill. Dancing, as a part of masquerades or elaborate spectacles, still drew performers and audience alike from the ranks of the nobility, and their leisured associates, and it was close on another century before the courtier with a flair for dancing gave place to the professional performer. Indeed, in the wider field of theatrical entertainment, Arbeau himself has harsh words for those who "for gain admit all indiscriminately to witness their plays and farces."

But Arbeau was no ordinary dancing master, compiling a manual for his fashionable patrons, and his interest in the art went far beyond the confines of its aspect as a passport to social success. Ancient legend and contemporary geography alike are gleaned in the exposition of his topic and Arbeau has the true Frenchman's attachment to the soil, which colours his perception of the rustic disporting himself in country dances with his wench. He continually stresses the valuable function of dancing in the life of the community, ranging, so he says, from a spur to action in battle to a precautionary measure prior to the selection of a husband or wife. He makes short shrift of prudish reformers, who would ban dancing on moral grounds, while permitting himself the role of censorious critic, in the immemorial pattern ,when he compares current dances with those of his youth.

Laure Fonta, in her informed preface to the reprint of the Orchesography,

published in Paris in 1888, suggests that Arbeau was animated to under-
take this work, at the ripe age of sixty-nine, by the re-introduction of religious dances into the Church in France. It seems equally probable that the
great wave of enthusiasm for masquerades and dancing, which swept France
in the wake of the famous Ballet Comique de la Reine,[1] aroused in Arbeau
an old love. It may well be that a rekindled interest in a pastime dear to
his youth led to this dialogue between the elderly Thoinot Arbeau and an
imaginary pupil not unlike the youthful Jehan Tabourot he once was. And
he gives the lad a deal of good robust general advice into the bargain.

The drawings, which I think it may be safely assumed were Arbeau's
own handiwork, are a diverting and often illuminating addition to the
Orchesography. These, together with the musical examples in the present
volume, are all facsimile reproductions of those in the original edition.
Of particular interest are the vertical musical examples, which were an
ingenious device to enable the pupil to see at a glance which notes and steps
corresponded by placing them opposite to one another on the page.[73]

Arbeau constantly emphasises the importance of musicality in a dancer
and the dependence of the dance upon music. This seems self-evident to
us but I believe we are sometimes inclined to overlook the enormous influence
which the dance had upon the early development of instrumental music.
The progression from free rhythm, as it existed in plainsong and early
harmonized music, to a steady two, three, four, five or six in a measured
rhythm is probably largely due to the dance, as was also the adoption of
equal and balanced phrases, contrasting passages followed by repetition
of what had gone before, and regularly recurring cadences. The actual
dance forms were used by instrumental composers and a musical association
of complementary dance-types arose, such as the pavan and the galliard,
which gave birth to the instrumental suite, and eventually to the sonata.

Arbeau's Orchesography is without literary pretensions. Had he fore-
seen its publication he would almost certainly have given it a final polish.
But, for all its simplicity, it is far from being a work hastily conceived,
and it has the cardinal virtue that it achieves precisely what it sets out to do.
No pains were spared to make the directions detailed and practical and it
abounds in touches which show the author's genuine affection for his subject. Yet, when it was finished, Arbeau thrust the manuscript away among
a batch of old papers destined for the dust heap, and there it remained

until after his death when it was rescued by a former pupil, to whom our gratitude is due for its preservation. What the worthy canon regarded as his serious contribution to learning, a work on astronomy, has long since faded into oblivion, whereas these "scribblings to kill time", as he called the discarded manuscript of the Orchesography, have found a place among the classics on the dance.

In this translation I have tried to respect both the archaic French text and the English language. On those occasions when the modern English rendering necessitated a choice between the spirit and letter, I have unhesitatingly followed the former.

MARY STEWART EVANS

ACKNOWLEDGMENTS

My thanks are due to my friend Henry Boddington for his translation into English of the Latin quotations in the Orchesography and for much valuable advice. Also to the personnel of the British Museum, the Bibliothèque Nationale and the Library of Congress for the courteous assistance I have been afforded in matters of research.

M. S. E.

BIBLIOGRAPHY

ORCHÉSOGRAPHIE. Et Traicte en forme de dialogue, etc.
Par Thoinot Arbeau, demeurant à Lengres.
Lengres, Imprimé par Jehan des Preyz (1589?)

ORCHÉSOGRAPHIE, METHODE ET TÉORIE EN FORME DE DISCOURS, ETC.
Par Thoinot Arbeau, demeurant a Lengres.
A Lengres, Par Jehan des Preyz des merciers dicte les Pilliers
M. D. XCVI.

DIE TÄNZE DES XVI. Jahrhunderts und die alte französische Tanzschule
vor der Einführung des Menuetts. Hrsg. von Albert Czerwinski.
Nach Jean Tabourot's Orchésographie.
Danzig 1878.

ORCHÉSOGRAPHIE, PAR Thoinot Arbeau—réimpression précédée d'une
notice sur les danses du XVIe siècle par Laure Fonta.
Paris, F. Vieweg, 1888.

LA PAVANE D'APRES L'ORCHÉSOGRAPHIE DE THOINOT ARBEAU (PSEUD.)
XVIe siècle.
Paris, E. Capiomont, 1889.

ORCHESOGRAPHY, A TREATISE IN THE FORM OF A DIALOGUE, ETC. by
Thoinot Arbeau (pseud.) Translated by Cyril W. Beaumont, with
a preface by Peter Warlock (pseud.)
London, C. W. Beaumont, 1925.

ORQUESOGRAFÍA, TRATADO SOBRE DANZAS EN FORMA DE DIÁLOGO, trans-
lated from the English of C. W. Beaumont by Teresa Vriburn de
Lavalle Cobo.
Buenos Aires, Centurion, 1946.

ORCHESOGRAPHIE.

ET TRAICTE EN FORME DE DIALOGVE,

PAR LEQVEL TOVTES PERSONNES PEVVENT

facilement apprendre & practiquer l'honnefte
exercice des dances

Par Thoinot arbeau demeurant a Lengres

Eccle. 3
Tempus plangendi, & tempus faltandi.

Imprimé audiᵭ Lengres par Iehan des preyz **Imprimeur**
& Libraire, tenant fa boutique proche l'ᴇglife
Sainᵭ Mammes dudiᵭ Lengres.

M. D. LXXXIX.

Translation of original title page : "ORCHESOGRAPHY./AND TREATISE
IN THE FORM OF A DIALOGUE,/WHEREBY ALL MAY/easily learn & practise the
honourable exercise of dancing/*By Thoinot Arbeau, residing at Langres*/Eccles. 3/*A
time to mourn and a time to dance.*/Printed at the aforesaid Langres by Jehan des Preyz,
Printer/& Bookseller, whose shop is near the Church of/Saint Mammès of the aforesaid
Langres./M. D. LXXXIX." Printer's motto: "Such is the glory of man."

The reproduction of The Tabourot coat of arms is taken from *L'Armorial Colorié d'Hozier.*

To Maître Guillaume Tabourot, Sieur of Agreements, son of that great man and wise teacher Etienne Tabourot counsellor to the King and Sire and his Procurator at the Bailiwick of Dijon.[a]

When I was last in Dijon and saw the coat of arms of your distinguished family, upon which appear a lion sable on a silver chief and three drums with a gold chevron on an azure field[2], I was reminded that among the discarded and unsorted papers which I gathered up long since[b] by Thoinot Arbeau of Langres, my first tutor, there were certain writings wherein the drum was mentioned. I resolved, forthwith, to send these to you straightway upon my return to the said Langres.

Upon closer perusal of these sheets, I found that they dealt principally with dancing and incidentally with the drum. I have printed them in their entirety to offer you despite the fact that the said Sieur Arbeau forbade me to do so, saying that such things as he had scribbled merely to kill time did not merit printing, much less presentation to you. However, I believed that in taking this liberty I might have the good fortune to convey to you my warm desire to be of greater service.

Your humble servant,

JEHAN des PREYZ.

DIALOGUE UPON THE DANCE AND THE MANNER OF DANCING
by THOINOT ARBEAU, residing at Langres.[a]

CAPRIOL

I come to pay you my respects, Monsieur Arbeau. You do not remember me, for it is six or seven years since I left this town of Langres to go to Paris and thence to Orleans.[b] I am an old pupil of yours, to whom you taught computation.

ARBEAU

Indeed at first glance I failed to recognize you because you have grown up since then, and I feel sure that you have also broadened your mind by manliness and learning. What do you think of the study of law? I pursued it in bygone days myself.

CAPRIOL

I find it a noble art and necessary in the conduct of affairs, but I regret that while in Orleans I neglected to learn fine manners, an art with which many scholars enriched themselves as an adjunct to their studies. For, on my return I have found myself in society, where, to put it briefly, I was tongue-tied and awkward, and regarded as little more than a block of wood.

ARBEAU

You took consolation in the fact that the learned professors excused this shortcoming in recognition of the learning you had acquired.

CAPRIOL

That is so, but I should like to have acquired skill in dancing during the hours between my serious studies, an accomplishment which would have rendered my company welcome to all.

ARBEAU

This will be an easy thing by reading French books in order to sharpen your wit and by learning fencing, dancing and tennis that you may be an agreeable companion alike to ladies and gentlemen.

CAPRIOL

I much enjoyed fencing and tennis and this placed me upon friendly terms with young men. But, without a knowledge of dancing, I could not please the damsels, upon whom, it seems to me, the entire reputation of an eligible young man depends.

11

You are quite right, as naturally the male and female seek one another and nothing does more to stimulate a man to acts of courtesy, honour and generosity than love. And if you desire to marry you must realize that a mistress is won by the good temper and grace displayed while dancing, because ladies do not like to be present at fencing or tennis, lest a splintered sword or a blow from a tennis ball should cause them injury. You remember Virgil's lines that tell of Turnus and his mistress, the beautiful Lavinia, daughter of King Latinus.[a]

Illum turbat amor, figitque in virgine vultus:
Ardet in arma magis[3] *etc.*

And there is more to it than this, for dancing is practised to reveal whether lovers are in good health and sound of limb, after which they are permitted to kiss their mistresses in order that they may touch and savour one another, thus to ascertain if they are shapely or emit an unpleasant odour as of bad meat. Therefore, from this standpoint, quite apart from the many other advantages to be derived from dancing, it becomes an essential in a well ordered society.

CAPRIOL

I have sometimes pondered what you have just said and deemed it not without cause that games and dances had received recognition by the State. But it has chagrined me to find that many have condemned dancing, have even judged it shameless and an effeminate pastime, unworthy of the dignity of a man. I have read that Cicero reproached the consul Gambinius for having danced. Tiberius drove the dancers from Rome. Domitian dismissed any member from the Senate who had danced. When Alphonse, King of Aragon, saw the Gauls delight in dancing he reprimanded them. The holy prophet Moses was provoked to wrath upon seeing the children of Israel dance.

ARBEAU

For everyone who has belittled dancing, scores of others have praised and esteemed it. The holy prophet, King David, danced before the Ark of the Lord and the holy prophet Moses was not angered to see dancing, but grieved that it should take place around a Golden Calf and become an act of idolatry. As for Cicero, he had varicose veins and swollen legs and condemned that which he was unable to do himself, saying that he disliked to see those dance who were fasting. Appius Claudius commended dancing after his triumph. Indians worship the sun with dances, and those who have travelled in the New World report that the savages dance when the sun appears upon the horizon. Socrates learned dancing from Aspasia. The Salii,[4] very noble priests of Mars, danced at their sacrifices. The Corybants[5] in Phrygia, the Lacedaemonians and the people of Crete always went into battle dancing. Vulcan engraved a dance upon a shield as a symbol of beauty.

Museus and Orpheus wished the hymns they had composed in honour of the gods to be sung to the accompaniment of dances. Bacchus conquered the Indies by three kinds of dance. In the primitive church there was a custom, which has survived into our own times, of dancing and swaying while chanting the hymns of our faith, and it may still be seen in several places.[a] Castor and Pollux taught the Carians to dance. Neoptolemus, son of Achilles, taught the Cretans a dance called the Pyrrhic to aid them in battle. Epaminondas used dances very skilfully in the clash of battle, so that his men marched as one against the enemy.[b] Xenophon tells us that dances and masquerades[6] were arranged to welcome the military leaders of Cyrus.[c] Kings and princes are wont to command performances of dancing and masquerades to salute, entertain and give joyous greeting to foreign nobles. We take part in such rejoicing to celebrate wedding days and in the rites of our religious festivals, in spite of the abhorrence of reformers, which latter deserve to be fed upon goat's meat cooked in a pie without bacon.[d]

CAPRIOL

You fill me with a longing to learn to dance and I regret that I have not devoted many idle moments to it, for one can take honest pleasure without becoming tainted by vice or evil habits. I remember that the poet numbers the dancers among the happy ones, saying in the sixth book of the Aeneid,

Pars pedibus plaudunt choreas et carmina dicunt.[7]

ARBEAU

You can moreover quote Our Lord (St. Matthew Chap. XI and St. Luke Chap. VIII) when he reproached the Pharisees for their obstinacy and ill will. 'We have piped unto you and ye have not danced'.

I suggest that you should do as Demetrius, who, though wont to condemn dancing, upon witnessing a masquerade representing Mars and Venus in love admitted that it was the most beautiful thing in the world. You can quickly regain the time you have wasted, especially as you are a musician and dancing depends upon music, one of the seven liberal arts, and its modulations.

CAPRIOL

Then I beg of you to teach me about these things, Monsieur Arbeau, because I know you are a musician, and in your youth won a reputation for good dancing and dexterity in a thousand sprightly steps.

ARBEAU

The noun dance comes from the verb to dance, which in Latin is called *saltare*. To dance is to jump, to hop, to skip, to sway, to stamp, to tiptoe, and to employ the feet, hands and body in certain rhythmic movements. These consist of leaping, bending the body, straddling, limping, flexing the knees, rising upon the toes, twitching the feet, with variations of these, and further postures of which Athenaeus,[a] Celius,[b] Scaliger[c] and others make mention. At one time masks were worn to accentuate the gestures of the character represented. Lucian has written a treatise on the subject where you can study his theories more fully.[d] Julius Pollux has also devoted a long chapter to the matter.[e]

CAPRIOL

I believe I have read these authors at some time and others like them. If I remember correctly, they refer to three kinds of dance, one grave called Emmeleia,[f] one gay, which was known as Kordax,[g] and another combining gravity with gaiety called the Sikinnis.[h] They speak also of the Pyrrhic dances[i] and divers others. I remember a reference to several kinds of masquerade, particularly to one they called the Trichoria[j] which consisted of three choirs, made up respectively of old men, youths and little children, who sang 'We have been, we are and we shall be'. I have a general notion of it all but I should like to be shown what steps and movements were used, pray teach me.

ARBEAU

Anthony of Arena, a native of Provence, has set down what you wish to know in macaronic verse.[k]

CAPRIOL

In the lines you mention he refers to the movements that must be followed in branles and basse dances only, and to the dancers' deportment, but the demands of metre have obscured his meaning which is why I ask you to enlighten me further.

ARBEAU

As regards ancient dances all I can tell you is that the passage of time, the indolence of man or the difficulty of describing them has robbed us of any knowledge thereof. Besides, there is no need to trouble yourself about them, as such manner of dancing is out of date now. Why, even the dances seen in our fathers' time were unlike those of today and it will always be so because men are such lovers of novelty. It is true that we can compare the Emmeleia to our pavans and basse dances, the Kordax to galliards, tordions, lavoltas, gavottes, branles of Champagne and Burgundy, gay branles and mixed branles, the Sikinnis to double or single branles, and the Pyrrhic to the dance we call buffens or mattachins.[a]

CAPRIOL

I foresee then that posterity will remain ignorant of all these new dances you have named for the same reason that we have been deprived of the knowledge of those of our ancestors.

ARBEAU

One must assume so.

CAPRIOL

Do not allow this to happen, Monsieur Arbeau, as it is within your power to prevent it. Set these things down in writing to enable me to learn this art, and in so doing you will seem reunited to the companions of your youth and take both mental and bodily exercise, for it will be difficult for you to refrain from using your limbs in order to demonstrate the correct movements. In truth, your method of writing is such that a pupil, by following your theory and precepts, even in your absence, could teach himself in the seclusion of his own chamber. And to begin with, I would ask you to tell me in what esteem dancing is held by the majority of honourable men.

ARBEAU

Dancing, or saltation, is both a pleasant and a profitable art which confers and preserves health; proper to youth, agreeable to the old and suitable to all provided fitness of time and place are observed and it is not abused. I mention time and place because it would bring contempt upon one who became over zealous like the tavern haunters. You know what Ecclesiasticus said.

Cum muliere saltatrice non sis assiduus[8]

The children of the Roman senators went to learn dancing upon leaving school. Homer bears witness that dancing is an integral part and adjunct to banquets, so much so that none could boast he had given a fine feast unless dancing accompanied it, which, if masquerades are also included, becomes as a sound body joined to a fair intellect. When tragedies, comedies and pastorals were enacted in the ancient theatre, dances and gestures were not forgotten and the part of the theatre reserved for them was called the *orchestra,* which in our French tongue we may call the *dançoir.*

CAPRIOL

Since dancing is an art, it must therefore belong to one of the seven liberal arts.

ARBEAU

As I have already told you, it depends upon music and its modulations. Without this rhythmic quality dancing would be dull and confused inasmuch as the movements of the limbs must follow the rhythm of the music, for the foot must not tell of one thing and the music of another. But, most of the authorities hold that dancing is a kind of mute rhetoric by which the orator, without uttering a word, can make himself understood by his movements and persuade the spectators that he is gallant and worthy to be acclaimed, admired and loved. Are you not of the opinion that this is the dancer's own language, expressed by his feet and in a convincing manner? Does he not plead tacitly with his mistress, who marks the seemliness and grace of his dancing, 'Love me. Desire me'? And, when miming is added, she has the power to stir his emotions, now to anger, now to pity and commiseration, now to hate, now to love. Even as we read of the daughter of Herodias, who obtained her wish from Herod Antipas by dancing before him at the magnificent banquet he offered to the princes of his realm on his birthday. So it was also with Roscius,[a] who proved to Cicero that, by his employment of gesture and dumb show he could move the spectators, in the judgment of the arbiters, as much or more than Cicero had been able to by his eloquent orations.

CAPRIOL

Roscius was an actor, and it seems to me that our laws brand such men as infamous.

ARBEAU

Roscius was held and reputed as a very honest and able man by the Senate and those Romans who frequented the theatre habitually. So much so, that when they wished to describe a perfect craftsman they referred to him as a Roscius in his art. Cicero pleaded for him in a legal action he brought against Fannius and won his case by the approval of the entire Senate, who loved, esteemed and honoured him. It is true that those who for gain admit all indiscriminately to witness their plays and farces are counted infamous. But the law has never included among them men who give of their talent without reward, for their own pleasure, or to entertain kings, princes and noblemen, the inhabitants of a town or some special company; either by playing tragedies, comedies or pastorals without masks, or by dancing to music, with beautiful costumes and settings to lend grace and gaiety. And thus the Emperor maintains in the eleventh section of the Code in the chapter on public games.

CAPRIOL

I firmly believe it should be so. Do not tantalize me by delaying any longer to grant my request to learn how the movements of the dance are performed, in order that I may master them and not be reproached for having the heart of a pig and the head of an ass, as Lucian did Craton.

ARBEAU

Lucian did not address this reproach to those who had no wish to dance, or to those who wished to but were unable to learn the art, but to those who condemned it and desired to abolish dancing as an evil practice without reflecting that dances are of two kinds. One of these is employed in war for the strength and the defence of the State, the other is recreative and has the virtue of attracting hearts and awakening love. It is a preliminary, and, as I have already told you, a useful device for ascertaining whether a person be deformed by the gout or otherwise defective of limb. Also whether they be comely and modest. We read that Clisthenes, having seen Hippoclides dancing and swaggering in an impudent manner, refused him his daughter in marriage, saying that he had danced his wedding away.

CAPRIOL

God be thanked, I have no such infirmities, and only a sister twelve years old whom I shall instruct when you have taught me.

ARBEAU

Galen says, in his book of rules for health, that all things have a natural desire for movement and that everyone should practice gentle and moderate exercise, such as the dances invented by the Ionians for this purpose.[a] These contribute greatly to health, even to that of young girls, who, leading sedentary lives, intent upon their knitting, embroidery and needlework, are subject to a variety of ill-humours which have need to be dispelled by some temperate exercise.

CAPRIOL

Dancing is a very suitable exercise for them since they are not free to take walks, or go here, there and everywhere about the town as we may without reprehension. In fact, we need to dance less than they, but for all that I am desirous of learning this art, which is at once so old, so honourable and so beneficial.

ARBEAU

To please you I will tell you what I know although it would ill become me, at my present age of sixty-nine, to practice the subject matter. Let us speak first, then, of martial dances, and afterwards of those for recreation. The instruments used for military marching are long trumpets, trumpets, bugles, clarinets, horns, cornets, flutes, fifes, pipes, drums and others resembling the said drums.[b]

The Persian drum (used by some Germans who carry it at the saddle bow) consists of a half sphere of leather closed with strong parchment, about two and a half feet[9] in diameter, and it makes a noise like thunder when the skin is struck with the sticks.

The drum used by the French, and familiar enough to everyone, is of hollow wood about two and a half feet deep, closed at each end with parchment skins secured by two bands, about two and a half feet in diameter, and bound with cords to keep them taut. It makes, as you have often heard, a great noise when the skins are beaten with two sticks which the drummer holds in his hands. The appearance is well known by all, nevertheless I shall place a picture here as we are dealing with the subject.

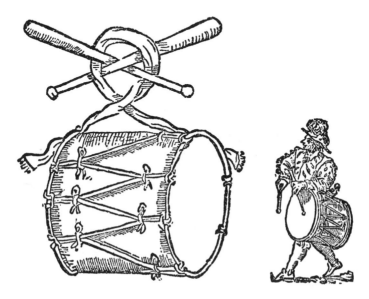

CAPRIOL

You have put little straps and buckles at each crossing of the cords on the drum.

ARBEAU

This is to tighten the skins when one wishes to beat the drum, by slipping the straps towards the centre, and to loosen them when the drum is not in use by slipping the straps towards the bands and edges. I do not know whether the Children of Israel made use of a drum with one parchment only, as was done at Rome in the sacrifice to the mother of the gods, but the fifteenth Chapter of Exodus tells us that Mary, sister of Moses and Aaron, played the drum exceedingly well. Virgil, in the sixth book of the Aeneid, speaking of Misenus, who was trumpeter to Hector and afterwards to Aeneas, uses these words,

Quo non praestantior alter

Aere ciere viros, martemque accendere cantu.[10]

and later: *Et lituo pugnas insignis obibat et hasta.*[11]

The sound of these various instruments serves as signal and warning to the soldiers, to break camp, to advance, to retreat, and gives them heart, daring and courage, both to attack the enemy and to defend themselves with manful vigour. Now, without them, the men would march in confusion and disorder, which would place them in peril of being overthrown and defeated by the enemy. This is why our Frenchmen are instructed to make the rankers and bondsmen of the squadrons march to certain rhythms.

CAPRIOL

How is that?   ARBEAU

You are a musician and well know that it is to the beats of time. Some are duple[12] others are triple[13], and either of these in their turn may be slow, moderate or quick.

CAPRIOL

That is true.

ARBEAU

You will concede that if three men are walking together and each one moves at a different speed they will not be in step, because to be so they must all three march in unison, either quickly, moderately or slowly.

CAPRIOL

There can be no doubt about it.   ARBEAU

That is why, in military marching, the French make use of the drum to beat the rhythm to which the soldiers must march, especially as the majority of soldiers are no better trained in this than they are in other branches of the military art. Wherefore, I shall not delay in setting down the methods.

The drum rhythm contains eight minims,[14] the first five of which are beaten and struck. The first four of these with one stick only and the fifth with both sticks at once. The other three beats are silent.

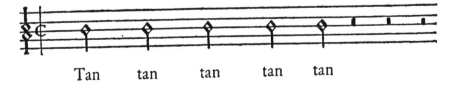

Tan   tan   tan   tan   tan

During the time occupied by the five minims and three rests the soldier takes one pace, that is to say, on the first note he places his left foot on the ground, and during the succeeding three notes raises his right foot so as to bring it down on the fifth note." During the three rests, which are the equivalent of three notes, he raises his left foot to recommence another pace as before. Consequently, if the march continues for two thousand five hundred drum beats, the soldier will have covered a league.

CAPRIOL

Why do you start off with the left foot?

ARBEAU

Because most men are right footed and the left foot is the weaker, so if it should come about that the left foot were to falter for any reason the right foot would immediately be ready to support it.

CAPRIOL

It seems to me that one pace, *passus*[15] in Latin, is said to be the span of the two arms extended and not the two feet.

ARBEAU

Look closely, and confirm by measuring, if one pace of the two feet is not the same span as both arms when extended, which geometricians estimate to be five feet.

CAPRIOL

Have you not miscalculated when you say that to march a league two thousand five hundred drum rhythms are sounded, as one league only contains two thousand paces which, allowing one pace to each rhythm as you say, would make two thousand?

ARBEAU

A single pace does in truth contain five feet, which would make two thousand to the league, but when successive paces are taken to the drum rhythm each pace is only four feet, inasmuch as the foot completing the first pace is already in position for the second and so on from pace to pace, so that the said paces contain four feet only, and thus it takes two thousand five hundred to cover a league, which is two thousand lengths of five geometric feet.

CAPRIOL

I quite understand now.

Besides this, you must reflect that when the drum beats are varied the sound
is more pleasing, wherefore the drummers sometimes use the five minims
and three rests noted above, and sometimes instead of the minims they employ two crotchets[16] or four quavers,[17] according to their fancy. However,
the fifth note must always be a minim, unless they wish to repeat the rhythm
two or three more times, in which case the three rests occur only at the end.

CAPRIOL

I come near to understanding that but I should very much like an example of
these various rhythms.

ARBEAU

The variations are obtained by different combinations of the minims, crotchets and quavers.

CAPRIOL

Let me see a list or tabulation of them.

ARBEAU

You are well aware that one minim is equal to two crotchets and that one
crotchet is equal to two quavers, therefore during the beat of one minim,
two crotchets or four quavers can be beaten. To understand it better, let us
call the sound of a minim, made by one tap of the stick, Tan or Plan and
the sound of two crotchets, made by two taps of the stick, we shall call Tere,
and the sound of four quavers, made by four taps of the stick, Fre. Let us
then combine these different beats and we shall find a great variety. Here is
a tabulation from which you may select those that please you most.

TABULATION CONTAINING ALL THE DIFFERENT DRUM RHYTHMS

The first manner is composed of five Tan only, as has been noted before.

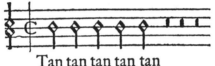

Tan tan tan tan tan

The other rhythms are composed of a combination of Tan with Tere, the said Tan with Fre, and of all three together, Tan, Tere and Fre. First of all, here is a combination of four Tan and one Tere which can be arranged in four different ways.

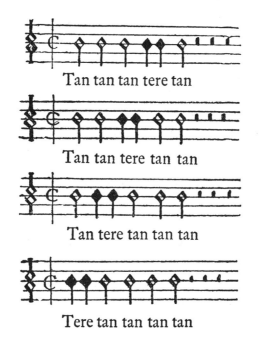

Tan tan tan tere tan

Tan tan tere tan tan

Tan tere tan tan tan

Tere tan tan tan tan

Combination of Three Tan and two Tere

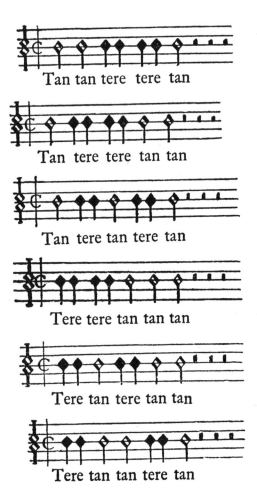

Tan tan tere tere tan

Tan tere tere tan tan

Tan tere tan tere tan

Tere tere tan tan tan

Tere tan tere tan tan

Tere tan tan tere tan

Combination of two Tan and three Tere

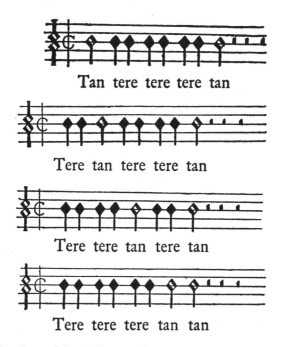

Tan tere tere tere tan

Tere tan tere tere tan

Tere tere tan tere tan

Tere tere tere tan tan

Another combination of four Tere and one Tan which can not be arranged otherwise because the Tan must be at the end to mark the cadence.

Tere tere tere tere tan

Combination of four Tan and one Fre

Tan tan tan fre   tan

Tan tan fre   tan tan

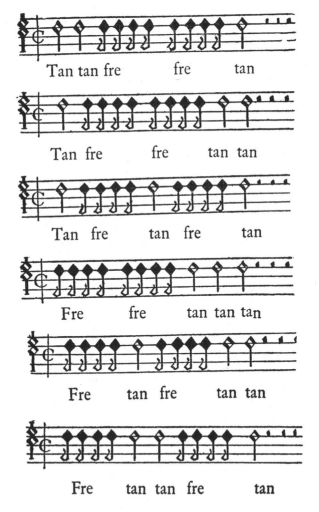

Combination of three Tan and two Fre, of which there are six variations, as follows:

Combination of two Tan and three Fre of which there are four different sorts.

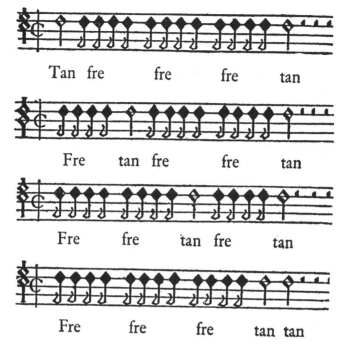

Another rhythm composed of four Fre and one Tan, which cannot be arranged otherwise.

Combination of three Tere and one Fre with the final Tan.

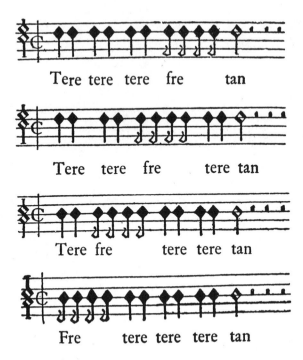

Tere tere tere fre tan

Tere tere fre tere tan

Tere fre tere tere tan

Fre tere tere tere tan

I do not believe the drum is capable of any further varieties of rhythm than those you have mentioned above.

The enumeration of them has wearied you, but there are still others and I must complete the list as I would not leave unfinished what I have begun.

Combination of two Tere and two Fre with the final Tan

Tere tere fre fre tan

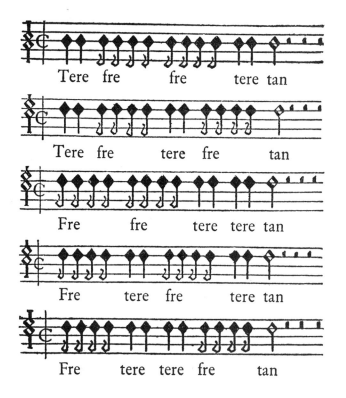

Combination of one Tere and three Fre with the final Tan, which can be varied in four ways, after which I will show you the remaining combinations.

Combination of three Tan, one Tere and one Fre, from which the following twelve variations can be made.

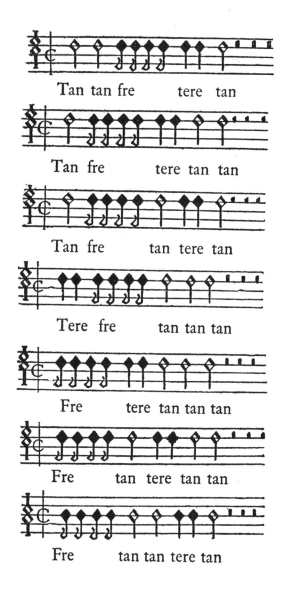

Tan tan fre   tere tan

Tan fre   tere tan tan

Tan fre   tan tere tan

Tere fre   tan tan tan

Fre   tere tan tan tan

Fre   tan tere tan tan

Fre   tan tan tere tan

Combination of two Tan, two Tere and one Fre, from which are made the variations that follow and which are twelve in number.

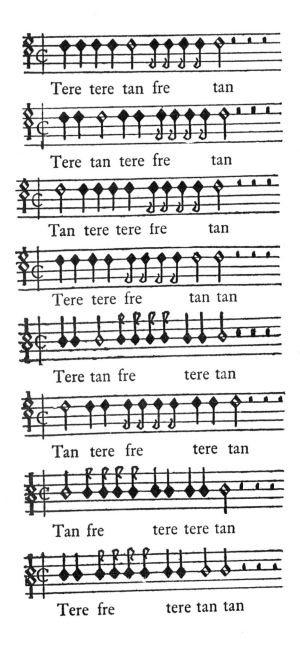

Tere tere tan fre tan

Tere tan tere fre tan

Tan tere tere fre tan

Tere tere fre tan tan

Tere tan fre tere tan

Tan tere fre tere tan

Tan fre tere tere tan

Tere fre tere tan tan

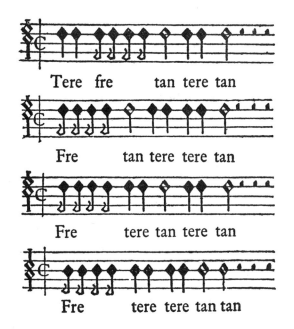

Tere fre tan tere tan

Fre tan tere tere tan

Fre tere tan tere tan

Fre tere tere tan tan

Combination of two Tan, one Tere and two Fre, from which are made the following eight variations

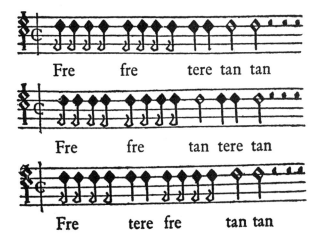

Fre fre tere tan tan

Fre fre tan tere tan

Fre tere fre tan tan

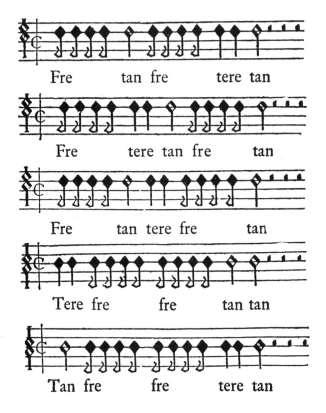

Fre   tan fre   tere tan

Fre   tere tan fre   tan

Fre   tan tere fre   tan

Tere fre   fre   tan tan

Tan fre   fre   tere tan

From all the above named varieties the drummer can choose those that seem
to him most pleasing and euphonious.

CAPRIOL

Why are the rests put down? Why should not the drummer use eight minims
for each step? Four for the left foot and four for the right.

ARBEAU

If the drummer did not use the rests the soldiers would fall out of step, because, as I have told you, the left foot must be brought down on the first
note and the right on the fifth, and if all the eight notes were struck a soldier
might bring his feet down on notes other than the first and fifth. This cannot

happen with pauses and rests because beaten thus he easily distinguishes
the first and fifth notes.

Can one only put a rest after the fifth note of a drum rhythm?

The Swiss drummers put a rest after the third note and three rests at the
end, but it comes to the same as the feet are always brought down on the
first and fifth note.

Colin   tan   plon   colin   tan   plon

CAPRIOL

This custom of marching to the drum looks very fine when well executed.

ARBEAU

It can be done otherwise in the said duple time, by putting only one rest after the five minim notes, and in this case the soldier brings his left foot down on the first note, then his right foot on the third note and again his left foot on the fifth. And in the bar that follows, he brings his right foot down on the first note, then his left foot on the third and again his right foot on the fifth, and so on for the distance to be covered.

CAPRIOL

According to this calculation each drum rhythm accounts for a greater distance than would be covered by a man's marching pace.

ARBEAU

Certainly, the first rhythm will cover seven feet and those that follow six feet only; and in this manner the soldiers will cover a league in one thousand six hundred and sixty six drum rhythms or thereabouts. It would also be possible to beat the said five minims and one rest and to march to them in triple time.[a]

In the said triple time the soldier brings down his left foot on the first note and then his right on the fourth note, and so on accordingly.

CAPRIOL

This triple time is very nice; as the paces are similar to those taken to duple time there is only one pause and rest.

ARBEAU

When the warriors draw near to the enemy they march in closer formation and must watch each step with care, always bringing down the left foot on the first note as I have told you.

CAPRIOL

Would it not be the same if the soldier brought his right foot down on the first note?

ARBEAU

Plainly not, because assuming most soldiers to be right footed they march with the left foot first. If any of them were to start with the right and finish with the left foot they would knock shoulders when in close formation and hinder one another, because we turn the shoulder slightly to the side of the foot that is leading. If, therefore, one soldier were to start on the left foot, his shoulder would swing towards the left and the shoulder of another who had started on the right foot would swing towards the right and they would collide. This does not happen when they march in step, as all the shoulders incline first to one side and then to the other without jostling or hindering one another, a thing you can easily prove for yourself by walking with some one. That is why the drummer beats a succession of repetitions of the rhythm, so that if confusion should occur, through a change in step, the soldiers can mend matters and easily get back on the left foot when they hear the pause or the three rests. And that is a great help in evolutions.

CAPRIOL

What does evolution mean?

ARBEAU

It is not our intention to deal with military art here. If you wish to know about evolution consult the book that Aelian[18] dedicated to the Emperor Hadrian. I shall only tell you this, that besides the marches, saltations and war dances already mentioned here, the drummer employs a succession of lighter and livelier crotchet beats, intermingled with loud blows of the sticks which sound like discharges of arquebus. This is done as the soldiers approach the enemy, and when they wish to join battle they close ranks to form a solid mass and lower their halberds and pikes, making them into a strong rampart difficult to force or break.

Meanwhile the drummer beats two crotchets in quick duple time, borrowed from the metrical foot that the poets call the Pyrrhic, and the soldiers advance, always leading with the left foot and bringing it down on the first note. And on the second note of the Pyrrhic they bring the right foot close up behind the left foot to brace it and serve as a buttress. And thus, leaping and dancing, they start to fight as if the drum were saying:—

Dedans dedans dedans dedans dedans dedans

CAPRIOL

It seems to me that by now I should be able to march and dance very well in military step to the beats and rhythms of the drum. But why is the drummer accompanied by one or two fifers?

ARBEAU

What we call the fife is a little transverse flute with six holes, used by the Germans and Swiss, and, as the bore is very narrow, only the thickness of a pistol bullet, it has a shrill note. In place of a fife some use a flageolet called an *arigot*,[19] which has a greater or lesser number of holes according to its size. The best ones have four holes in front and two behind and their sound is piercing; one might call them little *tibiae* as they were originally made from the shin bone and legs of the crane. The players of the said drum and fife are known by the name of their instrument, and we say of two soldiers that one is the drummer and the other the fifer of some captain.

CAPRIOL

Is there a particular way in which to play the fife or *arigot?*

ARBEAU

Those who play them improvise to please themselves and it suffices for them to keep time with the sound of the drum.[a] However, we are told that the Phrygian mode, which musicians call the third mode,[b] incites naturally to anger and that the Lydians used it when going to war. History records that when Timotheus played in it upon his *tibia,* Alexander the Great instantly arose like a madman raging for combat. Bacchus, that great leader called Dionysus, taught his soldiers, surrounded as they were by women camp followers, dancing and military marches to the sound of the drum and the Phrygian *tibia*. It was by this means that he subjugated the Indians who advanced in a disorderly mob, screaming and yelling, and consequently were thrown into confusion and easily scattered and vanquished.

CAPRIOL

Give me examples of the music for the fife or *arigot* as you have for the drum.

ARBEAU

As I have told you, the music for the fife or *arigot* is composed to the player's fancy. However, I will give you a little extract here that I have obtained from

M. Isaac Huguet, the organist. Its compass on his spinet extends from middle C or B up to high E. And for a bass accompaniment instead of the drum rhythm, he puts his left thumb on the C below and his little finger an octave lower and strikes them in turn, namely, the lower octave on the first beat and the middle C on the fifth, keeping his index finger on the G which makes a perfect fifth with the said lower octave, and a fourth with the upper C.

CAPRIOL

It seems to me, subject to your correction, that by the rules of music, this fourth should not be used as the bass.

ARBEAU

You are quite right, but that applies to voices singing in four parts. In this case we are concerned with the sound of the drum, serving as the bass, and because it has no definite pitch it blends with every thing and there is no objection to the spinet representing it in these euphonious discords. Before I give you the tabulation, you must remember that there are two ways of playing the flute, one by sucking, and the other by rolling the tongue. In the first case the player's tongue goes té, té, té, or teré, teré, teré, and in the second relé, relé, relé. I warn you of this because the example I wish to set down for you should be played té, té, and not rolled.

CAPRIOL

Why should one té, té, instead of rolling it?

ARBEAU

Because the sound of té, té, is shriller and harsher, consequently more war-like than the roll.

TABULATION FOR THE FIFE OR *ARIGOT* IN THE THIRD MODE[20]

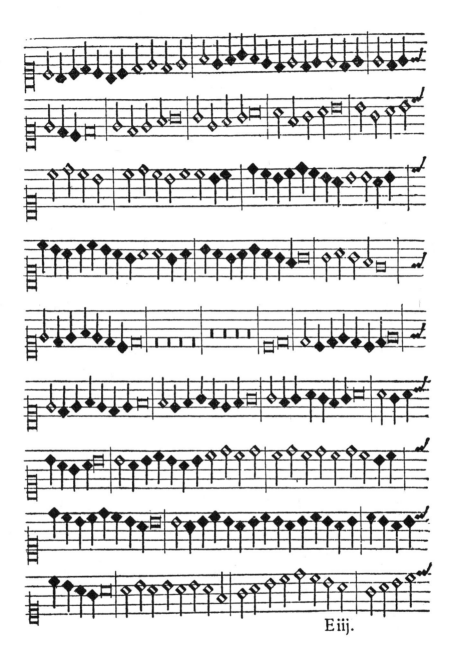

Eiij.

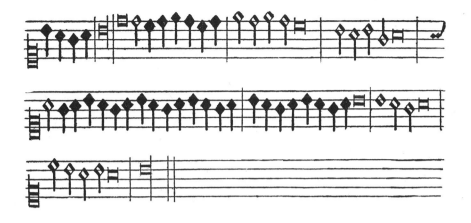

CAPRIOL

I am very pleased to have this tabulation. I have a little *arigot* and I shall try to play this tune on it.

ARBEAU

You can amplify this music to suit your pleasure and fancy. And if, for instance, you assume the drum is beaten in triple time, which consists of five minims and a rest, you can utilize the above music by subtracting two minims from each bar, sometimes at the end of the rhythm, sometimes at the beginning and sometimes in the middle, in such a way that the continuity is not broken.

CAPRIOL

Those who understand music can do it easily.

ARBEAU

I should like to give you an example in triple time which you can use without the trouble of abridging the above if you do not wish to; this you can also amplify as much as you wish.

CAPRIOL

Since it pleases you to take the trouble you will greatly oblige me.

TABULATION FOR PLAYING THE FIFE OR *ARIGOT* IN TRIPLE TIME[a]

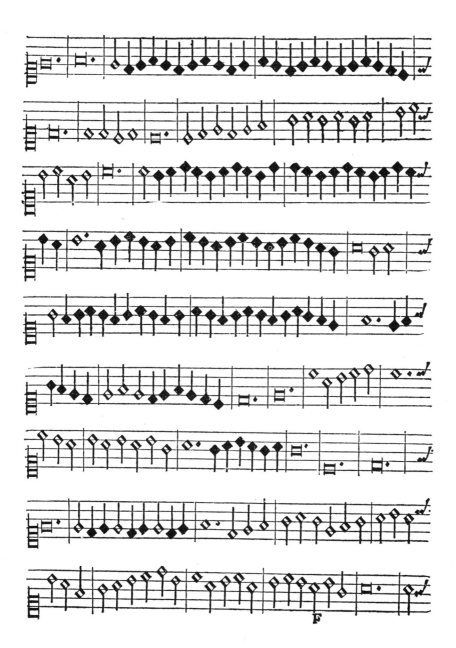

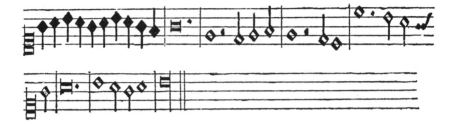

CAPRIOL

I have no inclination whatever to go to war, still what you have taught me about the dances of war may be of service to me when we engage in military exercises in the town of Langres. But for the moment let us pass on and tell me about recreative dances.

ARBEAU

I must first inform you that, in the likeness of the drum of which we have spoken above, a little one has been made called the tabor, about two small feet long and one foot in diameter, which Isidorus calls a half-symphony.[a] Twisted threads are placed at the extremities of both skins on the tabor, unlike the big drum where a double cord is placed across one of the skins only.[b]

CAPRIOL

What is the purpose of these twisted threads?

ARBEAU

It is due to them that when the tabor is struck by a stick or the fingers the sound is strident and throbbing.

CAPRIOL

Symphony means harmony and not a tabor.

ARBEAU

In truth the Greek word *symphonia* means harmony and from this word the Symphonic Musicians derive their name. But it is not inapposite that the tabor should have received the designation of symphony, or half-symphony as Isidorus calls it, because it is usually accompanied by one or more other musical instruments with which it blends, adding charm and serving as a bass and diapason*ᵃ* to all harmonies. It is very probably that which was used to accompany the instrument called the chorus*ᵇ* to give praise to God in rejoicing, and of which the Holy Royal Prophet speaks when he says— *Laudate Dominum in tympano et choro.*²¹ In the fifteenth chapter of St. Luke the elder son of the family was indignant when he learned that they were making great celebration with the fatted calf and the symphony and chorus to welcome his brother. Daniel relates in his third chapter that Nebuchad-nezzar proclaimed all should fall down and worship his statue when they heard the sound of the flute, the hautboy,²² the sackbut,²³ the harp, the psaltery,²⁴ the symphony and other musical instruments.*ᶜ*

CAPRIOL

I had understood this word chorus to mean a company of dancers.

ARBEAU

I have seen a picture of the said chorus in a book describing all the musical instruments and it was shown with the symphony as we should link the latter with the flute or large *tibia* today.*ᵈ* The Basques and Béarnais use another kind of tabor²⁵ which they hold suspended in the left hand while playing it with the fingers of the right. The wood is only half a foot deep and the skins a small foot in diameter. It is surrounded by tiny bells and little pieces of copper and makes a pleasant sound, not a horrible one as did the large drums filled with bells, used by the natives of India in battle, which Suidas describes. As for our tabor, we do not put any bells in it and usually accompany it with a long flute or large *tibia*. And the musician plays whatever songs he fancies on the said flute, holding it in his left hand while supporting the tabor by the same arm.

CAPRIOL

Is it possible that he can play a tune with his left hand alone? I cannot believe it, because I am at a loss to find so many different notes with both my hands on a flute with nine holes; and also it would seem impossible to me to play and hold it with the same hand.

ARBEAU

The mouth piece is held in the player's mouth and the lower end rests between the little finger and the third finger, besides which, in order that it should not slip through the player's hand, there is a little cord at the end of the flute through which the third finger is passed to support and hold it. It only has three holes, two in front and one behind, and is admirably fashioned as with the index and middle fingers touching the two holes in front and the thumb touching the one behind the notes of the scale are easily found.

CAPRIOL

This, then, is a secret I should like to learn by the way, after which I shall ask you to resume your discourse.

ARBEAU

You must know that pipes which are tall and long with a flat narrow mouthpiece like the flute in question will easily and naturally blow a fifth, and if one sounds them harder still they will reach the octave. Suppose the long flute is blown gently and all the holes are stopped, it sounds G, then if one opens the first hole, which was stopped by the middle finger, it will sound A, and if one opens the second hole, stopped by the index finger, it will sound B and if one opens the third hole, which is behind and stopped by the thumb, it will sound C. After which, with all the holes entirely stopped and blowing a little harder, it jumps to the fifth above and sounds D. With the same breath, if the middle finger be lifted, it will sound E, and F if the index finger be lifted. This done, by raising the thumb it will sound G, and continuing thus to lift the fingers and give it the appropriate blast, one can find many steps in the scale.

CAPRIOL

You sound this upper G octave on the hole used by the thumb, so by closing all the holes it should sound the A above it.

ARBEAU

When all the holes are stopped it sounds the octave also, because of the natural disposition of this type of flute, which jumps, when fully stopped, to the fifth and then to the octave.

CAPRIOL

When it is said in Terence that the comedy *Andria*[a] was performed to the unsurpassed *tibia* of Claudius, does it refer to these flutes of which you have been speaking?

ARBEAU

Indeed I believe so, because one finds in ancient sculpture that the same person played two flutes at once, one of which was larger with a deeper tone, and the other shorter and shriller. The larger was held in the left hand and the shorter in the right. And in my opinion they held them thus because the trills could be more effectively and easily played with the right hand. Once, while coming from Mount St. Claude, which Ptolemy calls Mount Ivras, I remember seeing a double flute played; one of the pipes was cut to about a third of the length of the larger one, and the person who played it, using both hands, brought the two parts into euphonious accord.

CAPRIOL

Valerius Maximus,[a] in the chapter on ancient institutions, speaks of the college of *tibia* players.

ARBEAU

The college resembled the bands of musicians that are found in towns. They played on a variety of *tibiae*, some like those we have been talking about, some with nine holes and others with reed tongues which make a sound rather like a trumpet,[b] as do the hautboys of which the poet Horace speaks, saying, *Tibia non ut nunc oricalcho cincta Tubaeque aemula*[26]

CAPRIOL

In truth hautboys have some resemblance to trumpets, and make quite an agreeable harmony when the large ones, sounding the octave in the bass, are combined with the little ones holding the high octave.

ARBEAU

This pair is excellent for making a tremendous noise, such as is required at village fêtes or large gatherings, but if they were played with the flute they would drown the sound of it. It combines well with the tabor or with the big drum.

CAPRIOL

Can one make use of the big drum for recreative dances?

ARBEAU

Yes, certainly, particularly with the said hautboys, which are harsh and wailing and are blown with force.

CAPRIOL

Let us return to the subject of the tabor and the dance.

ARBEAU

In our fathers' time, the tabor, accompanied by its long flute among other instruments, was used because a single musician could play them both together in symphony without necessitating the additional expense of other players, such as violins[27] and the like. Nowadays there is no workman so humble that he does not wish to have hautboys and sackbuts at his wedding.[a] Formerly there were a great variety of recreative dances.

CAPRIOL

Tell me about these dances and how they are performed.

ARBEAU

Our predecessors danced pavans, basse dances,[b] branles and corantos; the basse dance has been out of date some forty or fifty years, but I foresee that wise and dignified matrons will restore it to fashion as being a type of dance full of virtue and decorum.

CAPRIOL

How did our fathers dance the basse dance?[28]

ARBEAU

There were two kinds of basse dance, one common and regular, the other irregular.[c] The regular one was set to a tune in like form and the irregular one to an irregular tune.

CAPRIOL

What do you mean by common and regular tunes?

ARBEAU

The musicians of that time composed their ballads in sixteen bars which they repeated, making thirty-two bars for the beginning, and for the middle section they wrote sixteen bars, and for the end sixteen bars with a repetition. Thus, the common and regular basse dance contained eighty bars. And if it happened that the ballad exceeded these eighty bars the basse dance performed to it was called irregular.

CAPRIOL

What are the correct movements to be made to these bars?

ARBEAU

You should know beforehand that the music of the basse dance is played in triple time,[a] and in each bar the tabor also beats triple time to harmonize with the flute. In tapping the said eighty tabor rhythms with his little stick, each bar consists of one minim and four crotchets, thus:—

And to each bar the dancer moves his feet and body according to the rules of the dance.

CAPRIOL

How shall I execute these movements when I wish to dance a basse dance?

ARBEAU

In the first instance, when you have entered the place where the company is assmbled for the dance you will choose some comely damsel who takes your fancy, and, removing your hat or bonnet with your left hand, proffer her your right to lead her out to dance. She, being sensible and well brought up, will offer you her left hand and arise to accompany you. Then, in the sight of all, you will conduct her to the end of the room and give notice to the musicians to play a basse dance. Otherwise they might inadvertently play some other kind of dance. And when they begin to play you will begin to dance. And take note, that in requesting a basse dance they will understand you to mean a common or regular one. However, should the tune of some particular ballad, which is set to a basse dance, please you more than another, you could tell the musicians how it begins.

CAPRIOL

If the damsel refused me I should be deeply humiliated.

ARBEAU

A well-bred damsel will never refuse him who does her the honour of asking her to dance, and if she did she would be considered stupid, because unless she desires to dance she should not take her place among the others.

CAPRIOL

I quite agree, but nevertheless the shame would fall upon me.

ARBEAU

If you are assured of the good graces of another damsel in the company you should take her and leave the discourteous one after apologising for having importuned her. Still, there are many who would not endure it so patiently; but it is better to speak gently than with rancour, and thereby gain the reputation for kindliness and good humour and allow her own behaviour to brand her as haughty and unworthy of the honour you have paid her.

CAPRIOL

Here we are, then, standing at the end of the hall. The musicians begin to play a basse dance, what movements do we lead off with?

ARBEAU

The first movement is the *révérence*,[29] indicated by a capital R, the second movement is the *branle*,[30] indicated by a b. The third kind of movement comprises two *simples*,[31] indicated by ss. The fourth movement is the *double*, indicated by d, and the fifth movement is the *reprise*,[32] indicated by a small r.

CAPRIOL

Are these all the steps required to dance a common or regular basse dance?

ARBEAU

There are no other kinds of movement in the basse dance, nor in the *retour*[33] of the basse dance, although these are repeated several times.

CAPRIOL

What do you mean by this *retour* of the basse dance?

ARBEAU

The complete basse dance contains three parts. The first is called the basse dance, the second is called the *retour* of the basse dance and the third and last part is called the tordion. I have written them down in a memorandum for you to learn by heart.

MEMORANDUM OF THE MOVEMENTS FOR THE BASSE DANCE

R b ss d r d r b ss ddd r d
r b ss d r b c

CAPRIOL

What does the letter c that you have placed at the end mean?

ARBEAU

It represents the *congé*[34] which you must take of the damsel. You bow, still holding her by the hand, and return her to the place from which you started the dance in order to commence the second part or *retour* of the basse dance.

MEMORANDUM OF MOVEMENTS FOR THE *RETOUR* OF THE BASSE DANCE
b d r b ss ddd r d r b c

The final letter signifies the *congé* as before and there is no capital R at the beginning of the *retour* because it is begun without the *réverence*, which is deferred this time until after the *congé* and made before commencing the tordion.

CAPRIOL

Explain to me separately and in detail the gestures and movements signified by the letters in the memorandum.

ARBEAU

The *révérence*, the first gesture and movement, occupies four tabor rhythms accompanied by four bars of the tune on the flute.[a] In view of the fact that all dances begin with the left foot, Anthony Arena was of the opinion that the *révérence* should be made with the left foot; however in the end he seems to leave the matter in doubt, saying thus:

> *Bragardi certant et adhuc sub judice lis est*
> *De quali gamba sit facienda salus.*[35]

As for myself, I hold with my teacher, under whom I formerly studied at Poitiers,[b] that it should be done with the right foot.[c] In this way one is enabled to turn towards the damsel and throw her a courteous glance.

Reuerence

The *branle* follows the *révérence,* how should it be performed?

Arena calls the *branle* the *congedium,* and I think he has done so because from the gesture of the dancer it appears as if he were about to finish and take leave of the damsel, although in fact he proceeds with the steps and movements as set down in the memorandum.

The said *branle* is performed, in four tabor rhythms which accompany four bars of the melody on the flute, by keeping the heels together and turning the body gently to the left for the first bar; then to the right, glancing modestly the while at the spectators, for the second bar; then again to the left for the third. And for the fourth bar, to the right again with a discreetly tender sidelong glance at the damsel.

Two *simples* follow the *branle,* how should they be done?

You will take one step forward with the left foot for the first bar, then bring the right foot up beside the left for the second bar, then you will advance with the right foot for the third bar. And at the fourth bar and tabor rhythm you will bring the left foot up beside the right with the heels together, and thus the movement of two *simples* will be completed. And you must be careful not to take strides that suggest you wish to measure the length of the hall, as the damsel who is your partner cannot with decency take such long steps.

Arena, and others of his school, performed the *simple* with the same foot, bringing the left foot beside the right foot for the first bar and then advancing with the left foot again.[36] And doing likewise with the right foot. But I remember my teacher at Poitiers improved upon this, saying it was more seemly to finish the two *simples* with the feet together than with one foot in front of the other.

CAPRIOL

This appears sound reasoning to me and I shall be guided by your views. Let us now proceed to the *double*, how should this be performed?

ARBEAU

The *double* occupies four bars and tabor rhythms. In the first bar one must advance a step with the left foot, in the second bar a step with the right foot, while in the third one must advance with the left foot again. And in the fourth bar, the right foot must be placed beside the left with the heels together. Thus in four bars the *double* is completed. And if there are two *doubles* the succeeding one is done contrariwise to the first, by advancing the right foot first, then the left and again the right, and in the fourth bar the left foot must be placed beside the right with heels together. Thus in eight bars two *doubles* are accomplished. And to execute yet a third *double* the left foot must be advanced, then the right, then the left, and to conclude both heels brought together as in the first *double*. Thus the three *doubles* are completed in twelve bars and tabor rhythms.

CAPRIOL

It still remains for me to learn how a *reprise* is executed.

ARBEAU

The movement called *reprise* usually precedes the *branle*, and sometimes the *double*, and occupies four bars like all the other movements. You will perform it by moving the knees gently from side to side, or the feet, or the toes only, as if your feet were trembling.

To wit; on the first bar with the toes of the right foot, then again the toes of the said right foot on the second bar, then the toes of the left foot on the third bar, and the toes of the said right foot on the fourth bar. And in these four movements the *reprise* is accomplished and the dancer is ready to perform the *branle* or the other movements which follow.[a]

CAPRIOL

If we were to call the four bars of the tabor and flute a quaternion, or tetradion, I find by counting the characters in the memorandum you gave me that the basse dance contains twenty quaternions and the *retour* of the basse dance twelve.

ARBEAU

Your calculation is correct. And after the basse dance and the *retour* of the basse dance you can commence the tordion, which is in triple time like the basse dance. But it is lighter and more lively.

CAPRIOL

Is the tordion composed of the same movements as the basse dance and its *retour*, that is to say, of *simples, doubles, reprises* and *branles?*

ARBEAU

It contains another type of movement, comprising certain positions of the feet and a cadence, which I will explain to you more fully when we come to discuss the galliard, because the tordion is nothing other than a galliard danced with the feet kept close to the ground.

CAPRIOL

Teach me the movements of this galliard.

ARBEAU

We shall come to that after we have spoken of the pavan,[37] which is usually danced before the basse dance. The said pavan has not become obsolete or gone out of fashion, nor do I believe it ever will although in truth it is less popular than it was in the past. Our musicians play it when a maiden of good family is taken to Holy Church to be married or when they lead a procession of the chaplains, masters and brethren of some notable confraternity.

CAPRIOL

While awaiting your discourse upon the galliard tell me what movements are employed in the pavan.

ARBEAU

The pavan is easy to dance as it is merely two *simples* and one *double* forward and two *simples* and one *double* backward. It is played in duple time, you will take note that in dancing it the two *simples* and the *double* forward are begun with the left foot, and the two *simples* and one *double* backward are begun with the right foot.

CAPRIOL

Then the tabor and other instruments play eight bars while the dancers advance and eight bars while they move backwards.

ARBEAU

That is so, and if one does not wish to move backwards one may continue to advance all the time.

CAPRIOL

Are there no retreating steps in the basse dance?

ARBEAU

Sometimes the hall is so thronged with a multitude of guests that the space for dancing is limited and therefore when you near the end of the room you are faced with two alternatives, either you, and the damsel with whom you are dancing, must move backwards or you must make a *conversion.*[38]

CAPRIOL

What do you mean by a *conversion?*

ARBEAU

It means that upon approaching the end of the hall you continue to guide the damsel forward while you yourself move backwards as she advances, until you are facing in the opposite direction from which you started.

CAPRIOL

Which of these two seems to you the better course?

ARBEAU

In my opinion it is better to make a *conversion,* in order that the damsel may always see where she is going. Because if she were to meet with some hindrance while moving backwards she might fall, a mishap for which you would receive the blame and suffer a rapid decline in her good graces. And so, it seems to me this practice should always be followed in the pavan when one wishes to take two or three turns around the room.

CAPRIOL

Is the tabor rhythm the same for the pavan as it is for the basse dance?

ARBEAU

It is in duple time, consisting of one minim and two crotchets, in this manner.

CAPRIOL

I find these pavans and basse dances charming and dignified, and well suited to honourable persons, particularly ladies and maidens.

ARBEAU

A cavalier may dance the pavan wearing his cloak and sword, and others, such as you, dressed in your long gowns, walking with decorum and measured gravity. And the damsels with demure mien, their eyes lowered save to cast an occasional glance of virginal modesty at the onlookers. On solemn feast days the pavan is employed by kings, princes and great noblemen to display themselves in their fine mantles and ceremonial robes. They are accompanied by queens, princesses and great ladies, the long trains of their dresses loosened and sweeping behind them, sometimes borne by damsels. And it is the said pavans, played by hautboys and sackbuts, that announce the grand ball and are arranged to last until the dancers have circled the hall two or three times, unless they prefer to dance it by advancing and retreating.^a Pavans are also used in masquerades to herald the entrance of the gods and goddesses in their triumphal chariots or emperors and kings in full majesty.

CAPRIOL

Pray write down the tunes of a pavan and a basse dance for me.

ARBEAU

I shall do so willingly, in the hope that such honourable dances are reinstated and replace the lascivious, shameless ones introduced in their stead to the regret of wise lords and ladies and matrons of sound and chaste judgment. First I shall give you a pavan with the tabor rhythm in slow duple time, accompanied by the tenor, alto and bass, which will suffice to show you how to dance all the others; and if you wish it can be sung or played in four-part harmony without dancing it. Then, later, I shall give you a common basse dance with its *retour* and the tordion, which will likewise serve you as a pattern for all the others, provided that you know what I have written for you above by heart.

PAVAN IN FOUR PARTS WITH THE DRUM RHYTHM [a]

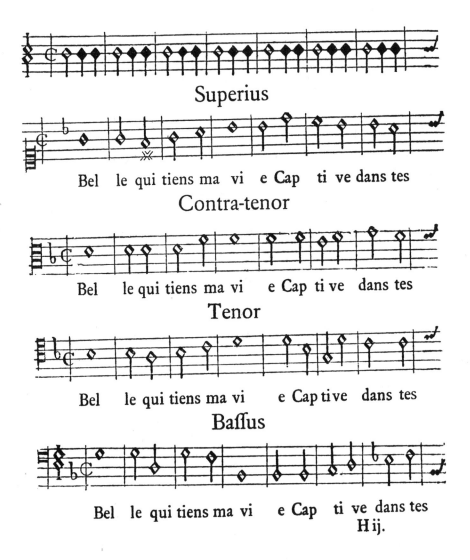

Superius

Bel   le qui tiens ma vi   e Cap ti ve dans tes

Contra-tenor

Bel   le qui tiens ma vi   e Cap ti ve dans tes

Tenor

Bel   le qui tiens ma vi   e Cap tive   dans tes

Baſſus

Bel   le qui tiens ma vi   e Cap   ti ve dans tes

H ij.

Battement du tambour

Superius

Contra-tenor

Tenor

Baſſus

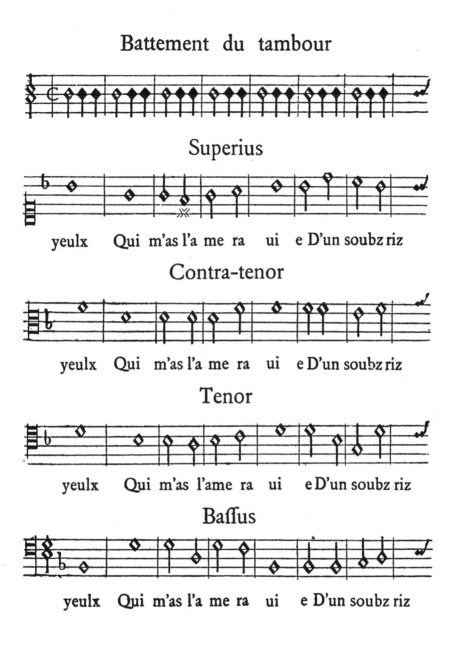

yeulx   Qui m'as l'a me ra   ui   e D'un soubz riz

Battement du tambour

Battement du tambour

Superius

me faul dra mou rir Viens toft me fecou rir

Contra-tenor [a]

me faul dra mou rir   Viens toft me fe cou   rir

Tenor

me faul dra mourir   Viens toft me fe cou   rir

Baffus

me faul dra mourir Viens toft me fecou   rir

Battement du tambour

Superius

Ou me faul dra mou rir

Contra-tenor

Ou me faul dra mourir

Tenor

Ou me faul dra mou rir

Baſſus

Ou me faul dra mou rir

The above pavan arranged in four parts contains two advancing and two retreating movements, indicated by their characters thus, ss d ss d ss d ss d, and comprises thirty-two bars and tabor rhythms. And to prolong it, these can be repeated as many times as the musicians or dancers please. Since you may feel inclined to sing the whole song some day, here are the words:

<table>
<tr><td>SONG</td><td>CHANSON[a]</td></tr>
<tr><td>

Fair one, who holds my heart
Captive within thine eyes,
Whose gracious smiles impart
Secrets of Paradise,
Give me hope to cherish
For without I perish.

Fly not, I entreat thee,
For in thy presence fair
I am lost completely
To myself and care.
Thy divine perfection
Claims my whole affection.

Such grace of form and face
Kindles a sweet desire,
My icy heart yields place
To a heart all afire,
Fanned by ardent yearning
Passionately burning.

I wandered fancy free,
Nor glance nor sigh I gave
Till love imprisoned me
And I became his slave,
Ready to die for him,
Sworn to his slightest whim.

Draw near, O mistress mine,
Come closer to me still.
Since I am wholly thine
Soften thy rebel will,
Mend my heart with the bliss
Of one sweet healing kiss.

</td><td>

Belle qui tiens ma vie
Captive dans tes yeux,
Qui m'as l'âme ravie
D'un souris gracieux,
Viens tôt me secourir
Ou me faudra mourir.

Pourquoi fuis tu, mignarde,
Si je suis près de toi
Quand tes yeux je regarde
Je me perds dedans moi,
Car tes perfections
Changent mes actions.

Tes beautés et ta grace
Et tes divins propos
Ont échauffé la glace
Qui me gelait les os,
Et ont rempli mon coeur
D'une amoureuse ardeur.

Mon âme voulait être
Libre de passion,
Mais l'amour s'est fait maître
De mes affections
Et a mis sous sa loi
Et mon coeur et ma foi.

Approche donc ma belle,
Approche toi mon bien,
Ne me sois plus rebelle
Puisque mon coeur est tien,
Pour mon mal appaiser
Donne moi un baiser.

</td></tr>
</table>

Angel, my life's eclipse	*Je meurs, mon Angelette,*
In thine embrace I die,	*Je meurs en te baisant*
The honey of thy lips	*Ta bouche tant doucette*
Sweetens my parting sigh,	*Va mon bien ravissant*
And my soul soars above	*A ce coup mes esprits*
Borne on the wings of love.	*Sont tous d'amour épris.*
Oceans shall surge no more	*Plutôt on verra l'onde*
And heaven's eye wax cold	*Contremont reculer,*
Full many a moon before	*Et plutôt l'oeil du monde*
My love for thee grows old,	*Cessera de brûler,*
Or wanes a single jot	*Que l'amour qui m'époint*
If thou forsake me not.	*Décroisse d'un seul point.*

CAPRIOL

This pavan is too solemn and slow to dance alone with a young girl in a room.

ARBEAU

The musicians sometimes play it more quickly to a lighter beat, and in this way it assumes the moderate tempo of a basse dance[a] and is called the *passamezzo.*[39] Recently another one has been introduced, called the Spanish pavan, in which the steps are rearranged with a variety of gestures, and, as it is somewhat similar to the dance known as the Canary, I shall not explain how it is performed until we are on the subject of the said Canary. Only you should be told now that some dancers divide up the *double* that follows the two *simples,* and instead of the *double* comprising only four bars with four semi-breves,[90] they introduce eight minims or sixteen crotchets, resulting in a great number of steps, passages[40] and embellishments, all of which fit into the time and cadence of the music. Such rearrangement and a sprightly execution of the steps, tempers the gravity of the pavan, added to the customary practice of following it by the galliard, which is a lively dance.

CAPRIOL

Teach me all these passages and divisions.

ARBEAU

What you wish to know in effect is how to divide up a *double.* Good dancers who are agile and lively can make whatever rearrangements seem desirable to them, provided they come down on the last beat with the foot ready to perform the two *simples* which follow the said *double*. And sometimes they anticipate their passages on the second *simple*. You will understand these passages and divisions when you have learned the various movements of the feet, which we shall speak of when we describe the dance known as the galliard. In the meanwhile I will write down the tune of a common basse dance, with the tabor rhythm in triple time, for you.

CAPRIOL

Must the tabor and flute necessarily be used for pavans and basse dances?

ARBEAU

Not unless one wishes it. One can play them on violins, spinets, transverse flutes, and flutes with nine holes, hautboys and all sorts of instruments. They can even be sung. But the tabor with its regular rhythm is an immense help in bringing the feet into the correct positions required by the movements of the dance.

BASSE DANCE CALLED 'I WILL GIVE YOU JOY',[41] WITH THE TABOR RHYTHM[a]

Air de la baſſe-dance

REVERENCE

Battement du tambour ou tabourin

Continuation de l'air

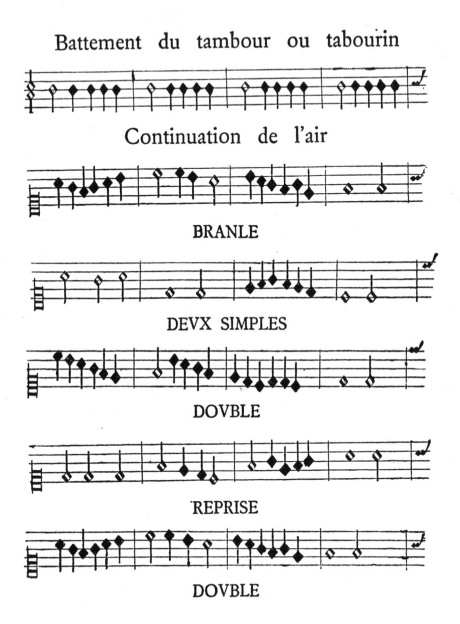

BRANLE

DEVX SIMPLES

DOVBLE

REPRISE

DOVBLE

Battement du tabourin

Continuation de l'air

REPRISE

BRANLE

DEVX SIMPLES

DOVBLE

DOVBLE

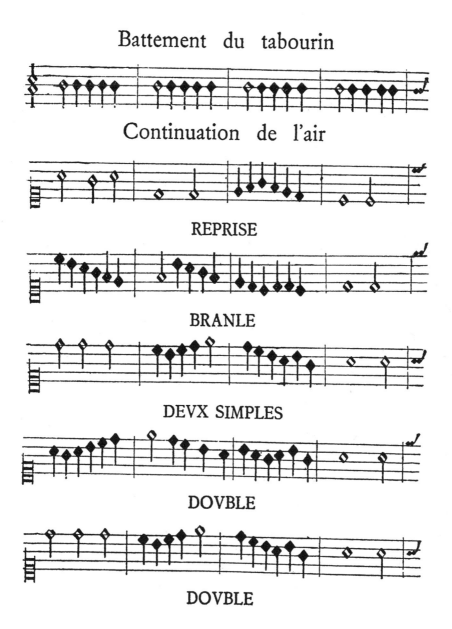

Battement du tabourin

Continuation de l'air

DOVBLE

REPRISE

DOVBLE

REPRISE

BRANLE

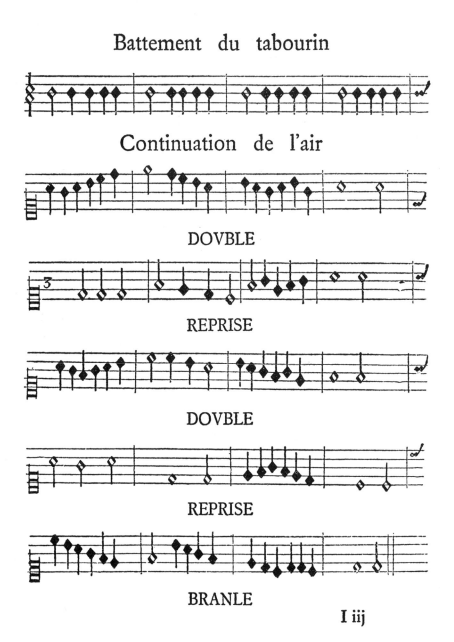

I iij

Battement du tabourin

Continuation de l'air

DEVX SIMPLES

DOVBLE

REPRISE

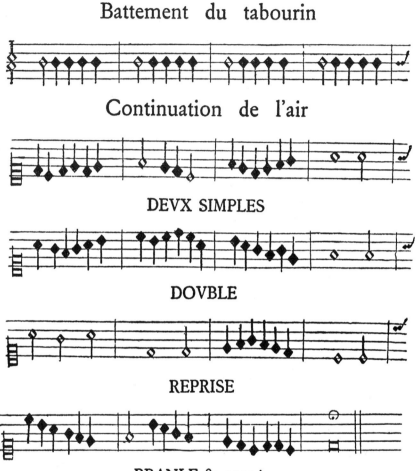

BRANLE & congé.

As soon as you hear the last beat of the *branle*, which precedes the *congé*, you will turn your body towards the damsel, and, removing your bonnet to bow, take your *congé* and accompany her to where you began the basse dance in order to commence the *retour* of the basse dance according to the tabor rhythms and movements which follow.

RETOUR OF THE BASSE DANCE WITH THE TABOR RHYTHM

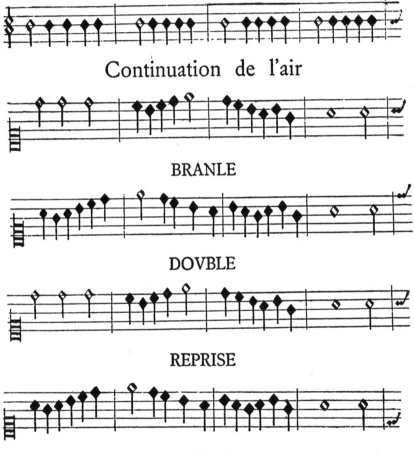

Continuation de l'air

BRANLE

DOVBLE

REPRISE

BRANLE

Battement du tabourin

Continuation de l'air

DEVX SIMPLES

DOVBLE

DOVBLE

DOVBLE

REPRISE

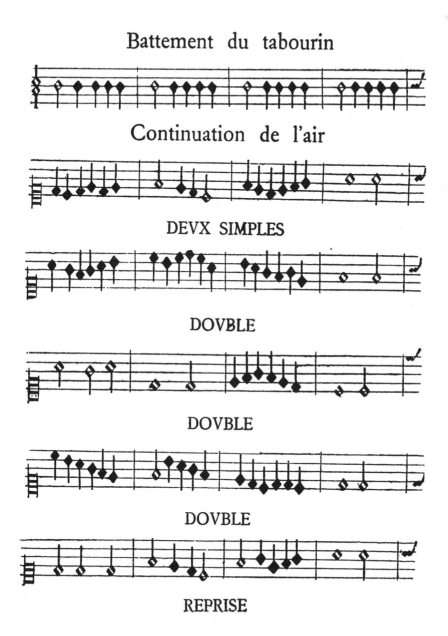

Battement du tabourin

Continuation de l'air

DOVBLE

REPRISE

BRANLE, & congé.

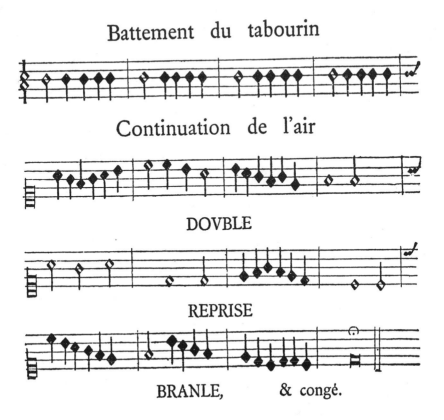

CAPRIOL

I should have liked you to inscribe five or six pavans and as many basse dances for me.

ARBEAU

You will find plenty in the books on dances printed by the recently defunct Attaignant, who lived near the church of St. Cosmo in Paris,[a] and in the books of the late Master Nicolas du Chemin,[b] printer in the said Paris at the sign of the Silver Lion. However you will have to put all those basse dances which are written in duple time into triple time.

CAPRIOL

What is to prevent you from rearranging them as you indicate and writing them down for me?

ARBEAU

When one knows the steps and movements of one pavan and one common basse dance one can dance all the others. Because although the melodies differ, and they may be either sung or played, they all have the same number of bars. It is therefore the musician's concern to learn a quantity of different ones and as for you it suffices that you should know how to dance them. This is easy for you now since you have learned and understood them.

CAPRIOL

You are forgetting to tell me about the uncommon and irregular basse dances.

ARBEAU

They contain no movements unlike those in the common basse dance, and differ only in that they are longer or shorter, or else of the same length but with the movements differently arranged, than the common basse dance. Arena made a list of them which I shall not enumerate here because they are seldom danced, and also because it is enough for the present that you should know the common one. I will merely write down three for you,[c] one of twenty-four quaternions, which is among the longest, and one of fourteen quaternions, which is among the shortest, and one of twenty quaternions like the common basse dance.

MEMORANDUM OF THE MOVEMENTS IN THE BASSE DANCE CALLED 'COMFORT ME'[42] OF TWENTY-FOUR QUATERNIONS, CONTAINING NINETY-SIX BARS.

R b ss d ss r b ss d ss r b

ss ddd ss r b ss d ss r b c

BASSE DANCE CALLED 'ALL FORLORN'[43] IN FOURTEEN QUATERN-IONS CONTAINING FIFTY-SIX BARS AND TABOR RHYTHMS.

R b ss d ss r b ss ddd ss r b c

BASSE DANCE CALLED 'PATIENCE', CONTAINING TWENTY QUATERNIONS AND EIGHTY BARS AS IN THE COMMON BASSE DANCE, BUT WHICH IS NEVERTHELESS IRREGULAR.

R b ss d r d ss r b ss ddd r b ss d ss r b c

I wanted to describe these three to you to cover all the rest, of which you need take little heed as few people danced them in the past, in fact only those who were vain and wished to show what good memories they had. By this means they often misled others who only knew how to dance the common basse dance, because whenever they saw that someone wished to dance with them they asked for one of these irregular ones.

CAPRIOL

Can several persons dance together?

ARBEAU

You can, if you wish, take two damsels. But one is enough and as the old proverb says "He who has two has one too many."[44] Also, when you have taken your place at one end of the hall with a damsel, another may take up his position with his mistress at the further end to dance opposite you. And when you approach one another you will have to go backwards or employ a *conversion*. I have explained to you already what is meant by a *conversion*.

CAPRIOL

You told me that after the basse dance and its *retour* one must dance the tordion, and that the tordion was a kind of galliard which you postponed explaining to me until you came to the subject of the galliard.[45]

ARBEAU

In the towns nowadays the galliard is danced regardless of rules, and the dancers are satisfied to perform the *five steps* and a few passages without any orderly arrangement so long as they keep the rhythm, with the result that many of their best passages go unnoticed and are lost. In earlier days it was danced with much more discernment. When the dancer had chosen a damsel and led her to the end of the hall, after making the *révérence*, they circled the room once or twice together simply walking. Then the dancer released the damsel and she went dancing away to the other end of the hall, and, once there, continued to dance upon the same spot. In the meanwhile, the dancer having followed her presented himself before her to perform a few passages, turning at will now to the right, now to the left. This done the damsel danced her way to the opposite end of the hall and her partner, dancing all the while, pursued her thither in order to execute more passages before her. And thus, continuing these goings and comings, the dancer kept introducing new passages and displaying his skill until the musicians stopped playing. Then, taking the damsel by the hand and thanking her, he performed the *révérence* and returned her to the place from whence he had led her forth to dance.[a]

CAPRIOL

This manner of dancing the galliard seems to me more laudable than the slipshod way in which I usually see it performed because when the dancer all but turns his back to the damsel she retaliates by doing the same thing to him while he is performing the passages.

ARBEAU

For some time now the galliard has been danced in a manner known as the Lyonnaise, in which the dancer, giving way to another, takes his *congé* of the damsel and withdraws. She, thus left alone, continues to dance a little while and then goes to choose another partner, and after they have danced together she takes her *congé* of him and withdraws. And these changes continue to take place as long as the galliard lasts.

CAPRIOL

If there are not enough young girls or dancers to make these changes may one choose among those who have danced already?

ARBEAU

You could do so, but this method was introduced to allow all the damsels present to participate in the dance and obviate the undesirable practice of those, indiscreet in their affections, who always wish to dance with their favourite. Also, by this means of changing over the less prepossessing damsels are afforded the opportunity of joining in the dance.

CAPRIOL

What movements are required in this dance which they call the galliard?

ARBEAU

The galliard is so called because one must be gay and nimble to dance it, as, even when performed reasonably slowly, the movements are light-hearted. And it needs must be slower for a man of large stature than for a small man, inasmuch as the tall one takes longer to execute his steps and in moving his feet backwards and forwards than the short one. The galliard comprises the tordion, which, as we have said above, should be danced after the *retour* of the basse dance. But the said tordion is danced more slowly and with less extreme movements and gestures.[a]

CAPRIOL

What movements are used in the galliard and tordion?

ARBEAU

The galliard should consist of six steps as it contains six minims played in two bars of triple time, thus:—

However, it consists of five steps only because the fifth and penultimate note is lost in the melody, as you see below where it is deleted and replaced by a rest of equivalent value. So there remain only five notes and, allowing one step for each note, you must count five steps and no more.

CAPRIOL

Then that is why I so often hear it said that he who dances the galliard must above all know his *five steps*.[46] But how are these five steps executed?

ARBEAU

There are many kinds of steps and by mingling these a variety of passages are constructed. From their nature springs the appropriate name by which each is known.

CAPRIOL

You have named and taught me them already. Are they not *révérence, branle,* two *simples, double* and *reprise,* which you have indicated in writing by the characters R b ss d r ?

ARBEAU

The steps of the galliard and tordion are different as I shall explain to you. And not without reason, because the steps and movements of the pavan and basse dance are slow and solemn whereas those of the galliard and tordion are quick and gay so that young men of your age are better suited to dance them than old ones like myself. To make the explanation clearer I will give you pictures of them with their names written above, if you think it well and feel the need.

CAPRIOL

Pray do whatever will enable me to understand more readily that which you are pleased to teach me. And do not be sparing with pictures because I find them very useful in following your explanation and fixing it in my memory.

ARBEAU

At the commencement of the galliard you must pre-suppose that the dancer, holding the damsel by the hand, makes the *révérence* as the musicians begin to play. The *révérence* made, he assumes a seemly modest attitude. To perform the *révérence,* you will keep the left foot firmly upon the ground and bending the right knee take the point of the toe behind the left foot, removing your bonnet or hat the while and bowing to your damsel and the company, as you see in the picture.

RÉVÉRENCE

After the *révérence* is completed straighten your body and replace your bonnet, then bring your right foot forward and place it beside the left, *pieds joints.*[47] This is considered to be the correct position when the feet are disposed side by side, as you see in the picture below, the toes in a straight line and the dancer's weight equally distributed on both feet.

PIEDS JOINTS

And if it happens that one foot is so placed as to support the whole weight of the body and the heel of the other foot is brought close to it with the toe at an oblique angle, this pose will be called *pieds joints oblique*, of which there are two kinds. To wit, *pieds joints oblique droit*, when the right foot is placed at an oblique angle and the left foot supports the body, and *pieds joints oblique gauche* when the left foot is at an oblique angle and the right foot supports the dancer's weight.

CAPRIOL

You have not told me the degree of this oblique angle, which I do not ask without cause as the geometricians hold that between two lines at right angles there are an infinity of oblique lines.

ARBEAU

The degree is left to the discretion of the dancer, so he may place the free foot at right angles to the foot supporting the body or at any other degree he pleases in relation to it, provided the feet touch one another. For the natural rotation of the leg will not permit it to exceed a right angle. You see here the pictures of the said movement *pieds joints oblique*.

PIEDS JOINTS OBLIQUE DROIT   PIEDS JOINTS OBLIQUE GAUCHE

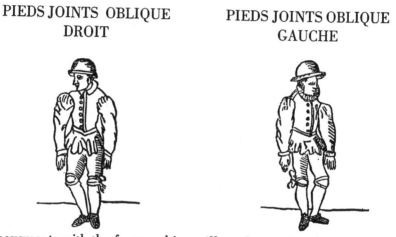

These movements with the feet touching will teach you that there are opposite movements, which we call *pieds largis*.[48] This is when both feet are on the ground with the weight of the body equally divided between them, but instead of touching one another they are separated. Not in an exaggerated and strained manner as were the feet of the colossus representing the statue of the sun, cast in copper by Colossus or Chares, pupils of Lysippus, and erected at Rhodes. It was seventy cubits[49] high, which is about one hundred and five of our Langres feet. This colossus had his legs as far apart as would be humanly possible and ships passed between them with ease.

CAPRIOL

It is not without reason, then, that it was counted one of the world's wonders and it was a great pity that fifty-six years later it collapsed as the result of an earthquake. I should like to have seen it to verify whether, as has been written, there were few people to be found who could encircle its thumb with their arms. But this tale aside, I quite understand how you wish the *pieds largis* to be placed, neither too far apart, nor too near nor touching one another.

PIEDS LARGIS*ᵃ*

ARBEAU

This position of *pieds largis* is also taken when one foot supports the weight of the body and the other rests at an oblique angle, which can be done in two ways. To wit; when, with the feet separated, the right foot rests at an oblique angle and the left foot supports the dancer's body, which is called *pied largi oblique droit,* and contrariwise when the left foot rests at an oblique angle and the right foot supports the body, which is called *pied largi oblique gauche.*

PIEDS LARGIS OBLIQUE DROIT   PIEDS LARGIS OBLIQUE GAUCHE

CAPRIOL

You have just described six positions and movements to me, which do you consider the most seemly?

ARBEAU

One of those in which the foot rests at an oblique angle would appear to me the most beautiful, because we observe in ancient medals and statues that figures resting upon one foot are more artistic and pleasing. As for feet close together, or toes too positively turned out, these have a feminine appearance. And in the same way that it ill becomes a damsel to assume a masculine bearing so we should avoid feminine poses. This is demonstrated in the *révérence*, because in making it the men cross one foot smartly to the rear of the other and the damsels bend both knees gently and arise in like manner. And while I am on the subject of the *révérence* I wish to tell you that those of salutation, which are made at the beginning, at the end and sometimes in the middle of dances, are not included among these lively movements although there are two kinds of passing *révérence* that are used in certain passages of the galliard.

CAPRIOL

What is the difference between these passing *révérences* and those of salutation?

ARBEAU

In the passing *révérence* the bonnet or hat must not be removed and although it is performed in almost the same way, by bending the leg and drawing the foot behind, it is done in a shorter space of time as you will understand more clearly later. There are two kinds; one, when the left foot supports the body and the right foot is crossed behind, is called *révérence passagière droite*,[50] the other, when the right foot supports the body and the left foot is crossed behind, is called *révérence passagière gauche*.[51]

RÉVÉRENCE PASSAGIÈRE   RÉVÉRENCE PASSAGIÈRE
DROITE   GAUCHE

To proceed with the description of steps and movements, I would say that there is a movement called *pied croisé*,[52] when the weight is thrown on one foot to support the body and at the same time the other foot is raised in the air in front of the shin. This is done in two ways, to wit; when the left foot supports the body and the right foot is raised and crossed in front of the left shin, which is called *pied croisé droit,* and contrariwise when the right foot supports the dancer's body and the left foot is raised and crossed in front of the right shin, which is called *pied croisé gauche.*

PIED CROISÉ DROIT   PIED CROISÉ GAUCHE

CAPRIOL

We have quite an assortment of gestures and movements already.

ARBEAU

You are restless, as I can well understand, to begin to perform the *five steps* but it cannot be helped, you must have patience to listen to how all the movements are executed. Because, you know in the art of grammar the pupil first amasses nouns, verbs and other components of speech and then learns to link them together with congruity. So it is in the art of dancing, you must first learn a variety of separate movements and then by means of the music you will be given, together with the tabular arrangements of movements, you will grasp it all.

CAPRIOL

Once I know the separate movements, may I not combine them to my own fancy?

ARBEAU

You could do so, but you would then have to explain them to good dancers and it is much better to learn the passages already invented and accepted, as there is a certain grace in some not to be found in others.

Continue with the rest of the movements, if you please.

Sometimes, when one foot has taken the body's weight and is placed in position to support it,[a] the toe of the other foot is brought close up against the foot on the ground. This movement is called *marque pied*,[53] to wit, *marque pied droit* when the right toe performs the movement and *marque pied gauche* when the left toe does.

MARQUE PIED DROIT   MARQUE PIED GAUCHE

When, on the other hand, one foot is placed in position to support the dancer's body and the heel of the other foot is brought close against the foot on the ground,[b] this sort of movement is called *marque talon droit*,[54] when the right heel is moved, and *marque talon gauche* when the left heel is used.

MARQUE TALON DROIT   MARQUE TALON GAUCHE

CAPRIOL

As for the name given the movement *marque talon* it seems to me most apposite, but you should then call the preceding movement *marque orteil*[55] instead of *marque pied*.

ARBEAU

You are right, and you can call it so if you wish. But I have changed it because the words *marque orteil* are more grating and difficult to articulate than the words *marque pied*.

CAPRIOL

The Poles, so I have heard said, invariably walk on their toes.

ARBEAU

Their heels are raised and supported by the cork and iron placed in their shoes, which prevents them from running as easily as we do. That is why the Poles give the appearance of being two or three fingers[56] taller than they are. If you watch animals closely you will find that with few exceptions they move on their toes.

To return to the subject of the movements of the galliard, you should also know that there is a certain movement and position of the feet which we call *coup de pied*,[57] or *grève*,[58] when the dancer throws his weight upon one foot to support his body and raises the other into the air in front of him as if he were about to kick someone. This movement is done in two ways, with the right foot when it is called *grève droite* and with the left foot when it is called *grève gauche*.

Sometimes the foot is only raised slightly off the ground and moved little, if at all, forward, and this is called *pied en l'air droit* if the right foot is lifted or *pied en l'air gauche* if it be the left. One picture will serve for both these movements, only you must remember that when you find the words *pied en l'air* in the tabulation the said movement must be performed barely off the ground and gently as a damsel might do it; it is thus the steps and movements are made in dancing the tordion. And when you find the word *grève* in the tabulation the foot must be raised very high and the movement made with vigour.

CAPRIOL

I shall take care to remember this advice and also the reason for it which you gave me above. Because in dancing the tordion one always holds the damsel by the hand and he who dances it boisterously causes needless discomfort and jolting to the said damsel.

ARBEAU

Nowadays, dancers lack these courteous considerations in their lavoltas[59] and other similarly wanton and wayward dances that have been brought into usage. In dancing them the damsels are made to bounce about in such a fashion that more often than not they show their bare knees unless they keep one hand on their skirts to prevent it.

CAPRIOL

This manner of dancing seems neither beautiful nor honourable to me unless one is dancing with some strapping hussy from the servants' hall.

ARBEAU

I shall not overlook to give you the tabulation for dancing it later on. In the meanwhile here are the pictures of the movements *grève* and *pied en l'air*.

<table>
<tr><td align="center">GRÈVE DROITE
OR
PIED EN L'AIR DROIT</td><td align="center">GRÈVE GAUCHE
OR
PIED EN L'AIR GAUCHE</td></tr>
<tr><td align="center"></td><td align="center"></td></tr>
</table>

Sometimes this movement *grève* is performed or results when the dancer transfers his weight from one foot to the other while the foot previously on the ground is raised in the air in front of him.[a] This movement is called *entretaille*[60] and there are two kinds just as there are two kinds of *grève*.

To wit, *entretaille gauche* resulting in *grève droite,* and *entretaille droite* resulting in *grève gauche.*

CAPRIOL

That I quite understand, it is the same movement except it commences with the *entretaille.*

ARBEAU

The opposite movement to the *grève* is made when the dancer throws his weight on one foot to support his body and raises the other foot behind him. This movement is called *ruade,*[61] to wit, *ruade droite* if the right foot is lifted behind and *ruade gauche* if it be the left foot.

RUADE DROITE   RUADE GAUCHE

If the foot is raised to the side, and neither in front as in the *grève* nor behind as in the *ruade,* this movement is called *ru de vache*[62] because cows kick in this way instead of behind as do horses. There are also two kinds, *ru de vache droit* when the left foot is used to support the body and the right foot is raised and *ru de vache gauche* when the weight is thrown upon the right foot to support the body and the left foot is raised.

CAPRIOL

I do not believe this *ru de vache* movement is often used.

ARBEAU

In truth it is seldom put into practice, but I could not omit it as nothing must be overlooked while we are on the subject of the movements and steps of the galliard. And these are not used in the galliard alone but also in other dances of which we shall speak later on.

CAPRIOL

Then it will be so much accomplished when we come to these other dances.

ARBEAU

There will be a few slight modifications.

CAPRIOL

What modifications?

ARBEAU

I will tell you when we come to them. For the present, observe the pictures of the two kinds of *ru de vache* that I have just been speaking about.

RU DE VACHE DROIT   RU DE VACHE GAUCHE

When the dancer springs off both feet and places one in front of the other,[a] each supporting the body equally, this attitude and movement is called *position* or *posture* and usually marks a cadence. It can be done in two ways, when the right foot is in front it is called *posture droite* and when the left foot is in front it is called *posture gauche*. Regarding these *postures* you should be forewarned that they are more graceful if the foot behind touches the ground a moment before the one in front. For when they both come down together it looks as if a sack of grain had been dumped on the ground.[b]

CAPRIOL

I have noticed that in all these above mentioned movements, one foot, or both, are on the ground.

ARBEAU

You are right, and certainly those in which only one foot is on the ground are more animated. But there is a movement called *saut*[63] which takes place when both feet are raised in the air and is livelier still. And you should understand that there are two kinds of *saut*, to wit, *saut majeur*[64] and *petit saut*.[65] As for the *petit saut* it is part and parcel of the movements and is not noted in the tabulation.

CAPRIOL

I do not in the least understand what you mean.

POSTURE DROITE   POSTURE GAUCHE

ARBEAU

Imagine you are in the position *pieds joints*. If the tabulation instructs you to perform a *grève droite*, how would you do so?

CAPRIOL

I should support my body on the left foot and raise the right foot in the air in front of me.

ARBEAU

It would be possible to perform the *grève droite* thus, but it would not be blithe. That is why, instead of leaving the left foot on the ground you must place it there anew; and to do this you are obliged to make a *petit saut* upon the said left foot and at the same moment perform the *grève* with the right foot. In so doing you will see plainly enough that the said leap is, as I have told you, a part of the movement of the *grève*. And in like manner the *petit saut* must be used in all the other steps and movements where one foot is raised in the air. Also, if you recall, I told you how you must spring to place your feet in position. Therefore when I give you the tabulation of the galliard in writing I shall not mention the *petit saut* and will only write down the steps and movements, inasmuch as they are understood to comprise it.

What is the *saut majeur?*

It is a separate movement that precedes the cadence and will be noted in the tabulation of the galliard by a rest which takes the place of one of the six minims of triple time of which the galliard consists, so that the said *saut majeur* is equivalent in duration to any of the other five steps or movements.

Then, to keep the correct beats of time in the five steps, one must execute four movements, followed by a *saut majeur* and the *posture.*

That is true when one makes the cadence which is called *clausula*[a] by musicians, and there are many dancers so agile that while executing the *saut majeur* they move their feet in the air[b] and such capering is called *capriole*[66] as you see in the picture below. But it must be done so dexterously that it does not interfere with the timing of the *posture* which usually follows the *saut majeur* to complete the said cadence.

CAPRIOLE

I shall willingly learn this *capriole* as it bears my name. But what do you mean by cadence?

Cadence is simply a *saut majeur* followed by a posture. You have observed in a musical composition how musicians pause for a moment after the penultimate chord before playing the final chord in order to make an agreeable and harmonious ending; thus, the *saut majeur,* which is almost like a silence of the feet and a pause in movement, enhances the grace of the succeeding *posture* and creates a more pleasing effect. Besides this, you can understand that if the dancer did not make this leap he would be obliged to make six movements to each of the six minims and thus his cadence would always fall on the same side. This is obviated by the said leap which makes the movements and steps uneven and consequently the cadence falls first on one side and then on the other.

What matter if the cadence always fell on the same side?

Are you not well aware that variety delights and that repetition is odious,[a] as the old adage *crambe repetita*[67] testifies? And the lines of Horace so often quoted:

Ridetur chorda qui semper oberrat eadem[68]

Does the cadence always fall on the sixth minim?

This is most frequently the case, although there are some qualifications to be made. But I will speak of these when we come to them. For the present I will tell you that the dancer takes six positions and movements of the feet, one on each of the six notes and disregards the cadence until the twelfth note, keeping the rest on the eleventh note for his leap, and thus the passage becomes one of eleven steps. And if the dancer so desires he can postpone the cadence until the eighteenth note and make the *saut majeur* on the rest which represents the seventeenth note, and thus the passage comprises seventeen steps. The dancer can further postpone the cadence and delay it until the twenty-fourth, thirtieth or thirty-sixth beat, in consequence making passages of twenty-three, twenty-nine and thirty-five steps. But I do not advise you to do so because the onlookers might find it wearisome waiting so long for the cadence and think you were out of your mind. And in truth, the memory might become confused in such long passages.

CAPRIOL

Are these all the steps, positions and movements used in the galliard?

ARBEAU

They are those that I call to mind at the moment. If, in watching good dancers you notice that they are executing others, you may write them down and give them what names you please.

CAPRIOL

Well, here am I holding a damsel by the hand, my bow made, my hat replaced and my bearing seemly. Where should I commence?

ARBEAU

You will perform your steps and movements according to the tabulation, which you will have committed to memory. But I advise you to be modest, that is to say dance close to the ground and execute the *five steps* quietly as if you were dancing the tordion. And furthermore, to circle the room first with your damsel and when you are ready to take your *congé*, letting her dance off alone while you commence dancing your *five steps* higher in the air, continuing thus until you are in front of her. And then execute what passages you please in a lively fashion. For if you leap too nimbly at the outset it would seem that you sought to break a chitterling across your knee,[69] as the saying goes.

CAPRIOL

I have seen many who spend their time preening themselves before beginning to dance.

ARBEAU

I do not approve of this fashion as such persons invite the poet's censure:

Quid dignum feret promissor hiatu[70]

CAPRIOL

First of all give me the tune of a tordion and then a galliard.

ARBEAU

The tune of a tordion and that of a galliard are the same, and there is no difference between them save that the tordion is danced close to the ground to a light, lively beat and the galliard is danced higher off the ground to a slower, stronger beat. But you do well to ask for the music of a tordion because when the melodies are familiar to a dancer and he sings them in his head as the musician plays them he cannot fail to dance well. You will take the following tune,[a] then, as a specimen for all the other tordions, which are countless.[71]

CAPRIOL

I know this tune well, but I do not see the cadences of which you spoke.

ARBEAU

I have marked the position of the cadences by bars or perpendicular lines, which you can reduce yourself, thus:

CAPRIOL

I understand it much better than I did, it only remains now for me to know what movements I should put to it.

Execute a *pied en l'air gauche* to the first minim for the first step.

Then a *pied en l'air droit* on the second minim for the second step.

Then a *pied en l'air gauche* on the third minim for the third step.

Then a *pied en l'air droit* on the fourth minim for the fourth step.

On the rest that replaces a minim execute a *saut moyen*,[72] as it is a tordion that you are dancing, and on the last minim execute a *posture gauche* for the fifth step.

Continuing your tordion, change over and perform everything to the right that you have just performed to the left and to the left that which you did to the right. To wit:

Pied en l'air droit on the first minim for the first step, then *pied en l'air gauche* on the second minim for the second step, then *pied en l'air droit* on the third minim for the third step, then *pied en l'air gauche* on the fourth minim for the fourth step.

On the rest that replaces a minim execute the *saut majeur* that precedes the *posture*, but you will make the leap moderate in view of the fact that you are dancing the tordion and not the galliard. On the final minim execute a *posture droite* for the fifth step.

Thus, as long as the musician continues to play you continue to permute and to make your cadences first on one side and then on the other, coming down alternately in *posture gauche* and *posture droite*. And in order that it may be easier for you to understand all this I will make a tabulation of what I have just said which will show you everything at a glance. Because I shall set down the tune of this tordion again for you, and opposite each note I shall inscribe the corresponding steps and movements. And I intend to do likewise with the tune of a galliard. The said tabulation will serve you for all the other galliards, which are also countless.

When the musician has finished the tordion, should one not make a *révérence* of salutation on taking leave of the damsel?

Yes, and you should quietly return her to the place from whence you led her forth, whilst thanking her for the honour she has done you.

TABULATION OF THE TORDION
TO BE DANCED IMMEDIATELY AFTER THE *RETOUR* OF THE
BASSE DANCE

Movements to be made by the dancer in executing the Tordion which is danced immediately after the basse danse.

a

Melody of the Tordion
arranged in minims [73]

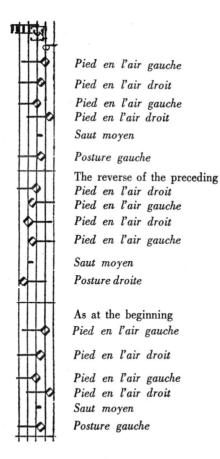

Pied en l'air gauche

Pied en l'air droit

Pied en l'air gauche
Pied en l'air droit

Saut moyen

Posture gauche

The reverse of the preceding
Pied en l'air droit
Pied en l'air gauche

Pied en l'air droit

Pied en l'air gauche

Saut moyen
Posture droite

As at the beginning
Pied en l'air gauche

Pied en l'air droit

Pied en l'air gauche
Pied en l'air droit
Saut moyen
Posture gauche

Melody of Tordion   Movements of Tordion
                                   Reverse

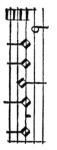

Pied en l'air droit
Pied en l'air gauche
Pied en l'air droit
Pied en l'air gauche
Saut moyen
Posture droite

The movements *marque pied* and *marque talon* are made quite quietly and you could use them instead of *pieds en l'air*, thus:

Melody of Tordion   Movements for the *five steps* of the Tordion

Marque pied gauche
Marque talon gauche

Marque pied droit
Marque talon droit

Saut moyen
Posture gauche

Marque pied droit
Marque talon droit
Marque pied gauche

Marque talon gauche
Saut moyen
Posture droite

CAPRIOL

I find the arrangement of the cadences troublesome. Would it not be as well to divide the tune up by perpendicular lines, each section comprising two bars of triple time, and allowing a step, a *saut majeur* and a *posture* to the last bar?

ARBEAU

It all comes to the same and I only suggested the said arrangement to explain your *five steps* more clearly to you. I shall therefore not use it again and will leave the galliard in its normal form without omitting anything. But remember to employ the steps according to the time indicated in the staff margin, and note that the cadence will fall as it does in the examples below, the third of which is reduced.

CAPRIOL

Cannot the second bar of triple time, which you call the cadence, be comprised of music other than one of the three examples given above?

ARBEAU

It may be of several other sorts, as the composer pleases and the melody of the galliard dictates. But inevitably the cadence must be made in the second bar or be delayed until the fourth bar, which we call a passage of eleven steps, or until the sixth, which we call a passage of seventeen steps.

CAPRIOL

It is time that you gave me the tabulation of the steps of the galliard.

ARBEAU

So many galliards have been composed that I do not know which one to choose for you to begin on. When I started learning to dance at Poitiers, our master played one that he called 'Because of the Traitor I Die', which was held to be among the loveliest melodies of them all. I will set it down for you in music here.

MELODY OF THE GALLIARD CALLED 'BECAUSE OF THE TRAITOR I DIE '[74]

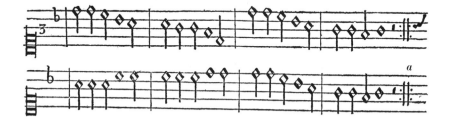

CAPRIOL

I deem that melody marvellously pleasing. When we gave our aubades[75] at Orleans we always played a galliard called 'Romanesque'[b] on our lutes[c] and cithers[76] but I found it hackneyed and trite. I learned one on the lute which I enjoyed seeing danced by my companions as I knew how to play and sing it. And it also seemed to me that the steps were well accented by those who danced it. It was called 'Antoinette'. Here is the music:

MELODY OF THE GALLIARD CALLED 'ANTOINETTE'

ARBEAU

Verily, that is a light hearted melody and as you have it at hand we shall take it to perform the first step and make it the basis of the tabulated steps and movements of the galliard.

CAPRIOL

Since all the galliard tunes are related it is the same to me whether you begin with galliard 'Antoinette' or with any other that may please you.

ARBEAU

I shall commence my tabulation with your galliard, then I will give you others as I chance to call them to memory.

TABULATION OF THE *FIVE STEPS* OF THE GALLIARD, WHEREIN THE MOVEMENTS ARE LIKE THOSE OF THE *TORDION* EXCEPT THAT THEY ARE PERFORMED HIGHER AND MORE VIGOROUSLY, AND INSTEAD OF *PIEDS EN L'AIR* THE DANCER PERFORMS *COUP DE PIEDS* OR *GRÈVES*

Melody of the Galliard 'Antoinette'

Movements to be made by the dancer in dancing the galliard

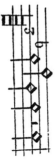

Grève gauche
Grève droite
Grève gauche

Grève droite
Saut majeur
Posture gauche

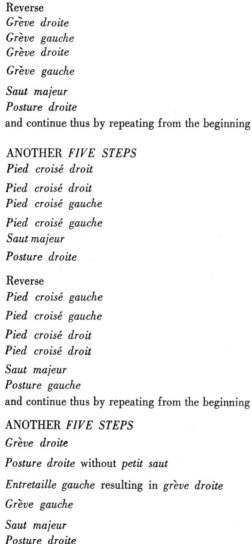

Reverse
Grève droite
Grève gauche
Grève droite

Grève gauche

Saut majeur
Posture droite
and continue thus by repeating from the beginning

ANOTHER *FIVE STEPS*
Pied croisé droit

Pied croisé droit
Pied croisé gauche

Pied croisé gauche
Saut majeur

Posture droite

Reverse
Pied croisé gauche

Pied croisé gauche

Pied croisé droit
Pied croisé droit

Saut majeur

Posture gauche
and continue thus by repeating from the beginning

ANOTHER *FIVE STEPS*
Grève droite

Posture droite without *petit saut*

Entretaille gauche resulting in *grève droite*

Grève gauche

Saut majeur
Posture droite

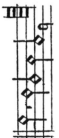

Reverse

Grève gauche

Posture gauche without *petit saut*

Entretaille droite resulting in *grève gauche*
Grève droite
Saut majeur
Posture gauche
and continue by repeating from the beginning.

CAPRIOL

Why have you placed a *posture droite* without *petit saut* on the second minim for the second step?

ARBEAU

One must surmise that dancers have found that the introduction of a few pleasing variations lends grace; and, further still, instead of placing the soles of both feet on the ground for the said *posture* they support themselves on the heel of the foot in front and keep the knee rigid, not bent, believing this to be more graceful.

Melody of the galliard called 'Love Let us Kiss'[77]

Movements to be made by the dancer in dancing this galliard

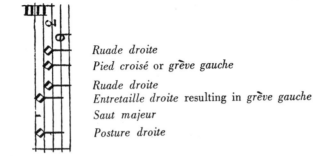

Ruade droite
Pied croisé or *grève gauche*

Ruade droite
Entretaille droite resulting in *grève gauche*
Saut majeur
Posture droite

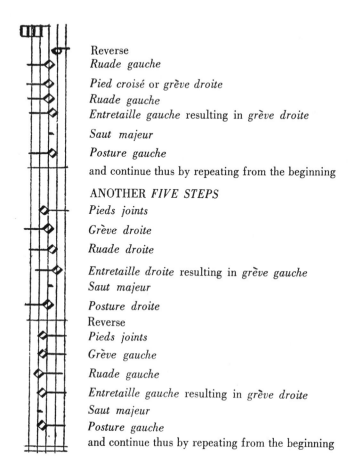

Reverse
Ruade gauche

Pied croisé or *grève droite*
Ruade gauche
Entretaille gauche resulting in *grève droite*

Saut majeur

Posture gauche

and continue thus by repeating from the beginning

ANOTHER *FIVE STEPS*

Pieds joints

Grève droite

Ruade droite

Entretaille droite resulting in *grève gauche*
Saut majeur

Posture droite
Reverse
Pieds joints

Grève gauche

Ruade gauche

Entretaille gauche resulting in *grève droite*
Saut majeur
Posture gauche
and continue thus by repeating from the beginning

You can substitute *postures* for the *pieds joints* in the above *five steps*, and, furthermore, make the said *postures* sideways as if they were *pieds largis*, instead of forward.

CAPRIOL

You tell me to continue by repeating from the beginning but in so doing one would execute only one sequence of *five steps* in each galliard.

ARBEAU

This is left to the dancer's choice as if he wishes he may proceed to a new variety of *five steps* instead of repeating from the beginning, and in this he cannot err provided always that he has completed the reverse of his first *five steps*. And if the dancer finds himself pressed for room and in a place where he cannot advance in a direct line, he can dance the said *five steps* in a circle and by turning around seek to regain his position in front of the damsel.

CAPRIOL

Must I always dance my *five steps* in a straight line when there is enough room?

ARBEAU

When I speak of moving straight ahead I only mean not to turn the body completely, because you will dance more gracefully by inclining first your right side then your left side towards the damsel as though you were fencing, the *grève droite* displaying the right side and the *grève gauche* the left.[a]

CAPRIOL

I am of the opinion that by combining the different movements you have shown me I could compose many *five steps* to my own fancy.

ARBEAU

Certainly you could. But you must take note that there are some sequences of *five steps*, so called because they occupy the same musical time as the true *five steps*, yet which contain either more or less than five movements. And this is brought about by extending or shortening the beats. For, as there are two bars of triple time to a phrase and the said two bars contain six minims each, one of which is replaced by a rest leaving four with the *posture*, it clearly follows that if each of the first four notes are divided in two there will be eight crotchets instead of four minims. And in adapting a movement to each note there will be eight steps (before the *posture*) instead of four, and all told, the posture included, nine steps.

Melody of the galliard[b] called 'Whether I Love or No'[78]   *Five steps* in two movements, which can be made by the dancer in executing the galliard

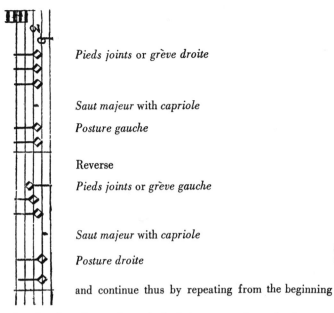

Pieds joints or *grève droite*

Saut majeur with *capriole*

Posture gauche

Reverse

Pieds joints or *grève gauche*

Saut majeur with *capriole*

Posture droite

and continue thus by repeating from the beginning

Observe that in the above the *pieds joints* or *grève droite* occupies the same time as the three minim beats and the *saut majeur* with the *posture* occupies the remainder of the time. To bring this about the fourth minim is replaced by a rest and the *saut majeur* anticipated by making it fall upon the fourth instead of the fifth note.

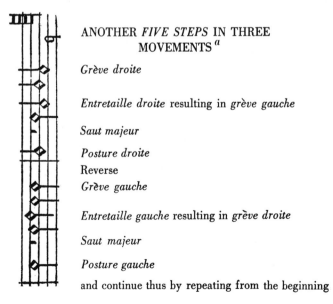

ANOTHER *FIVE STEPS* IN THREE
MOVEMENTS [a]

Grève droite

Entretaille droite resulting in *grève gauche*

Saut majeur

Posture droite
Reverse
Grève gauche

Entretaille gauche resulting in *grève droite*

Saut majeur

Posture gauche

and continue thus by repeating from the beginning

Observe from the above that the *grève* occupies two minim beats and the *entretaille*, resulting in a *grève*, occupies two more minim beats. The *saut majeur* occupies the rest equivalent to a minim and the *posture* the time of another minim. And thus, all these *five steps* are reduced to three steps, equivalent in time to five.

ANOTHER ABRIDGED *FIVE STEPS*

Révérence gauche

Pied croisé gauche

Saut majeur
Posture droite

Reverse
Révérence droite

Pied croisé droit

Saut majeur
Posture gauche
and continue thus by repeating from the beginning

ANOTHER ABRIDGED *FIVE STEPS*
Pied croisé droit

Entretaille droite resulting in *grève gauche*

Saut majeur
Posture droite

Reverse
Pied croisé gauche

Entretaille gauche resulting in *grève droite*

Saut majeur
Posture gauche
and continue thus by repeating from the beginning

CAPRIOL

You should give me an example of a cadence containing more than five steps and movements.

ARBEAU

There are an infinity of varieties, which you will obtain and learn from those of your own generation. For the present, take the following seven steps, which are equivalent and reduced to the two bars of triple time employed for all *five steps*. Because, as you see in the notation, the first and third minims, which should only require one step apiece, are allotted two and replaced by two crotchets in the tabulation. And you will notice that the two crotchets and one minim, to which the dancer executes two *pieds en l'air* and one *greve* without *petit saut*, are called a *fleuret*, so that two *fleurets*, a *saut majeur* and a *posture* comprise *five steps*.

Melody of   Movements which can be made by the dancer in
the galliard[a]   this galliard

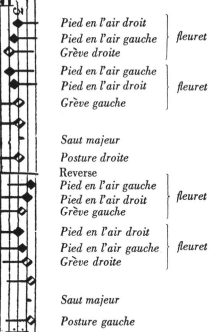

Pied en l'air droit
Pied en l'air gauche } *fleuret*
Grève droite

Pied en l'air gauche
Pied en l'air droit } *fleuret*
Grève gauche

Saut majeur

Posture droite
Reverse
Pied en l'air gauche
Pied en l'air droit } *fleuret*
Grève gauche

Pied en l'air droit
Pied en l'air gauche } *fleuret*
Grève droite

Saut majeur

Posture gauche
and continue by repeating from
the beginning

I recently attended a wedding where I saw a young man execute *five steps* that seemed to me very graceful. He danced them thus:—

Melody of the galliard called 'Weariness'[79]

Another sequence of movements to be made by the dancer in performing this galliard

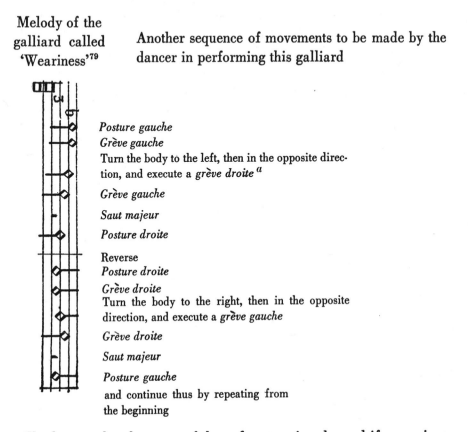

Posture gauche
Grève gauche
Turn the body to the left, then in the opposite direction, and execute a *grève droite* [a]

Grève gauche

Saut majeur

Posture droite

Reverse
Posture droite
Grève droite
Turn the body to the right, then in the opposite direction, and execute a *grève gauche*

Grève droite

Saut majeur

Posture gauche
and continue thus by repeating from the beginning

You will take note that the grace of these *five steps* is enhanced if you mince them.[b]

CAPRIOL

What do you mean by mincing steps?

ARBEAU

You will be making mincing steps when you replace the five minims by ten crotchets, and, instead of taking a step with its *petit saut* all at once, you divide it into two parts by anticipating slightly the *petit saut*, thus making it fall on the first crotchet and taking the step immediately afterwards on the second crotchet. In point of fact, these mincing steps only equal five normal steps but they are lighter and more graceful, as instead of one's whole weight coming to the ground at once it falls gradually.

CAPRIOL

If the music should happen to contain only minims could one introduce *fleurets?*

ARBEAU

Yes, certainly, because by imagining the last minim to be divided into two crotchets you would make the first two steps into three and by doing likewise with the third minim add yet another step.^a Hence your phrase would contain seven steps and movements as if the music were written thus. In this way you can make what divisions you please and increase or decrease the number of steps to the music as you see fit.

CAPRIOL

The *saut majeur* and the *posture* occupy the time of two minims. By substituting two crotchets for the rest, I could then make another *fleuret* and thus the two bars of triple time would be covered by three *fleurets.*

ARBEAU

You are right, but there would be no cadence and you would have to make it on the fourth bar, which is what is called making a passage because you would pass over a cadence intending to introduce it later on. And suppose that in the two following bars you made two *fleurets* and one *posture* your whole passage would contain sixteen steps. To wit; nine steps for the first three *fleurets* and seven steps for the two *fleurets, saut majeur* and *posture* of the cadence, making sixteen in all. And if you again wished to pass over and postpone your cadence until the sixth bar of triple time your passage would contain twenty-five steps and movements.

CAPRIOL

You have already told me that the first passage, after the *five steps*, consists of eleven steps finishing in the fourth bar, and of seventeen finishing in the sixth bar, and twenty-three in the eighth bar. Thus you count six steps for the two bars where the cadence is passed over and five steps for the two bars where the cadence is made.

ARBEAU

I did tell you so and that applies when one step is danced to each minim. But the number of steps is altered when we divide a minim into two crotchets and wish a step to correspond to each crotchet. Also, when the passages are less than eleven, seventeen or twenty-three steps, and when we make use of two or three minims to a single step. You will remember what I told you about a dancer's action only attaining beauty when the movements of his feet are in perfect time with the beats of the music. This you can test in the melody of the galliard called 'The Girl from Milan' which you see below. It consists of a passage of eleven steps extended to fifteen by five *fleurets,* followed by *five steps* abridged to three.

CAPRIOL

Can one perform *fleurets* in dancing the galliard even when the music is without a minim divided into two crotchets?

ARBEAU

Easily, by imagining the said division even though it is not written thus. And generally speaking either in writing or your mind's eye you can arrange your bars with whole or divided notes as you wish.

CAPRIOL

I am eager for this tune, 'The Girl from Milan', and the tabulation of steps and movements to be adapted to it.

ARBEAU

Melody of the galliard called 'The Girl from Milan'[80]	Movements to be made by the dancer in executing the galliard [a]

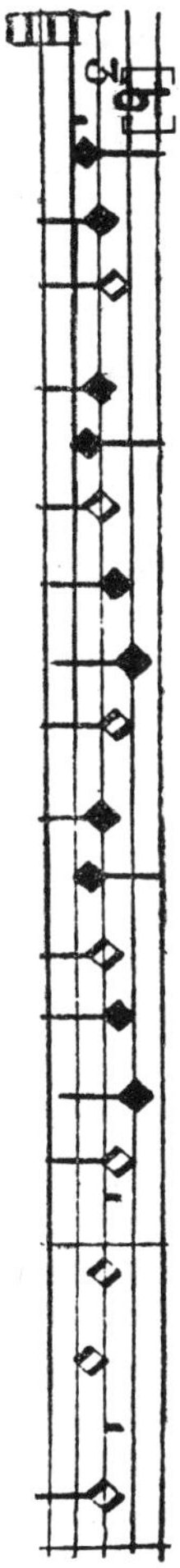

Pied en l'air droit without *petit saut*
Pied en l'air gauche without *petit saut*   } *fleuret*
Grève droite

Pied en l'air gauche without *petit saut*
Pied en l'air droit without *petit saut*   } *fleuret*
Grève gauche

Pied en l'air droit without *petit saut*
Pied en l'air gauche without *petit saut*   } *fleuret*
Grève droite

Pied en l'air gauche without *petit saut*
Pied en l'air droit without *petit saut*   } *fleuret*
Grève gauche

Pied en l'air droit without *petit saut*
Pied en l'air gauche without *petit saut*   } *fleuret*
Grève droite

Pied croisé droit without *petit saut*

Révérence passagière droite, or *entretaille droite* resulting in a *grève gauche*
Saut majeur

Posture droite

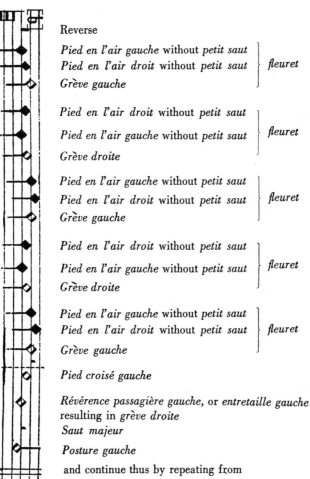

Reverse

Pied en l'air gauche without *petit saut* ⎫
Pied en l'air droit without *petit saut* ⎬ *fleuret*
Grève gauche ⎭

Pied en l'air droit without *petit saut* ⎫
Pied en l'air gauche without *petit saut* ⎬ *fleuret*
Grève droite ⎭

Pied en l'air gauche without *petit saut* ⎫
Pied en l'air droit without *petit saut* ⎬ *fleuret*
Grève gauche ⎭

Pied en l'air droit without *petit saut* ⎫
Pied en l'air gauche without *petit saut* ⎬ *fleuret*
Grève droite ⎭

Pied en l'air gauche without *petit saut* ⎫
Pied en l'air droit without *petit saut* ⎬ *fleuret*
Grève gauche ⎭

Pied croisé gauche

Révérence passagière gauche, or *entretaille gauche*
resulting in *grève droite*
Saut majeur

Posture gauche

and continue thus by repeating from
the beginning

CAPRIOL

Let us pass on from this and give me the tabulation of a passage of eleven steps.

ARBEAU

Passages of eleven steps can be formed by linking together two phrases of *five steps* or such equivalent to them as you choose. Provided that for the *saut majeur* which falls upon the rest in the first phrase you substitute another movement, or else convert the said rest and the *posture* into a *fleuret*, or two steps, to break up this first cadence. And if you do not wish to take this trouble the following tabulation will help you until such time as you have picked up others from good dancers, for practice will teach you more than precept. And you will notice that these passages of eleven steps or more are, by their nature, appropriate to the conclusion of galliards and are more graceful when made while turning the body.*

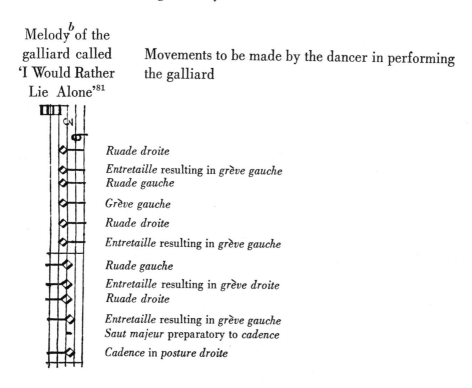

Melody*b* of the galliard called 'I Would Rather Lie Alone'[81]

Movements to be made by the dancer in performing the galliard

Ruade droite

Entretaille resulting in *grève gauche*
Ruade gauche

Grève gauche

Ruade droite

Entretaille resulting in *grève gauche*

Ruade gauche

Entretaille resulting in *grève droite*
Ruade droite

Entretaille resulting in *grève gauche*
Saut majeur preparatory to *cadence*

Cadence in *posture droite*

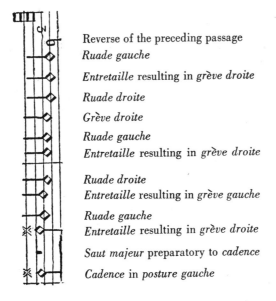

Reverse of the preceding passage
Ruade gauche

Entretaille resulting in *grève droite*

Ruade droite

Grève droite

Ruade gauche
Entretaille resulting in *grève droite*

Ruade droite
Entretaille resulting in *grève gauche*

Ruade gauche
Entretaille resulting in *grève droite*

Saut majeur preparatory to *cadence*

Cadence in *posture gauche*

You must turn the body twice in the course of the eleven steps, and as many times in dancing the reverse, as a single turn of the body will not suffice.

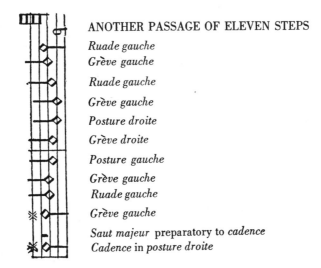

ANOTHER PASSAGE OF ELEVEN STEPS
Ruade gauche
Grève gauche

Ruade gauche

Grève gauche

Posture droite

Grève droite

Posture gauche

Grève gauche
Ruade gauche

Grève gauche

Saut majeur preparatory to *cadence*
Cadence in *posture droite*

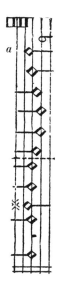

Reverse of the preceding passage

Ruade droite

Grève droite

Ruade droite

Grève droite

Posture gauche
Grève gauche
Posture droite

Grève droite

Ruade droite
Grève droite

Saut majeur preparatory to *cadence*

Cadence in *posture gauche*

Melody of the galliard [b] called 'The Grief That Tortures Me'[82]

Movements to be made by the dancer in executing this galliard

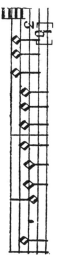

ANOTHER PASSAGE OF ELEVEN STEPS

Grève droite
Grève droite

Ruade gauche

Grève gauche
Posture droite

Grève droite

Posture gauche

Grève gauche

Ruade gauche

Grève gauche

Saut majeur preparatory to *cadence*
Cadence in *posture droite*

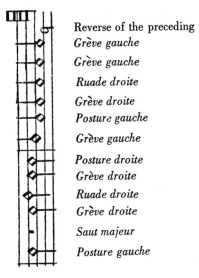

Reverse of the preceding
Grève gauche

Grève gauche

Ruade droite

Grève droite
Posture gauche

Grève gauche

Posture droite
Grève droite

Ruade droite
Grève droite

Saut majeur

Posture gauche

CAPRIOL

God be thanked, I now have enough grounding to practice the galliard. Just the same, I beg you to give me a couple more passages if it does not weary you.

ARBEAU

ANOTHER PASSAGE OF ELEVEN STEPS

Ruade droite
Entretaille resulting in *grève gauche*

Ruade droite
Entretaille resulting in *grève gauche*
Posture droite

Grève droite

Posture gauche

Grève gauche
Ruade gauche

Grève gauche

Saut majeur

Posture droite

Reverse of the preceding passage
Ruade gauche

Entretaille resulting in *grève droite*

Ruade gauche
Entretaille resulting in *grève droite*

Posture gauche
Grève gauche

Posture droite

Grève droite
Ruade droite
Grève droite

Saut majeur
Posture gauche

ANOTHER PASSAGE OF ELEVEN STEPS WHERE THE SIXTH STEP IS DIVIDED INTO TWO AND THE SEVENTH ALSO, MAKING THIRTEEN STEPS INSTEAD OF ELEVEN [a]

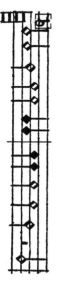

Pieds joints
Grève droite

Entretaille resulting in *grève gauche*

Entretaille resulting in *grève droite*
Posture droite

Grève gauche
Posture droite

Grève droite
Posture gauche
Grève droite

Grève droite

Grève droite

Saut majeur
Posture gauche

Another passage of eleven steps

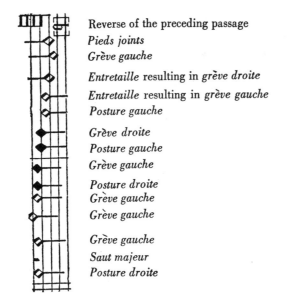

Reverse of the preceding passage
Pieds joints
Grève gauche

Entretaille resulting in *grève droite*
Entretaille resulting in *grève gauche*
Posture gauche

Grève droite
Posture gauche
Grève gauche

Posture droite
Grève gauche
Grève gauche

Grève gauche
Saut majeur
Posture droite

To make passages of seventeen steps you must link together three phrases of five steps and pass over the first two cadences. Or else, link a passage of eleven steps with a phrase of five steps and omit the cadences until you come to the last one. To make passages of twenty-three steps you must link together four phrases of five steps or two passages of eleven steps and disregard all the cadences except the last one. And so on in the same manner.

CAPRIOL

That is quite easy, witness whether I perform this first passage of eleven steps properly.

ARBEAU

You have executed your steps and movements nicely and kept the rhythm well, but when you dance in company never look down at your feet to see whether you are performing the steps correctly. Keep your head and body erect and appear self-possessed. Spit and blow your nose sparingly, or if needs must turn your head away and use a fair white handkerchief. Converse affably in a low, modest voice, your hands at your sides, neither hanging limp nor moving nervously. Be suitably and neatly dressed, your hose well secured and your shoes clean; and remember this advice not only when you are dancing the galliard but in performing all other kinds of dance as well.

We have discussed the galliard enough and I shall leave the subject, except to point out that you will now perceive it is easy to divide the *double* of a pavan by extending it with what movements you choose. These will be calculated by six minims, a rest for the *saut majeur* and a *posture*. Or else, by extensions or abridgements of these combined containing the same number of beats required to perform the *double* that you wish to divide. There are some persons so nimble in the air that they have invented numerous leaps, sometimes doubling or tripling them as a substitute for the *five* or eleven *steps*, and upon completing these leaps they have finished so neatly on the cadence as to gain the reputation of being very fine dancers. But it has often come to pass that in performing these feats of agility they have fallen down, when laughter and jeers have ensued. Wherefore the prudent have always advised against such leaps, unless they are performed so easily that no ill consequence could befall the dancer.

CAPRIOL

That is now quite clear to me. Besides I should be happy not to overlook the lavolta since it is coming into current usage.

LAVOLTA

ARBEAU

The lavolta[83] is a kind of galliard familiar to the people of Provence, which, like the tordion, is danced in triple time. The movements and steps of this dance are made while turning the body and consist of two steps, a rest for the *saut majeur*, a *pieds joints* and finally two rests or pauses. To understand the above place yourself, hypothetically, facing me with *pieds joints*. For the first step, make a rather short *pied en l'air* while springing on your left foot and at the same time turning your left shoulder towards me. Then take a rather long second step with your right foot, without springing, and in so doing, turn your back to me. Then make the *saut majeur*, while turning your body, and alight *pieds joints* with your right shoulder towards me. Thus the first turn is accomplished.

By your account one does not turn the body around completely.

If you were to turn the body completely you would find yourself back where you had started. After this first turn, which is a three quarter one, you will make the second turn by a *pied en l'air*, rather short as before, while springing on your left foot, and in so doing turn facing me. Then you will take a rather long second step with your right foot, without springing, and at the same time turn your left shoulder towards me. Then you will make the *saut majeur*, while turning your body, and alight *pieds joints* with your back towards me.

For the third turn and cadence you will make a rather short *pied en l'air* for the first step while springing on your left foot and turning your right side towards me. Then take a rather long step on the right foot, without springing, and in so doing face me. Then you will make the *saut majeur*, while turning your body, and alight *pieds joints* with your left shoulder towards me.

For the fourth turn and cadence you will execute a rather short *pied en l'air* for the first step, springing on your left foot and in so doing turn your back to me. Then you will make the second step, rather long, on your right foot, without springing, at the same time turning the right shoulder towards me. Then you will make the *saut majeur*, while turning your body, and alight *pieds joints* facing me as you were at the beginning. And, to conclude, you see that in four phrases you can return to the same place and position in which you were when you commenced. However, this is not an inflexible rule because it may happen that you will turn either more rapidly or more slowly. But I have invented this hypothetical case to make it clearer to you.

If I held the damsel by the hand it would be impossible for her to turn with me inasmuch as she is further from the centre.

Your point is a good one, presuming, as is in fact true, that the damsel makes the same steps and movements as you. For this reason, he who dances the lavolta must regard himself as the centre of a circle and draw the damsel as near to him as possible when he wishes to turn because by this means the said damsel will find the steps shorter and easier to perform. To bring her nearer to you proceed as follows:

Make your *révérence* (holding the damsel by the hand) and before you begin turning take a few steps around the room, by way of preparation, as if you were dancing the tordion. Here you should note that some dance this first part by making *five steps* to the right and then *five steps* to the left alternately, or else by *five steps* abridged to two steps, a *saut majeur* and a *posture,* and the same for the reverse and so on. Others dance the beginning, like the rest of the lavolta, by a *pied en l'air,* a *saut majeur* and the position *pieds joints* as has been explained above.

CAPRIOL

Which way commends itself to you?

ARBEAU

The latter, because by this means the lavolta remains uniform in all its parts, the same at the outset as at the end. When you wish to turn release the damsel's left hand and throw your left arm around her, grasping and holding her firmly by the waist above the right hip with your left hand. At the same moment place your right hand below her busk to help her to leap when you push her forward with your left thigh." She, for her part, will place her right hand on your back or collar and her left hand on her thigh to hold her petti-coat and dress in place, lest the swirling air should catch them and reveal her chemise or bare thigh. This done, you will perform the turns of the lavolta together as described above. And after having spun round for as many cadences as you wish return the damsel to her place, when, however brave a face she shows, she will feel her brain reeling and her head full of dizzy whirlings; and you yourself will perhaps be no better off. I leave it to you to judge whether it is a becoming thing for a young girl to take long strides and separations of the legs, and whether in this lavolta both honour and health are not involved and at stake. I have already given you my opinion.

CAPRIOL

The dizziness and whirling head would annoy me.

ARBEAU

Then dance some other kind of dance. Of if you dance this first to the left, begin anew to the right and thus unwind in the second stage what you have wound up in the first.

Melody of the Lavolta	Movements to be made by the dancers in performing the lavolta[a]

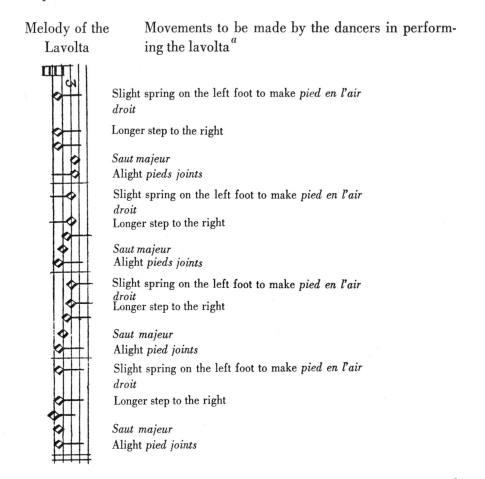

Slight spring on the left foot to make *pied en l'air droit*

Longer step to the right

Saut majeur
Alight *pieds joints*

Slight spring on the left foot to make *pied en l'air droit*
Longer step to the right

Saut majeur
Alight *pieds joints*

Slight spring on the left foot to make *pied en l'air droit*
Longer step to the right

Saut majeur
Alight *pied joints*

Slight spring on the left foot to make *pied en l'air droit*
Longer step to the right

Saut majeur
Alight *pied joints*

You will continue to turn by cadences to the left as long as it pleases you.[b] And if another time you wish to dance the lavolta to the right, you must place your right hand on the damsel's back and the left below her bust, and, by pushing her with your right thigh under her buttocks, turn her in the opposite direction to that shown in the above tabulation. And take heed that dexterity is required to seize and press the damsel close to you as this must be accomplished in two bars of triple time. On the first bar you step before her, at the end of the second bar you should have one hand placed on her hip and the other below her bust, in readiness, by the third bar, to resume turning according to the steps contained in the tabulation.

CAPRIOL

How should one dance the coranto,[84] is it very unlike the lavolta?

THE CORANTO

ARBEAU

It differs greatly from the lavolta and is danced in a light duple time. It consists of two *simples* and a *double* to the left and the same to the right, either moving forwards, to the side, or sometimes backwards, as it pleases the dancer. And you will take note that the steps of the coranto must be executed with a spring which is not the case in the pavan or the basse dance. Therefore, to perform a *simple à gauche* in the coranto, you, with seemly bearing, will spring off the right foot and alight on the left foot for your first step, then you will spring off the right foot again and alight *pieds joints* for the second step and thus the *simple à gauche* will be accomplished. Do the same in reverse for the *simple à droite*. For the *double à gauche* you will spring off the right foot and alight on the left foot for the first step of the said *double à gauche*, then spring off the left foot making the second step with your right foot, then spring off the right foot making the third step with the left foot. Then you will spring off the right foot and alight *pieds joints* for the fourth step. And, thus, the *double à gauche* will be accomplished. Do the same in the reverse manner for the two *simples* and the *double à droite*.

In my youth there was a kind of game or mime arranged to the coranto. Three young men would choose three young girls, and, having ranged themselves in a row, the first dancer would lead his damsel to the other end of the room and then return alone to his companions. The second dancer would do the same, then the third, so that the three girls were left segregated at one end of the room and the three young men at the other. And when the third dancer had returned, the first one, playing the fool and making amorous grimaces and gestures while pulling up his hose and adjusting his shirt, went off to claim his damsel who refused his suit and turned her back upon him, until, seeing the young man was returning to his place, she feigned despair. The other two did the same. Finally they all three advanced together, each to claim his own damsel and to implore her favour upon bended knee with clasped hands. Whereupon the damsels fell into their arms and they all danced the coranto helter-skelter.

CAPRIOL

Do they no longer dance the coranto in this fashion?

ARBEAU

As for the steps, they are bound to be the same. But young men who have never been taught what a *simple* is, nor yet a *double,* dance it according to their caprice and are satisfied as long as they alight on the cadence. They turn the body in dancing, releasing the damsel's hand, and, the turn made, still dancing they again take the damsel by the hand and resume. And when a dancer's companions perceive that he is weary they go and steal his damsel and dance with her themselves. Or else they provide him with a fresh partner if they see the first one is fatigued. Here is a tabulation of the coranto.

Melody of
the   Movements to be made in dancing the Coranto
Coranto

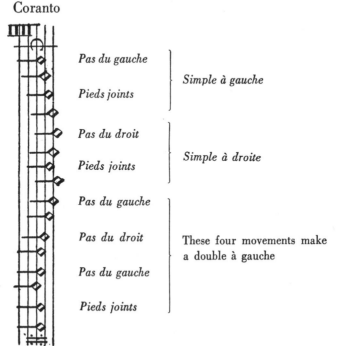

Pas du gauche

Pieds joints   } Simple à gauche

Pas du droit

Pieds joints   } Simple à droite

Pas du gauche

Pas du droit   These four movements make
                    a double à gauche
Pas du gauche

Pieds joints

You will do the same for the reverse and continue by repeating the beginning. None of the minims in the above tabulations are omitted and upon the alternate beats you will make the little springs which accompany the movements. Or, when you are tired and disinclined to spring, you may use them as if they were rests.

CAPRIOL

What is the dance known as the Alman?[85]

THE ALMAN

ARBEAU

The Alman is a simple,rather sedate dance, familiar to the Germans, and, I believe, one of our oldest since we are descended from them. You can dance it in company, because when you have joined hands with a damsel several others may fall into line behind you, each with his partner. And you will all dance together in duple time, moving forwards, or if you wish backwards, three steps and one *grève*, or *pied en l'air* without *saut;* and in certain parts by one step and one *grève* or *pied en l'air*. When you have reached the end of the hall you can dance while turning around without letting go of your damsel, and the dancers who follow you will do the same. When the musicians finish this first part each dancer stops and engages in light converse with his damsel and then you will begin all over again for the second part. When you come to the third part you will dance it to a quicker, more lively duple time with the same steps but introducing little springs as in the coranto. You will grasp this easily by the tabulation which is scarcely necessary in view of the fact that there are no variations in the movements. However, in order that the whole may be quite clear, I shall not spare myself the pains of giving it to you in writing.

Melody of the first and second parts of the Alman.[a]

Movements to be made in dancing the Alman

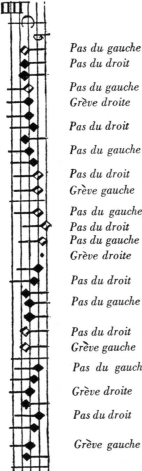

Pas du gauche
Pas du droit

Pas du gauche
Grève droite

Pas du droit

Pas du gauche

Pas du droit
Grève gauche

Pas du gauche
Pas du droit
Pas du gauche
Grève droite

Pas du droit

Pas du gauche

Pas du droit
Grève gauche

Pas du gauche

Grève droite

Pas du droit

Grève gauche

Note that in the last two bars there is only one step and one *grève* in each, because the melody requires this.

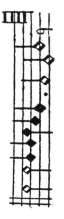

Pas du gauche
Pas du droit

Pas du gauche
Grève droite

Pas du droit

Pas du gauche

Pas du droit
Grève gauche

Tabulation of the third part of the Alman, which is danced in duple time, like the coranto, with *petits sauts* between each step [a]

Pas du gauche

Pas du droit

Pas du gauche

Grève droite
Reverse
Pas du droit

Pas du gauche

Pas du droit

Grève gauche

and continue thus by repeating from the beginning

The minims omitted here are replaced by rests and pauses, or the little springs, that, as has been said, are used in the coranto. In dancing the Alman the young men sometimes steal the damsels from their partners and he who has been robbed seeks to obtain another damsel. But I do not hold with this behaviour because it may lead to quarrels and heart burning.

CAPRIOL

I have noticed that in good society they usually begin the dancing with a *branle*.[86] Tell me how these should be danced.

THE DOUBLE BRANLE

ARBEAU

Since you already know how to dance the pavan and the basse dance it will be easy for you to dance branles in the same duple time, and you should understand that the branle is danced by moving sideways and not forward. To begin with, in what is called the double branle[87] you will perform one *double* to the left and then one *double* to the right; you are well aware that a *double* consists of three steps and a *pieds joints*. To perform these sideways, you will assume a proper bearing after the *révérence* of salutation, and, while keeping the right foot firmly in position, throw your left foot out to the side which will make a *pieds largis* for the first bar. Then for the second bar, keep the left foot firmly in position, bringing the right foot near to the left which will make a *pieds largis* that is almost a *pieds joints*. For the third bar, keep the right foot firm and throw the left foot out to the side which will make a *pieds largis*, and for the fourth bar keep the left foot firm and bring the right foot close to it which will make a *pieds joints*. These four steps, made in four bars or tabor rhythms, we shall call a *double à gauche*, and you will do the same in the opposite direction for a *double à droite*. Namely, while keeping the left foot firmly in position you will throw the right foot out to the side, which will make a *pieds largis* for the fifth bar. Then for the sixth bar keep the right foot firm and bring the left foot near to the right, which will make a *pieds largis* that is almost a *pieds joints*. For the seventh bar, while keeping the left foot fast, you will throw the right foot out to the side, which will make a *pieds largis*. Finally, for the eighth bar, you will keep the right foot fast and bring the left foot close to it, which will make a *pieds joints*, and these last four steps we call *double à droite*. And thus, in these eight steps and bars the double branle will be accomplished as you will see in the tabulation, and you will repeat from the beginning making a *double à gauche* and then a *double à droite*.

CAPRIOL

I hear Master Guillaume with his violin down in your little room. Give me the tabulation for a double branle and I will practise it to see if I perform it aright.

ARBEAU

This is most timely, let us go down and make him play his violin. All musicians are in the habit of opening the dancing at a festival by a double branle which they call the common branle, and afterwards they play the single branle and the gay branle and at the end the branles of Burgundy, which some people call branles of Champagne. The order of these four varieties of branle is determined by the three different groups taking part in a dance; the elderly who dance the double and the single branle sedately, the young married folk who dance the gay branle and the youngest of all, like yourself, who nimbly trip the branles of Burgundy. And every dancer acquits himself to the best of his ability, each according to his years and his degree of skill.

TABULATION FOR DANCING DOUBLE BRANLES

Melody of a
double branle

Movements for dancing
the double branle

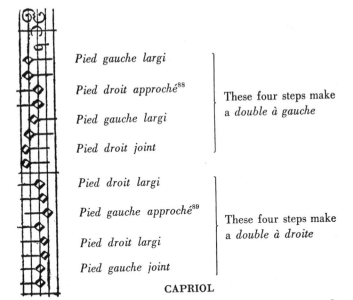

Pied gauche largi	
Pied droit approché[88]	These four steps make
Pied gauche largi	a *double à gauche*
Pied droit joint	
Pied droit largi	
Pied gauche approché[89]	These four steps make
Pied droit largi	a *double à droite*
Pied gauche joint	

CAPRIOL

This double branle is very easy to dance, but it seems to me that the dancers never move from one place, inasmuch as they make four steps to the left which they cancel by another four steps to the right.

ARBEAU

To obviate that they make the *double à droite* shorter and thus they gradually move towards the left. In some places, instead of the *double à droite*, they make a *reprise* or a *branle.*[a]

CAPRIOL

I like branles because a number of persons can enjoy them together.

ARBEAU

When you commence a branle several others will join you, as many young men as do damsels, and sometimes the damsel who is the last to arrive will take your left hand and it will thus become a round dance.

CAPRIOL

Does he who leads the dance always remain in the front when it is not a round dance?

ARBEAU

Yes, usually, because another dancer and his damsel would not care to usurp his place, albeit that other were a renowned nobleman of whom none would care to fall foul.

CAPRIOL

What place should he take who wishes to join in the dancing?

ARBEAU

He should place himself at the tail end, holding his damsel by his right hand, or else, if agreeable to the others, find a place among those who are dancing.[a]

CAPRIOL

Do I make no divisions in dancing these branles?

ARBEAU

It has always been held that the more sedately and slowly double branles were danced the better. All the same, it is not improper to make a *pied en l'air gauche* on the first minim of the seventh bar, and on the second minim of the seventh bar a *pied en l'air droit*. And on the first minim of the eighth and last bar a *pied en l'air gauche* in readiness to resume and repeat from the beginning, holding the said *pied en l'air gauche* through the last minim beat.

Continuation of the melody for a double branle   Movements divided as described above

Pied gauche largi	
Pied droit approché	These four steps make
Pied gauche largi	a *double à gauche*
Pied droit joint	
Pied droit largi	
Pied gauche approché	These five steps make
Pied en l'air gauche	a divided *double à droite*
Pied en l'air droit	
Pied en l'air gauche	
Pause	

CAPRIOL

Are there no other divisions made in double branles?

ARBEAU

Young men of exceptional agility make divisions at their pleasure but I advise you to dance them soberly.

THE SINGLE BRANLE

You will dance the single branle to the same duple time and with the same steps as those I have just described for the double branle, making a *double* to the left to commence with. But here is where they differ, instead of following the above with a *double à droite* you will perform a *simple* only, by making a *pied largi* with the right foot and to conclude a *pied joint* with the left foot. In this *simple* you may divide the four minims into three *pieds en l'air* and one rest, as we have just explained in reference to the double branle.

TABULATION OF THE SINGLE BRANLE

Melody of a single branle   Movements for dancing the single branle

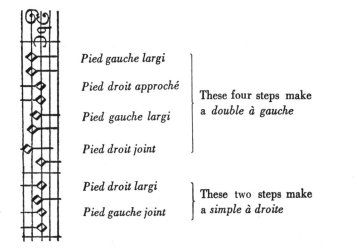

Pied gauche largi	
Pied droit approché	These four steps make
Pied gauche largi	a *double à gauche*
Pied droit joint	
Pied droit largi	These two steps make
Pied gauche joint	a *simple à droite*

Movements divided as in the double branle

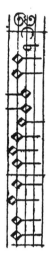

Pied gauche largi

Pied droit approché

Pied gauche largi

Pied droit joint

These four steps make a *double à gauche*

Pied en l'air gauche
Pied en l'air droit
Pied en l'air gauche
Pause

These three steps make a *simple à droite*

THE GAY BRANLE

After the single branle comes the gay branle which you will dance to the left only, with four steps and a pause in two bars of triple time." To do this, step sideways on the left foot, and, as it receives your weight, make a *pied en l'air droit* for the first step on the first minim. Then bring the right foot close to the left and make a *pied en l'air gauche* for the second step on the second minim. Then, step sideways on the left foot, and, as it receives your weight, make a *pied en l'air droit* for the third step on the third minim. Then bring the said right foot close to the left and make a *pied en l'air gauche*, and hold this position, preparatory to repeat from the beginning, during the two minim beats which are equivalent to two rests or a pause. And if you meet with any semi-breves[90] in the tabulation think of them as divided into two minims each to suit the steps proper to the gay branle.

Melody of the
Gay branle

Movements suitable for dancing this branle

Pied en l'air droit

Pied en l'air gauche
Pied en l'air droit

Pied en l'air gauche

Pause

Pied en l'air droit
Pied en l'air gauche

Pied en l'air droit

Pied en l'air gauche
Pause

Pied en l'air droit
Pied en l'air gauche

Pied en l'air droit
Pied en l'air gauche

Pause

Pied en l'air droit
Pied en l'air gauche
Pied en l'air droit

Pied en l'air gauche
Pause

CAPRIOL

This branle is not called gay for nothing because it looks to me as if one foot is always in the air. But proceed and tell me of the dance which you call the branle of Burgundy.

THE BURGUNDIAN BRANLE

ARBEAU

After the gay branle the musicians play the Burgundian branle, which is danced in duple time first to one side and then to the other, to a lighter, livelier beat. There is no difference in the steps except that, instead of the *pieds joints*, one makes *grèves* or *pieds en l'air* for the fourth and eighth steps.

TABULATION OF THE BURGUNDIAN BRANLE

Melody of the Burgundian branle[a]

Movements suitable for dancing the Burgundian branle

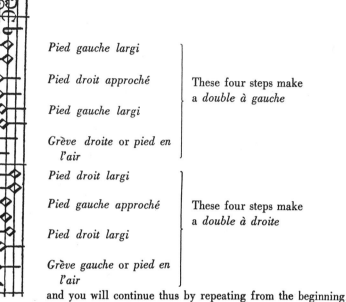

Pied gauche largi

Pied droit approché

Pied gauche largi

Grève droite or pied en l'air

⎫
⎬ These four steps make a *double à gauche*
⎭

Pied droit largi

Pied gauche approché

Pied droit largi

Grève gauche or pied en l'air

⎫
⎬ These four steps make a *double à droite*
⎭

and you will continue thus by repeating from the beginning

THE BRANLE OF HAUT BARROIS[b]

There is another kind of branle called the Haut Barrois,[91] which is danced like the double branle or the Burgundian branle. But there is a difference, because in this branle the shoulders and arms, as well as the feet, must be made to move with the *petits sauts* to a light, vivacious duple time. To dance it you will proceed thus:— spring sideways off both feet, moving towards the left, and alight *pied largi gauche*. Then spring sideways off both feet again, moving towards the left, and alight *pied droit approché*. Then spring sideways to the left off both feet again and alight *pied largi gauche*. Then spring sideways off both feet, moving to the left, and alight *pieds joints*, or else upon the left foot followed by a *grève droite* or *pied en l'air droite;* and thus the *double à gauche* will be completed. You will do the same in the opposite direction, towards the right, to execute a *double à droite*. And if the tune of the Haut Barrois is like the single branle, you will divide the two penultimate bars to perform the simple. This branle is danced by lackeys and serving wenches, and sometimes by young men and damsels of gentle birth in a masquerade, disguised as peasants and shepherds, or for a lark among themselves at some private gathering. The foregoing tabulation for the double or single branle should suffice you, but I might give you one arranged to the tune of a branle of Montierandal.[92]

CAPRIOL

This branle seems to me to be more rousing than those preceding it and would be the very dance to keep one warm in the winter. Since you have begun to give me tabulations, pray let me have one for this particular branle.

ARBEAU

TABULATION OF THE HAUT BARROIS BRANLE

Melody of an
Haut Barrois   Movements for dancing the Haut Barrois
    branle

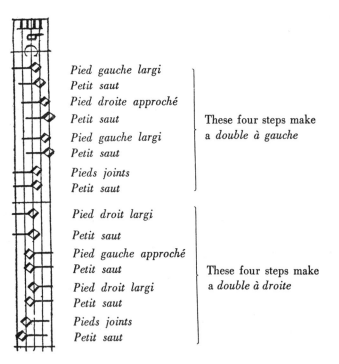

Pied gauche largi
Petit saut
Pied droite approché
Petit saut   These four steps make
Pied gauche largi   a *double à gauche*
Petit saut
Pieds joints
Petit saut

Pied droit largi
Petit saut
Pied gauche approché
Petit saut   These four steps make
Pied droit largi   a *double à droite*
Petit saut
Pieds joints
Petit saut

and you will continue thus by repeating it from the beginning.

The various branles noted above represent the source from whence are derived certain other branles composed of a combination of *doubles, simples, pieds en l'air, pieds joints* and *sauts,* sometimes varied by the insertion of miscellaneous bars, in slow or quick time, as it pleases the composers or inventors. The musicians call them mixed branles[93] of Champagne, and, with a view to orderly classification, these branles have been arranged in numbered series. Our musicians in Langres play ten in succession which they call mixed branles of Champagne; they play another number in sequence known as Camp branles and yet others they have named branles of Hainaut and branles of Avignon. And, as fresh compositions and novelties appear, so they devise new series and bestow upon them what names they wish.

CAPRIOL

Give me the tabulation of all these suites.

ARBEAU

I shall not give you any tabulations but will leave you to memorize them yourself under the guidance of the master musicians or from your companions. And when you are proficient enough to wish to dance them at some festival you will ask the musicians for the suite you require by name and they will play it for you. In the meanwhile, I will warn you that if you aspire to dance these branles well you must know the tunes by heart and sing them in your head with the violin.

CAPRIOL

Give me the tabulation of at least two or three, because, in this way, it will be easier for me to understand the others.

ARBEAU

Very well, here are the tabulations for the branles of Cassandra and Pinagay, first and second in the suite of the mixed branles of Champagne, which are danced in duple time, lightly and without *sauts,* (as are also those of Camp, Hainaut, and Avignon). Or you may dance them like the branles of Haut Barrois with little springs.

TABULATION OF THE MIXED BRANLE CALLED
CASSANDRA

Melody of the
mixed branle
called
Cassandra

Movements suitable for dancing the mixed
branle called Cassandra

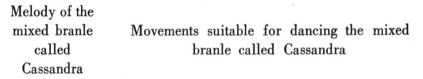

Pied gauche largi
Pied droit approché | These four steps make
                            | a *double à gauche*
Pied gauche largi
Pieds joints

Pied droit largi | These four steps make
                           | a *double à droite*
Pied gauche approché

Pied droit largi
Pieds joints

Pied gauche largi
Pied droit approché | These four steps make
                           | a *double à gauche*
Pied gauche largi
Pieds joints

Pied droit largi | These four steps make
                           | a *double à droite*
Pied gauche approché

Pied droit largi

Pieds joints

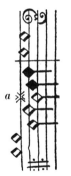

Pied gauche largi	These two steps make a
Pieds joints	*simple à gauche*
Pied droit largi	
Pied gauche approché	These four steps make
	a *double à droite*
Pied droit largi	
Pieds joints	

TABULATION OF THE BRANLE CALLED PINAGAY

Melody of the branle called Pinagay

Movements for dancing the branle called Pinagay

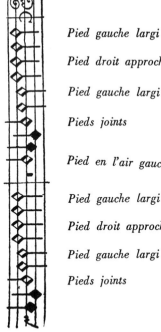

Pied gauche largi	
Pied droit approché	These four steps make
	a *double à gauche*
Pied gauche largi	
Pieds joints	
Pied en l'air gauche	
Pied gauche largi	
Pied droit approché	These four steps make
	a *double à gauche*
Pied gauche largi	
Pieds joints	

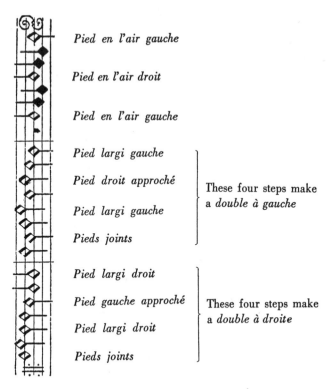

Pied en l'air gauche

Pied en l'air droit

Pied en l'air gauche

Pied largi gauche

Pied droit approché

Pied largi gauche   These four steps make a *double à gauche*

Pieds joints

Pied largi droit

Pied gauche approché

Pied largi droit   These four steps make a *double à droite*

Pieds joints

CAPRIOL

I believe you know all the movements of the mixed branles.

ARBEAU

When I first came to live in this town of Langres people talked only of dancing and masquerades and gaiety. We had Master Claudin, who played exquisitely upon several instruments and made us eager to practise. But for some time now I have met with nothing but sorrow and it has made me old and dull. In those days of yore we danced, among other mixed branles, the branle of war, the branles of Aridan and of Charlotte and an infinity of others.

CAPRIOL

How were these branles you mention danced?

ARBEAU

You will see by their tabulations.

TABULATION OF THE MIXED BRANLE, CHARLOTTE

Melody of the
mixed branle   The correct movements for dancing this branle
Charlotte

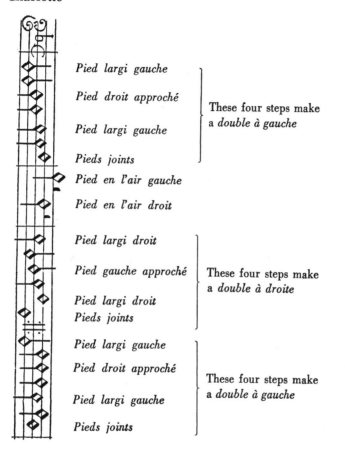

Pied largi gauche

Pied droit approché

Pied largi gauche

Pieds joints

} These four steps make
a *double à gauche*

Pied en l'air gauche

Pied en l'air droit

Pied largi droit

Pied gauche approché

Pied largi droit
Pieds joints

} These four steps make
a *double à droite*

Pied largi gauche

Pied droit approché

Pied largi gauche

Pieds joints

} These four steps make
a *double à gauche*

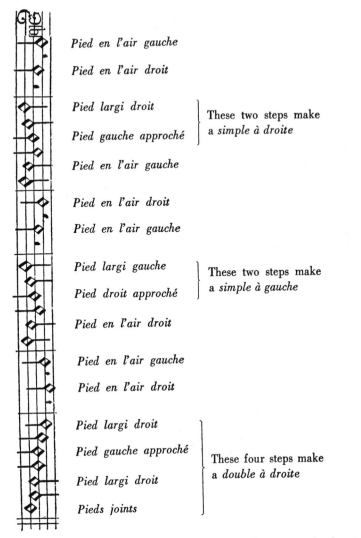

Pied en l'air gauche

Pied en l'air droit

Pied largi droit   ⎫ These two steps make
Pied gauche approché ⎬ a *simple à droite*

Pied en l'air gauche

Pied en l'air droit

Pied en l'air gauche

Pied largi gauche   ⎫ These two steps make
Pied droit approché ⎬ a *simple à gauche*

Pied en l'air droit

Pied en l'air gauche

Pied en l'air droit

Pied largi droit

Pied gauche approché   These four steps make
a *double à droite*
Pied largi droit

Pieds joints

and continue by repeating as at the beginning. Note that if you wish to dance this like the Haut Barrois you must make *petits sauts* or leave some of the minim beats empty.

TABULATION OF THE MIXED BRANLE OF WAR[a]

Melody of the
mixed branle of   The correct movements for dancing this branle
war

Pied largi gauche

Pied droit approché   These four steps make
                               a *double à gauche*
Pied largi gauche
Pieds joints

Pied largi droit

Pied gauche approché   These four steps make
                               a *double à droite*
Pied largi droit

Pieds joints

Pied largi gauche
Pied droit approché   These four steps make
                               a *double à gauche*

Pied largi gauche
Pieds joints

Pied largi droit

Pied gauche approché   These four steps make
                               a *double à droite*

Pied largi droit
Pieds joints

Pied largi gauche

Pied droit approché

Pied largi gauche

Pieds joints

These four steps make a *double à gauche*

Pied largi droit

Pied gauche approché

Pied largi droit

Pieds joints

Pied largi gauche

These four steps make a *double à droite*

Pieds joints

Pied largi droit

Pieds joints

Pied largi gauche

Pied droit approché

Pied largi gauche

Pieds joints

Pied largi droit

These four steps make a *double à gauche*

Pieds joints

Pied largi gauche

Pieds joints

Pied largi droit

Pied gauche approché

Pied largi droit

Pieds joints

Pied largi gauche

These four steps make a *double à droite*

Pieds joints

Grève gauche

Grève droit

Grève gauche

Pieds joints

Saut majeur with capriole

TABULATION OF THE MIXED BRANLE CALLED ARIDAN

Melody of the
mixed branle   Correct movements for dancing this branle
called Aridan

Pied largi gauche	
Pied droit approché	These four steps make
Pied largi gauche	a *double à gauche*
Pieds joints	
Pied en l'air gauche	
Pied en l'air droit	
Pied en l'air gauche	
Pied largi gauche	
Pied droit approché	These four steps make
Pied largi gauche	a *double à gauche*
Pieds joints	
Pied largi droit	These two steps make
Pieds joints	a *simple à droite*
Pied largi gauche	These two steps make
Pieds joints	a *simple à gauche*
Pied largi droit	These two steps make
Pieds joints	a *simple à droite*

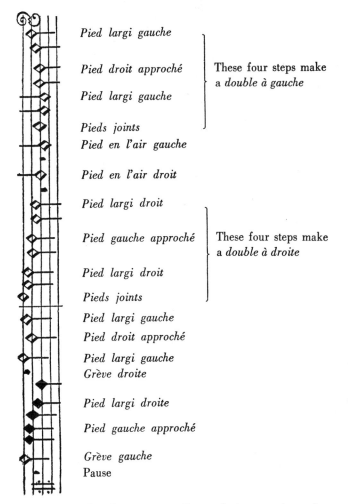

Pied largi gauche	
Pied droit approché	These four steps make a *double à gauche*
Pied largi gauche	
Pieds joints	
Pied en l'air gauche	
Pied en l'air droit	
Pied largi droit	
Pied gauche approché	These four steps make a *double à droite*
Pied largi droit	
Pieds joints	
Pied largi gauche	
Pied droit approché	
Pied largi gauche	
Grève droite	
Pied largi droite	
Pied gauche approché	
Grève gauche	
Pause	

Many branles take their name from the countries where they are customarily danced. The Poitevins dance their branles of Poitou,[94] the Scots, their branles of Scotland and the Bretons branles which they call the Trihory or papsy.[95]

CAPRIOL

I look forward to the tabulations of these.

THE BRANLE OF POITOU

ARBEAU

Some ignoramuses have corrupted the movements of the branle of Poitou

but I will not be a party to this and I shall give you a tabulation of the manner in which I danced it of yore with the maidens of Poitiers. This branle is
danced in triple time always moving to the left without deviation to the
right. I shall only give you the beginning of the tune, because the rest of it,
and indeed all the other numerous branles, have the same movements.

Melody of the
branle of   Movements of this branle
Poitou[a]

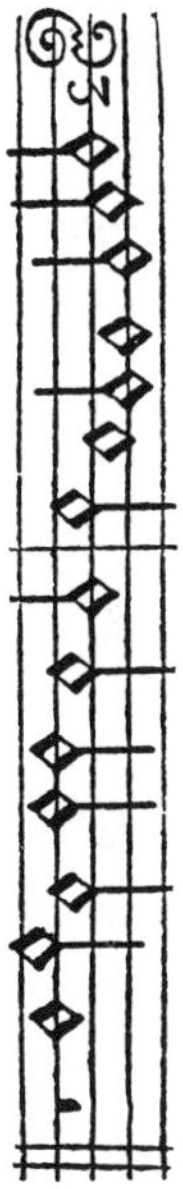

Pied en l'air droit

Pied en l'air gauche
Pied en l'air droit

Pied en l'air gauche

Pied en l'air droit
Pied en l'air gauche
Pied en l'air droit
Pied en l'air gauche
Pause

CAPRIOL

Do they no longer make divisions in this branle of Poitou? I have heard it
said that the young women of Poitou divide it by means of an agreeable
noise they make with their wooden shoes.

ARBEAU

In truth they do still stamp their feet in the second and third bars of triple
time, which contain six minims upon each of which they make a *pied en l'air*
from side to side as you see below.

Con. of the same melody	Movements further divided

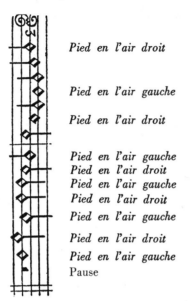

Pied en l'air droit

Pied en l'air gauche

Pied en l'air droit

Pied en l'air gauche
Pied en l'air droit
Pied en l'air gauche
Pied en l'air droit
Pied en l'air gauche

Pied en l'air droit
Pied en l'air gauche
Pause

THE SCOTTISH BRANLE

The Scottish branles were in fashion about twenty years ago. The musicians have a suite comprising a number of these branles, all differing in their movements, which you can learn from the said musicians or from your companions. They are danced in quick duple time as you see in the tabulation of the two following branles, which are the first and second in the suite.

TABULATION OF THE SCOTTISH BRANLE

Melody of the first Scottish branle   **Movements for dancing this first branle**

Pied largi gauche	
Pied droit approché	These four steps are equivalent to a *double à gauche*
Pied largi gauche	
Pied croisé droit	

Pied largi droit	
Pied gauche approché	These four movements are equivalent to a *double à droite*
Pied largi droit	
Pied croisé gauche	

Pied largi gauche	These two steps are equivalent to a *simple à gauche*
Pied croisé droit	

Pied largi droit	These two steps are equivalent to a *simple à droite*
Pied croisé gauche	

Pied largi gauche	
Pied droit approché	These four steps are equivalent to a *double à gauche*
Pied largi gauche	
Pied croisé droit	

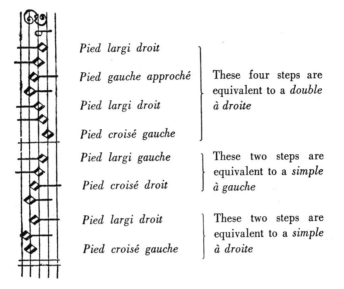

Pied largi droit	
Pied gauche approché	These four steps are equivalent to a *double*
Pied largi droit	*à droite*
Pied croisé gauche	
Pied largi gauche	These two steps are equivalent to a *simple*
Pied croisé droit	*à gauche*
Pied largi droit	These two steps are equivalent to a *simple*
Pied croisé gauche	*à droite*

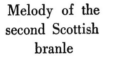

Melody of the second Scottish branle   **Movements for dancing the second Scottish branle**

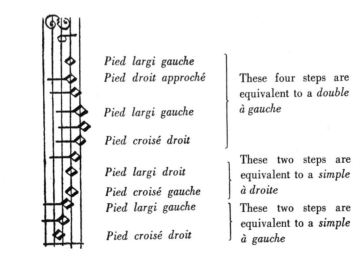

Pied largi gauche	
Pied droit approché	These four steps are equivalent to a *double*
Pied largi gauche	*à gauche*
Pied croisé droit	
Pied largi droit	These two steps are equivalent to a *simple*
Pied croisé gauche	*à droite*
Pied largi gauche	These two steps are equivalent to a *simple*
Pied croisé droit	*à gauche*

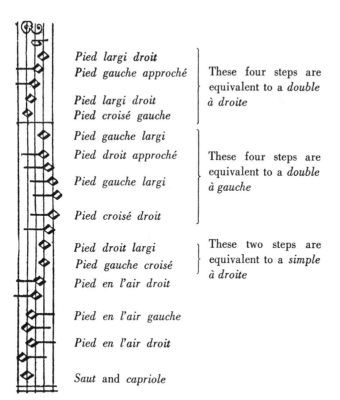

Pied largi droit	
Pied gauche approché	These four steps are equivalent to a *double à droite*
Pied largi droit	
Pied croisé gauche	
Pied gauche largi	
Pied droit approché	These four steps are equivalent to a *double à gauche*
Pied gauche largi	
Pied croisé droit	
Pied droit largi	
Pied gauche croisé	These two steps are equivalent to a *simple à droite*
Pied en l'air droit	
Pied en l'air gauche	
Pied en l'air droit	
Saut and *capriole*	

THE TRIHORY OF BRITTANY

This branle is seldom if ever performed in these parts. Should it befall you to dance it some day it will be in light duple time as the tabulation shows you. I learned it long ago from a young Breton who was a fellow student of mine at Poitiers.

CAPRIOL

I should be very glad to learn this trihory. One cannot do better than to have a knowledge of many things.

TABULATION OF THE BRANLE CALLED TRIHORY

Melody of the branle | Movements for dancing this branle called Trihory

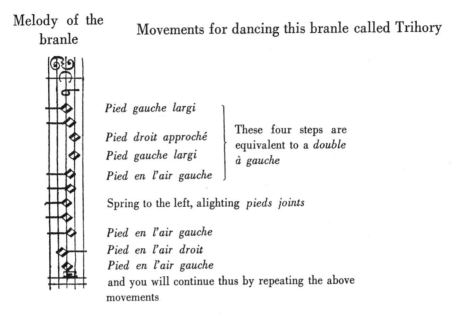

Pied gauche largi

Pied droit approché   These four steps are equivalent to a *double à gauche*

Pied gauche largi

Pied en l'air gauche

Spring to the left, alighting *pieds joints*

Pied en l'air gauche
Pied en l'air droit
Pied en l'air gauche
and you will continue thus by repeating the above movements

In place of the three *pieds en l'air* at the end of the trihory, you will hold yourself firmly on the tips of your toes, and, bringing your heels together, turn them both to the right instead of the *pied en l'air gauche* and to the left instead of the *pied en l'air droit.* And in place of the last *pied en l'air gauche,* you will turn your heels to the right raising your left foot in the air at the same moment. In order that you may see it clearly at a glance, I will give you a tabulation for the last three notes of the above melody.

Talons haussés droit [96]

Talons haussés gauche
Talons haussés droit
In this last movement of the heels, you must make
a *pied en l'air gauche* at the same moment

There are still several kinds of branle of which I am minded to give you the tabulations since you have such a thirst for knowledge. And I must tell you that whenever a new branle, termed a ballet and intended for use in a masquerade at some festival, is composed, the young people immediately introduce it into the ballroom and bestow what name they please upon it. The branles in the tabulations which follow belong in this category and of these the majority are danced with miming and gestures and therefore may be called mimed branles. We shall commence with the Maltese branle.

THE MALTESE BRANLE[a]

Some of the Knights of Malta devised a ballet for a Court masquerade in which an equal number of men and damsels, dressed in Turkish costume, danced a round branle, comprising certain gestures and twisting movements of the body, which they called the Maltese branle. It was some forty years ago that this branle was first danced in France. The melody and movements are in slow duple time as you will see by this tabulation.

CAPRIOL

Perhaps this dance is native to the Maltese and not merely a fanciful invention for a ballet.

ARBEAU

I cannot believe it to be other than a ballet, because it is performed with certain gestures and facial expressions that are peculiar to it and have been preserved ever since it came into fashion. Be that as it may, the following tabulation will assist you.

TABULATION OF THE MALTESE BRANLE

Melody of the
Maltese branle

Movements for dancing this branle

Melody	Movements for dancing this branle	
	Pied largi gauche	
	Pied droit approché	These four first steps make a *double à gauche*
	Pied largi gauche	
	Pieds joints	
	Pied largi droit	These two steps make a *simple à droite*
	Pieds joints	
	Pied gauche avancé[97]	During these movements the dancers gesticulate and advance in close formation to the centre of the circle as if they wished to parley together
	Pied droit avancé	
	Pied gauche avancé	
	Pied droit avancé	
	Pied gauche avancé with *grève droite*	
	Pied droit avancé	At this point they let go of each other's hands and commence turning round to the left
	Grève gauche	
	Pied gauche avancé	
	Grève droite	

 *Pied en l'air gauche*

Pied en l'air droit

Pied en l'air gauche

Pieds joints

After the dancers have completed the turn and fallen into the position of *pieds joints* they join hands again to repeat the dance from the beginning

You should note that in each repetition of this branle new facial expressions and gestures are made, such as touching the hands, or, on another occasion, raising them in mock praise with the head thrown back and eyes lifted heavenwards. And so on, in such fashion as the dancers please to vary them.

THE WASHERWOMEN'S BRANLE

This mimed branle called the Washerwomen's branle is danced in duple time and is thus designated because by clapping their hands the dancers make a noise like the women beating the washing on the banks of the Seine.

CAPRIOL

Are there many different kinds of miming in this Washerwomen's branle of which you speak?

ARBEAU

You will see by the notes I shall place in brackets beside the tabulation what these are. But they remain the same throughout and are not changed when the branle is repeated from the beginning, which I should have explained to you earlier.

TABULATION OF THE WASHERWOMEN'S BRANLE

Melody of this
branle[a]
Movements for dancing this branle

Pied largi gauche

Pied droit approché   These four steps make
a *double à gauche*

Pied largi gauche

Pieds joints

Pied largi droit

Pied gauche approché   These four steps make
a *double à droite*

Pied largi droit

Pieds joints

During these two *sim-
ples* the women place
their hands upon their

Pied largi gauche   hips and the men shake
their fingers at them,

Pieds joints   and in the repetition
of the *simples* the men

Pied largi droit   hold their sides and
the women shake their

Pieds joints   fingers at them

Pied largi gauche

Pied droit approché   During this *double à
gauche* all the dancers

Pied largi gauche   clap their hands

Pieds joints

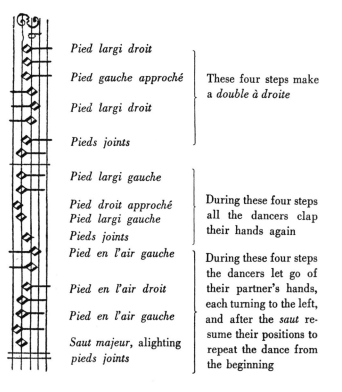

Pied largi droit	
Pied gauche approché	These four steps make a *double à droite*
Pied largi droit	
Pieds joints	
Pied largi gauche	
Pied droit approché	During these four steps all the dancers clap their hands again
Pied largi gauche	
Pieds joints	
Pied en l'air gauche	During these four steps the dancers let go of their partner's hands, each turning to the left, and after the *saut* resume their positions to repeat the dance from the beginning
Pied en l'air droit	
Pied en l'air gauche	
Saut majeur, alighting *pieds joints*	

THE PEASE BRANLE

Among the branles with mimic gestures is the Pease branle, otherwise known as the Margueritotte, which is danced in light duple time either like the common branle or the Haut Barrois, as one prefers. An equal number of men and women take part and they dance it in the manner you will see described in the tabulation which follows. I have placed notes in brackets showing you the suitable gestures and miming, neither of which is difficult.

TABULATION OF THE BRANLE CALLED PEASE [a]

Melody of this branle   **Movements for dancing this branle**

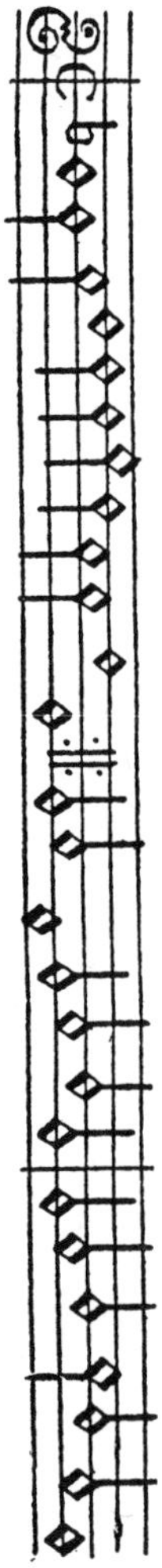

Pied largi gauche
Pied droit approché

These four steps make a *double à gauche*

Pied largi gauche
Pieds joints

Pied largi droit

Pied gauche approché

These four steps make a *double à droite*

Pied largi droit
Pieds joints

Saut majeur, by the men

During these two steps the women do not move

Pieds joints

Saut majeur, by the women

During these two steps the men do not move

Pieds joints

Pied largi gauche
Petit saut
Pieds joints

While the men make these three *sauts* the women do not move

Petit saut
Pieds joints

Petit saut

Pieds joints

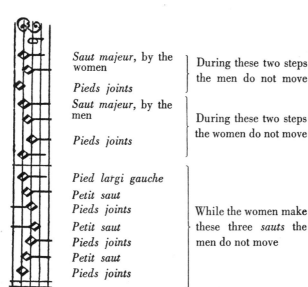

Saut majeur, by the women	During these two steps the men do not move
Pieds joints	
Saut majeur, by the men	During these two steps the women do not move
Pieds joints	
Pied largi gauche	
Petit saut	
Pieds joints	While the women make these three *sauts* the men do not move
Petit saut	
Pieds joints	
Petit saut	
Pieds joints	

THE HERMITS' BRANLE

I shall include the Hermits' branle, so called because it contains gestures resembling those made by hermits in greeting, among the mimed branles. I believe that it originally derived from some masquerade in which the young men were dressed in garments like those worn by hermits. But I do not advise you to wear such habits for fancy dress, nor to mimic the behaviour of a Religious Order, because one should respect both their cloth and their persons.[a] On this occasion, however, I shall hold my peace.

CAPRIOL

I will gladly follow your advice but do not be loth to give me the tabulation showing how it was danced.

ARBEAU

I am quite willing to gratify your wish since your sole intent is to gain information. This branle was danced in moderate duple time in the manner shown below.

THE HERMITS' BRANLE

Melody of this branle

Movements for dancing this branle

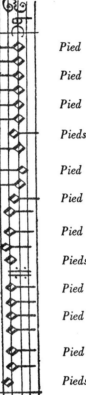

Pied largi gauche

Pied droit approché

Pied largi gauche

Pieds joints

These four steps make a *double à gauche*

Pied largi droit

Pied gauche approché

Pied largi droit

Pieds joints

These four steps make a *double à droite*

Pied en l'air droit

Pied en l'air gauche

Pied en l'air droit

Pieds joints

During these four steps the dancers make a half turn to the left and face outwards

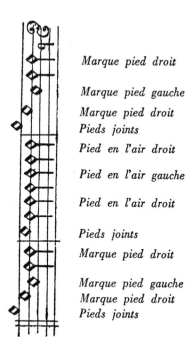

Marque pied droit	During these four steps the dancers cross their arms and bow their heads as young novices do
Marque pied gauche	
Marque pied droit	
Pieds joints	
Pied en l'air droit	During these four steps the dancers make a half turn to the left and face inwards as they did at the beginning
Pied en l'air gauche	
Pied en l'air droit	
Pieds joints	
Marque pied droit	During these four steps the dancers bow their heads as we have said above
Marque pied gauche	
Marque pied droit	
Pieds joints	

THE CANDLESTICK BRANLE[a]

This branle, otherwise known as the Torch branle, is danced in moderate duple time like the Alman and with the same steps. Those who wish to dance it take a candlestick with a lighted candle, or a torch or link, and make one or two turns around the room walking or dancing forwards and looking to right and to left the while for the partner of their choice. Each selects the damsel he fancies and they dance together for a little while, after which he disposes her at the end of the hall and making a *révérence* hands her the lighted candlestick or torch or link and retires dancing to his place. The damsel holding the candlestick then repeats what she has seen the young man do and dances off to choose another partner. In due course they change places, when she hands the candlestick to him, and in this manner all are invited in turn to join in the dance.

TABULATION OF THE TORCH BRANLE

Melody of
this branle^a

Movements for dancing this branle

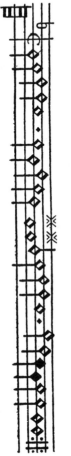

Pied gauche avancé

Pied droit avancé

Pied gauche avancé
Grève droite

Pied droit avancé

Pied gauche avancé

Pied droit avancé
Grève gauche
Pied gauche avancé

Pied droit avancé

Pied gauche avancé
Grève droite

Pied droit avancé

Pied gauche avancé

Pied droit avancé
Grève gauche

During these steps and movements the dancer makes one or two turns of the hall seeking the damsel he will choose to receive the candlestick

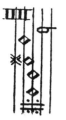

Pied gauche avancé	During these four steps
Grève droite	the dancer looks here
Pied droit avancé	and there to espy the
Grève gauche	partner of his choice

CAPRIOL

This is a dance where all the assembled company may take part just as you told me was the case in the Lyonnaise galliard.

ARBEAU

THE CLOG BRANLE

Rosinus[a] in his book on Roman antiquities relates that, according to the seventh book of Dionysius Halicarnassensis,[98] dancers carrying tibiae, harps and barbitons[99] marched in procession amid the pomp and splendour of the Public Games at Rome. One of their number led the others, walking in front and demonstrating to them certain set dances and mimings which all those who followed tried to imitate as if they were playing at puppets. A masquerade was given in our town of Langres after this fashion in which a Mother Folly led three clowns and showed them certain gestures. Then she would turn around to see if her brood of three was copying her faithfully. They danced the Clog branle which they had adapted to their purpose.

CAPRIOL

How is this Clog branle[b] danced?

ARBEAU

In duple time, like the double branle, by making four steps to the left and then four to the right, then two *simples* and three taps of the foot, all of which is repeated.

TABULATION OF THE CLOG BRANLE

Melody of
this branle[a]

Movements for dancing this branle

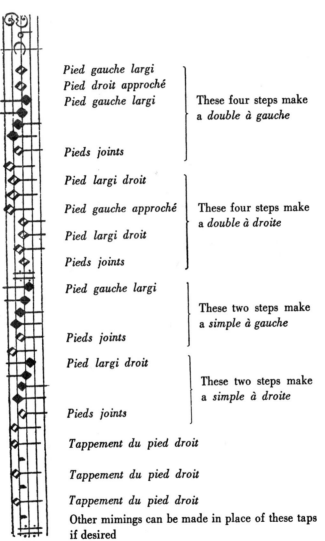

Pied gauche largi
Pied droit approché
Pied gauche largi

These four steps make
a *double à gauche*

Pieds joints

Pied largi droit

Pied gauche approché

These four steps make
a *double à droite*

Pied largi droit

Pieds joints

Pied gauche largi

These two steps make
a *simple à gauche*

Pieds joints

Pied largi droit

These two steps make
a *simple à droite*

Pieds joints

Tappement du pied droit

Tappement du pied droit

Tappement du pied droit

Other mimings can be made in place of these taps
if desired

If one wishes, in this Clog branle the men can make the first three taps and in the meanwhile the women should not move, and in the repetition the women will make the three taps and the men remain still. Then they all recommence the branle together, those who wish introducing new miming.

CAPRIOL

These tappings remind me of horses when they want water or of palfreys when they are kept waiting for their peck of oats.

ARBEAU

THE HORSES BRANLE

Apropos of that I have seen them dance a branle in this town called the horses branle in which they tap the feet as in the preceding branle. I believe the tune is the same or very similar to the one you see in the following tabulation. This was danced in duple time, like the common branle, and the young man held the damsel by both hands. The tune of the said branle began as you see it noted here and was danced by four *doubles à gauche,* and four *doubles à droite.*

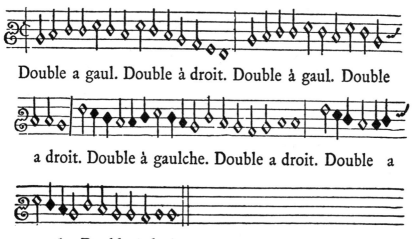

Double a gaul. Double à droit. Double à gaul. Double

a droit. Double à gaulche. Double a droit. Double a

gaul. Double à droit.

TABULATION FOR THE REST OF THIS BRANLE

Continuation of Melody	Continuation of movements

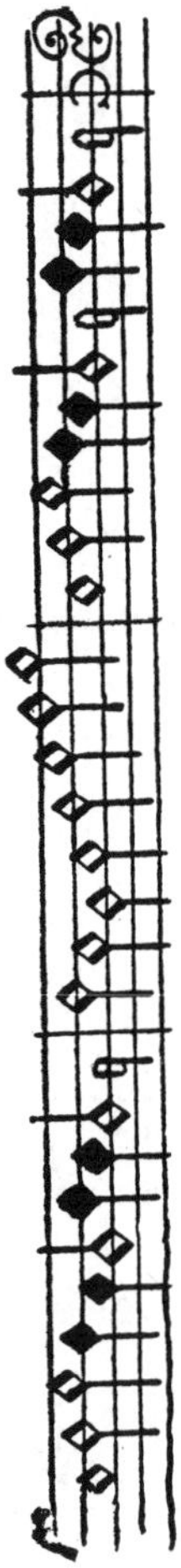

Two *tappements droits* by the man — During these taps and the turn made by the man the woman does not move

Pied *largi droit*

Pieds *joints* — These two steps make a *simple à droite*

Pied *largi gauche*

Pied *droit approché*

Pied *largi gauche* — During these four steps the man makes a turn to the left

Pieds *joints*

Two *tappements droits* by the woman — During these taps and the turn made by the woman the man does not move

Pied *largi droit*

Pieds *joints* — These two steps make a *simple à droite*

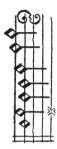

Pied largi gauche

Pied droit approché

Pied largi gauche

Pieds joints

During these four steps the woman makes a turn to the left

This done, the dancers join both hands again and repeat from the beginning

THE MONTARDE BRANLE

In bygone days we used to dance a mimed branle called the Montarde. It was danced in duple time, with little springs as in the Haut Barrois, and always moving to the left without any deviation to the right. An equal number of men and women take part, one of the men leading and one of the women bringing up the rear, and they all dance four *doubles à gauche* together. This done, the leader, detaching himself from the others, makes a turn alone, then the second makes a turn and joins the first. The third does likewise, joining the second, and so on until all those partaking in the dance have made their turn. And when the last dancer has finished her turn the first one makes a hay,[100] passing in front of the women and behind the men, and places himself at the tail end taking the last woman by the hand. And while he is making this hay all those before and behind whom he has passed join hands and repeat the branle as at the beginning. Thus, the woman who was at the end now finds herself leading and must follow the example of the original leader. In this way each dancer becomes leader and last in turn. And after the final one has reached the front and made her hay she is back once again at the end where she started. Then the musicians conclude the branle. Here is the tabulation.

TABULATION OF THE MONTARDE BRANLE

Melody of this branle[a]	Steps and movements for this branle

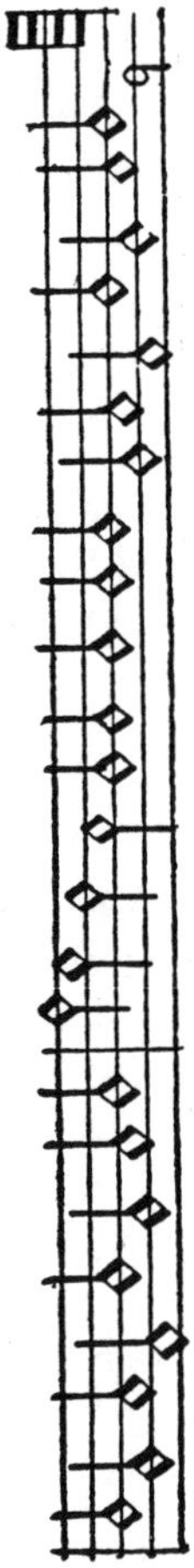

Pied largi gauche
Petit saut

Pied droit approché
Petit saut   These four steps make
Pied largi gauche   a *double à gauche*
Petit saut
Pieds joints

Petit saut
Pied largi gauche
Petit saut

Pied droit approché   These four steps make
Petit saut   another *double à
Pied largi gauche   gauche*

Petit saut

Pieds joints
Petit saut

Pied largi gauche
Petit saut

Pied droit approché

Petit saut   These four steps make
Pied largi gauche   another *double à
Petit saut   gauche*

Pieds joints
Petit saut

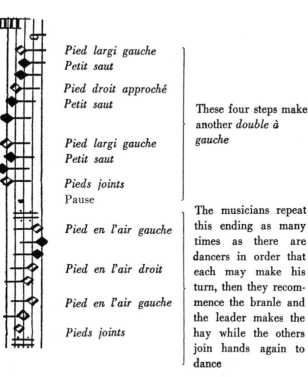

Pied largi gauche
Petit saut

Pied droit approché
Petit saut

These four steps make another *double à gauche*

Pied largi gauche
Petit saut

Pieds joints
Pause

Pied en l'air gauche

Pied en l'air droit

Pied en l'air gauche

Pieds joints

The musicians repeat this ending as many times as there are dancers in order that each may make his turn, then they recommence the branle and the leader makes the hay while the others join hands again to dance

CAPRIOL

To be sure, this Montarde branle must be the one that damsels call the hay.

ARBEAU

THE HAY BRANLE

The dance of the hay[101] to which you refer is another. It is danced in duple time like the coranto. The dancers begin, one at a time in succession, by dancing the melody in the manner of the coranto and at the end they interweave and make the hay.[a] In the first place I will give you the melody of the said coranto which, as you know, consists of two *simples* and a *double*. Then I will give you the melody played by the musicians at the end when the dancers interweave.

TABULATION OF THE HAY DANCE

Tabulature de la dance de la haye

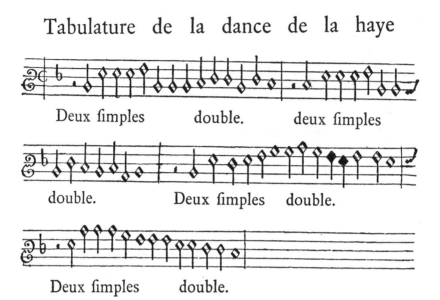

Deux ſimples　　　double.　　　deux ſimples

double.　　　Deux ſimples　　double.

Deux ſimples　　　double.

Melody and movements of the hay

Pied gauche avancé	D u r i n g these four
Pied droit avancé	steps, and others simi-
	lar that follow, the
Pied gauche avancé	dancers make the hay
	by changing p l a c e s
Pieds joints.	with one another
Pied droit avancé	During these four steps
	the leader of the dance
Pied gauche avancé	continues the hay until
	he reaches the last per-
Pied droit avancé	son and the musicians
	continue to play until
Pieds joints	the hay is finished

CAPRIOL

I do not fully understand what you tell me about this hay.

ARBEAU

You will understand it quite easily thus. Suppose there are three dancers, which is the minimum number there can be, and think of them as represented by the letters A, B and C.

A B C

In the first four steps of the hay A and B change places, passing to their left, then in the second four steps A and C change places, passing to their right, so that they are now placed as you see here.

B C A

This done B and C change places as above, then B and A do likewise so that in the third four steps of the hay they will be disposed thus:

C A B

In the four following steps C changes places with A, then the said C with B and thus they find themselves placed as they were at the beginning.

A B C

CAPRIOL

If perchance there were more than three dancers would they still change places in the manner you have just indicated?

ARBEAU

One might conclude so but you must have regard to what I am about to tell you. Suppose the dancers to be seven in number, A, B, C, D, E, F and G. When A who is first has changed with B who is second and when the said A has also changed with C, who is the third, and is about to change with D who is fourth, then B who is now first must begin to hay and change places with C who is now second and so on.

CAPRIOL

From what you say, I gather that C is now the first and so he must begin his hay by changing with D who is now second at the same moment that B changes and makes the hay with E who is now fourth and so on accordingly.

ARBEAU

You have grasped it very well. The Official branle will not be so difficult for you.

THE OFFICIAL BRANLE[a]

This branle, which has only recently received recognition, is danced in duple time with little springs like the Haut Barrois and it commences with a *double à gauche* and a *double à droite*. Then the dancers move continuously to the left for six *simples* at the end of which the musicians make the cadence. Whereupon the men take the women by the waist and assist them to leap into the air and alight upon the said cadence. Meanwhile the men remain firmly upon both feet to support their partners and are much hindered in these circumstances if they perforce must lift a damsel who will make no effort herself.

TABULATION OF THE OFFICIAL BRANLE

Melody of this branle   **Movements for dancing this branle**

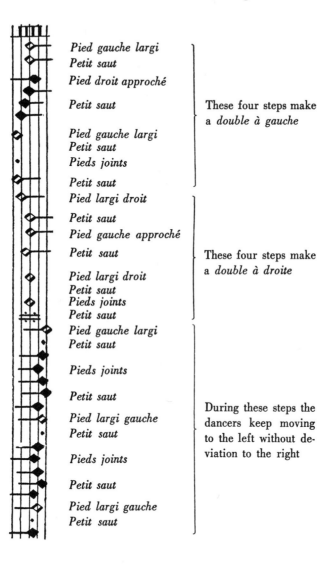

Pied gauche largi
Petit saut
Pied droit approché

Petit saut   } These four steps make
                       a *double à gauche*
Pied gauche largi
Petit saut
Pieds joints

Petit saut
Pied largi droit

Petit saut
Pied gauche approché

Petit saut   These four steps make
                     a *double à droite*
Pied largi droit
Petit saut
Pieds joints
Petit saut

Pied gauche largi
Petit saut

Pieds joints

Petit saut

Pied largi gauche   During these steps the
Petit saut   dancers keep moving
                          to the left without de-
Pieds joints   viation to the right

Petit saut

Pied largi gauche
Petit saut

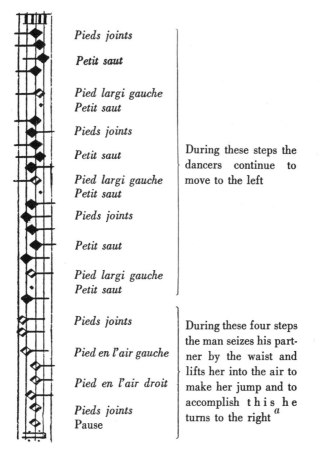

Pieds joints	
Petit saut	
Pied largi gauche *Petit saut*	
Pieds joints	
Petit saut	During these steps the dancers continue to move to the left
Pied largi gauche *Petit saut*	
Pieds joints	
Petit saut	
Pied largi gauche *Petit saut*	
Pieds joints	During these four steps the man seizes his part- ner by the waist and lifts her into the air to make her jump and to accomplish t h i s h e turns to the right [a]
Pied en l'air gauche	
Pied en l'air droit	
Pieds joints Pause	

CAPRIOL

I quite understand that this branle is continued by repeating from the beginning but it seems to me very toilsome. Besides which, its proper execution depends partly upon the dexterity and agility of the damsel whom one
must assist to jump and some damsels would attempt to dance it who lacked
the requisite proficiency.

ARBEAU

You will not find the gavotte[102] branles, where there is no need to lift but
only to kiss the damsels, so toilsome.

CAPRIOL

That is something I would do with ease and good grace, wherefore I am
anxious to hear more about these and to learn them.

ARBEAU

THE GAVOTTE [a]

Gavottes are a miscellany of double branles, selected by musicians and arranged in a sequence, which you can either learn from them or from your companions. They have named this suite the gavotte. It is danced in duple time with little springs in the manner of the Haut Barrois, and, like the common branle, consists of a *double à droite* and a *double à gauche*. But the dancers divide up the *doubles,* both those to the right and those to the left, by passages borrowed at will from the galliard. When those taking part have danced a little while, one couple detaches itself from the rest and executes a few passages in the centre of the room within view of all the others. Then, this first dancer proceeds to kiss all the damsels in the room and his partner kisses all the young men, after which they return to their rightful places. This accomplished, the second couple do likewise and so on throughout the company. Some confer this prerogative of kissing upon the host and his partner only and at the conclusion the said damsel, who carries a garland or bouquet, presents it to the dancer who must be host and pay the musicians at the next gathering. He will then avail himself of the same prerogative and thus it is taken in turn. I will give you the melody of the first branle and some divisions, which you can vary to please yourself.

TABULATION OF A GAVOTTE

Melody of the Gavotte   Movements for dancing the gavotte [a]

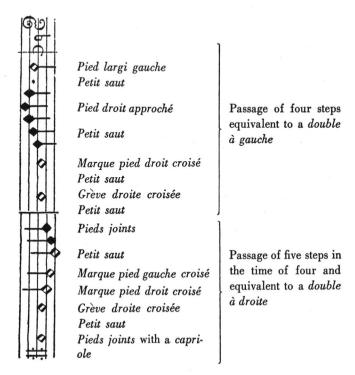

	Pied largi gauche	
	Petit saut	
	Pied droit approché	Passage of four steps
		equivalent to a *double*
	Petit saut	*à gauche*
	Marque pied droit croisé	
	Petit saut	
	Grève droite croisée	
	Petit saut	
	Pieds joints	
	Petit saut	Passage of five steps in
	Marque pied gauche croisé	the time of four and
	Marque pied droit croisé	equivalent to a *double*
	Grève droite croisée	*à droite*
	Petit saut	
	Pieds joints with a *capriole*	

Here is the rest of the melody of the first branle in the suite of gavottes played by our Langres musicians. You will adapt the above divisions to it or such others as it pleases you to select or devise, or to copy from accomplished and nimble dancers. If this sort of dance had been fashionable when I had a young pair of legs I should not have failed to make notes upon it.

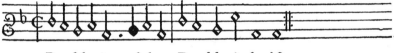

Double à gaulche. Double à droiĉt.

MORRIS DANCES [a]

In fashionable society when I was young, a small boy, his face daubed with black and his forehead swathed in a white or yellow kerchief, would make an appearance after supper. He wore leggings covered with little bells and performed a morris,[103] wherein he advanced the length of the room, made a kind of passage and then moving backwards retraced his steps to the place from whence he had started. Then he executed a new passage and he continued thus making various passages which delighted the spectators. Macrobius,[b] in his fourteenth chapter of the third book of the Saturnalia, makes Horus declare that the high born children and young girls of good family in Rome danced with crotala,[104][c] which the commentator Badius translates as meaning little bells. But this interpretation does not satisfy me and I believe it to be more likely that the crotalum was a Basque tabor[105] surrounded with tiny bells, such as the mother of the gods is represented as carrying. Or else it was what we call cymbals, triangular metal plates furnished with loops, which when played make a pleasing sound to accompany the vielle.[106] Whatever it may have been, the ability to perform this dance well was held in high esteem.

CAPRIOL

These lines of Virgil confirm your opinion. *Crispum sub crotalo docta movere latus.*[107] If the poet had meant bells he would have written *cum* not *sub.* Meanwhile I beg you to give me a short tabulation of these dances and I will teach them to my lackey.

ARBEAU

Morris dances are performed in duple time. Originally they were executed by striking the feet together, but because the dancers found this too painful they tried striking the heels only while keeping the toes rigid. Others wished to dance them with *marque pieds* and *marque talons* intermixed. The practise of any of these three methods, especially the one involving tapping the feet, has been proven by experience to lead eventually to podagra[108] and other gouty affections, wherefore this dance has fallen into disuse. I will only give you the melody and movements of one passage. As for the others you can learn them from those who are schooled therein although few such persons are to be found nowadays.

TABULATION OF MORRIS DANCES

Melody of the Morris[a]   Movements for dancing these[109]

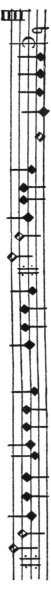

Frappe talon droit[110]
Frappe talon gauche
Frappe talon droit
Frappe talon gauche

Frappe talons
Pause
Frappe talon droit
Frappe talon gauche
Frappe talon droit

Frappe talon gauche
Frappe talons
Pause

Frappe talon droit
Frappe talon gauche
Frappe talon droit
Frappe talon gauche

Frappe talon droit
Frappe talon gauche
Frappe talon droit
Frappe talon gauche
Frappe talon droit
Frappe talon gauche
Frappe talon droit
Frappe talon gauche
Frappe talons
Pause

The dancer keeps the tips of his toes rigid and close t o g e t h e r while he strikes his heels to sound his bells, and when both heels are tapped (i.e. *frappe talons*) the position is tantamount to *pieds joints*

CAPRIOL

From what I can gather of the movements of this morris it would seem that the dancer always remains in one place.

ARBEAU

He must, in fact, advance continuously until he reaches the end of the room. And to do this you will note that after the tap by both heels, which corresponds to a *pieds joints* and cadence, the dancer moves both feet lightly forward and at the same time makes the *frappe talon droit*. Because, when you consider it, the *frappe talon droit* follows the *pieds joints*. Take note also that this morris melody is divided into crotchets and upon each of these both heels must be tapped as shown below.

CAPRIOL

I have noticed, Monsieur Arbeau, that in all the dances whereof you have given me the movements you have not yet mentioned the *ru de vache*, in spite of the fact that earlier you included it among the other movements.

ARBEAU

You are right, but the reason is that dancers almost never use it unless it be in the Canary,[111] a dance which I was about to describe to you.

THE CANARY

Some say this dance is common in the Canary Isles. Others, whose opinion I should prefer to share, maintain that it derives from a ballet composed for a masquerade in which the dancers were dressed as kings and queens of Mauretania, or else like savages in feathers dyed to many a hue. This is how the canary is danced. A young man takes a damsel and to the rhythm of the appropriate tune they dance together to the far end of the hall. This done, he withdraws to the place from whence he started, continuing the while to gaze at the damsel; then he regains her side anew and performs certain passages after which he withdraws again. The damsel now advances, does likewise before him and then withdraws to her former place, and they both continue to sally and retreat as many times as the variety of passages permits. And take note that these passages are gay but nevertheless strange and fantastic with a strong barbaric flavour. You will learn them from those who are practised in them and you can invent new ones for yourself. But I will give you the tune for this dance and some of the movements customarily performed by the dancers in which the onlookers take pleasure.

TABULATION OF THE CANARY DANCE

Melody of the Canary[a] Movements for this dance

Tappement du pied gauche resulting in pied en l'air droit[112]

Marque talon droit
Marque pied droit
Tappement du pied droit, resulting in pied en l'air gauche

Marque talon gauche
Marque pied gauche
Tappement du pied gauche, resulting in pied en l'air droit

Marque talon droit
Marque pied droit
Tappement du pied droit resulting in pied en l'air gauche

Marque talon gauche
Marque pied gauche

This tune is continued, and danced as shown above, during the time the dancer advances, performs before his partner and withdraws to his original position.

And note that for a second passage, instead of the tappements du pied made on the minims, one can make a very high grève and finish it by scraping the foot backwards along the ground as if one were treading down spittle or killing a spider.

You promised before to give me the Spanish pavan after the Canary. How should it be danced?

THE SPANISH PAVAN

The Spanish pavan is danced in moderate duple time to the tune and movements in the tabulation which follows. And after it has been danced moving forwards in the first passage one must then move backwards and retrace one's steps. Afterwards a second passage with new movements is performed to the same melody and the remaining passages, which you can learn at your leisure, follow in turn.

Melody *a*   Movements of the Spanish Pavan *b*

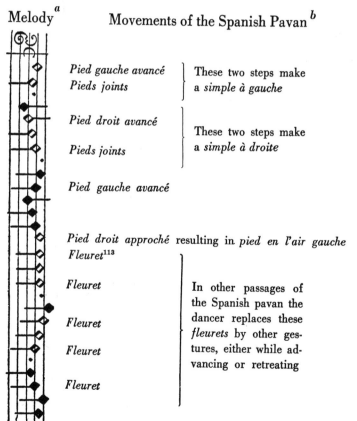

Pied gauche avancé ⎱ These two steps make
Pieds joints   ⎰ a *simple à gauche*

Pied droit avancé
                      These two steps make
Pieds joints   a *simple à droite*

Pied gauche avancé

Pied droit approché resulting in *pied en l'air gauche*
Fleuret[113]

Fleuret   In other passages of
                 the Spanish pavan the
                 dancer replaces these
Fleuret   *fleurets* by other ges-
                 tures, either while ad-
Fleuret   vancing or retreating

Fleuret

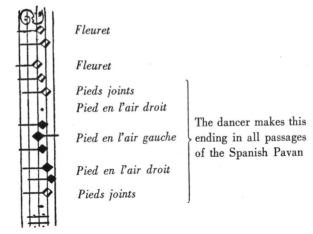

Fleuret

Fleuret

Pieds joints
Pied en l'air droit

Pied en l'air gauche   The dancer makes this
                         ending in all passages
                         of the Spanish Pavan

Pied en l'air droit

Pieds joints

I think that I have now fulfilled your wish, my good friend Capriol, by recounting all I can remember both of martial and recreative dances. Is it not ample considering how long it is since I myself have danced and that most of the dances are new?

CAPRIOL

I do not believe, Monsieur Arbeau, that it would be possible to treat of them more fully or more clearly. But truth to tell you have again forgotten to speak of the buffens.[114]

ARBEAU

Verily, and since you have reminded me I shall tell you what I have been able to learn of them.

THE BUFFENS[a]

The Salii, or dancers, initiated by King Numa[115] to celebrate the sacred festival of Mars, were twelve in number. They were attired in painted tunics with rich baldrics and pointed caps, a short sword at their side, little batons in the right hand and in the left a shield, one of which was said to have fallen from heaven. They danced to the sound of the *tibiae* and made martial gestures, sometimes in turn and sometimes all together.

CAPRIOL

Was this not the armed dance called the Pyrrhic which Minerva danced for joy after the Titans were vanquished?

ARBEAU

Legend has it that the Curetes invented the Pyrrhic dance to amuse the infant Jupiter by their gestures and the noise they make by striking their swords against their shields.[116] From these two types of dance there has been evolved one which we call the buffens or mattachins. The dancers are dressed in small corslets, with fringe epaulets and fringe hanging from beneath their belts over a silken ground. Their helmets are made of gilded cardboard, their arms are bare and they wear bells upon their legs and carry a sword in the right hand and a shield in the left. They dance to a special tune played in duple time and accompanied by the clash of their swords and shields. To understand this dance one must be familiar with the different gestures employed. One of these is called *feinte*,[117] when the dancer leaps upon both feet, sword in hand but without striking. Another gesture is called *estocade*,[118] when the dancer draws back his arm and thrusts his sword forward to strike that of his companion. Another gesture is called *taille haute*,[119] when the dancer strikes at his companion cutting downwards from the right hand, in which the sword is held, to the left. Another gesture is called *revers haut*,[120] when, contrariwise, the dancer strikes at his companion cutting downwards from left to right. Yet another gesture is called *taille basse*,[121] when the dancer strikes at his companion cutting upwards from right to left. And another *revers bas*,[122] when the dancer strikes at his companion cutting upwards from left to right. To the end that you may better understand the tabulation I propose to give you I shall not spare myself the pains of drawing pictures of these gestures for you.

Feincte

Eftocade

Taille haulte

Reuers hault

You see above four pictures of the gestures I have described to you, to wit; *feinte, estocade, taille haute* and *revers haut*. There remain the pictures of the other two gestures which you see below. Besides these there are several other body movements but it seems to me it will suffice for you to have them in writing without necessitating pictures.

Taille basse   Reuers bas

CAPRIOL

Fencing has already acquainted me with all these gestures. Now tell me how to dance the buffens.

ARBEAU

Suppose that A, B, C and D represent four persons suitably attired, either as soldiers or Amazons, or two of each, and that they are about to enter the hall.

CAPRIOL

I visualize them as you depict. What would they do?

ARBEAU

First, A would enter alone and brandishing his sword in time to the music circle the hall, then returning to the entrance place the point of his sword on the ground as if he desired to challenge his companions to combat. This done, he would again circle the hall and B would follow him, and when they had completed the round B would summon his companions. Now

A and B would begin once more to circle the hall and C would follow them repeating what the other two had done. Then, all three would make a round and D, who is the fourth, would join them. And when this fourth round is finished and none remain to enter they circle the hall in the opposite direction, and, upon the conclusion of this reversed round, find themselves in formation to begin the passages of their sword play with the left foot leading as it was in the first round.

D   C

A   B

The tune of the buffens is known to all. Here it is in its entirety, and the musicians always repeat it during the rounds as well as the passages.

TUNE OF THE BUFFENS [a]

CAPRIOL

What movements will the dancers make placed as they now are?

ARBEAU

You have yet to be told, that, just as the musicians continue to play the above tune throughout, so also the four dancers continue to perform the same movements whether they be circling the room or halted for their sword play.

CAPRIOL

Are the movements difficult?

ARBEAU

You will find them very easy. They are shown in the tabulation below, which is danced in light duple time:

Melody of the buffens   Movements for dancing the buffens

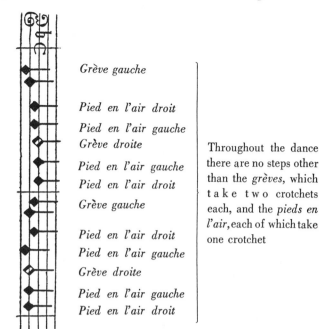

Grève gauche

Pied en l'air droit
Pied en l'air gauche
Grève droite

Throughout the dance
there are no steps other
than the *grèves*, which
take two crotchets
each, and the *pieds en
l'air*, each of which take
one crotchet

Pied en l'air gauche
Pied en l'air droit
Grève gauche

Pied en l'air droit
Pied en l'air gauche
Grève droite

Pied en l'air gauche
Pied en l'air droit

You have the steps and movements of the buffens, now you will learn
the gestures employed in the passages of sword play which must follow immediately after the rounds. And you will bear in mind that at the end of
each passage one round must be made with the left foot leading and then
one in the reverse manner before commencing the next passage. This is very
useful to the four dancers because while they are circling the hall they can
think over the next passage and collect their wits. As A, B, C and D are
now disposed, A is opposite D and will engage him in combat, and sometimes B, who is placed on A's right. And similarly C finds himself opposite B and will engage him in combat and sometimes D. And you will
take note that the gestures made by A are also made by C and therefore
the same tabulation will serve for them both as you will see below.

A combats D and B   C combats B and D
      Tune   Gestures of the first passage

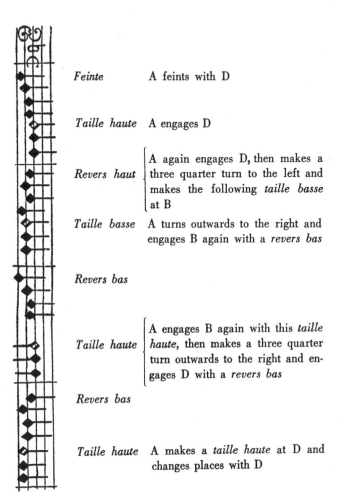

Feinte   A feints with D

Taille haute   A engages D

Revers haut | A again engages D, then makes a three quarter turn to the left and makes the following *taille basse* at B

Taille basse   A turns outwards to the right and engages B again with a *revers bas*

Revers bas

Taille haute | A engages B again with this *taille haute*, then makes a three quarter turn outwards to the right and engages D with a *revers bas*

Revers bas

Taille haute   A makes a *taille haute* at D and changes places with D

After A and D have changed places, and C and B have done likewise simultaneously, the four dancers will be disposed thus:

     A   B
     D   C

A will now combat B and sometimes D; and C will combat D and sometimes B, employing the same gestures and cuts as above, and when they have changed places they will be disposed thus:

B   A

C   D

A will make the gestures which we described at the beginning against D and sometimes against B, as C will also do against B and when they have changed places they will be disposed thus:

C   D

B   A

A will combat B and sometimes D; and C will do likewise with D and sometimes B and when they have changed places the dancers will be disposed thus:—

D   C

A   B

You observe that the four dancers are placed as they were at the beginning, which means their first passage is completed. And, without pause, they must make their round and the reverse round in readiness to commence the second passage, which is called the three cuts passage.

CAPRIOL

I could perform the gestures made by A and C well enough but you have not told me what gestures D and B have to make.

ARBEAU

The same as A and C; there is no difference between them save that when A and C make a three quarter turn outwards to the left, D and B must make a quarter turn only to the right; and when A and C make a turn outwards to the left D and B must make the said turn to the right. The other passages you can learn at your leisure.

CAPRIOL

I shall find but few tutors or companions able to instruct me in the other passages as they could in other branles. Wherefore I beg you to teach me them as I hope some day to devise a pretty masquerade for my mistress's entertainment.

I will gladly do so. Let us suppose, then, that after their round the four dancers are disposed as they were at the beginning. They would then make the following passage called the three cuts passage.

A combats D and
C combats B

THE THREE CUTS PASSAGE

Tune   Gestures of the second passage

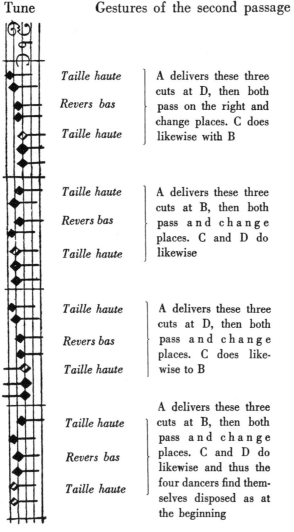

Taille haute	A delivers these three cuts at D, then both
Revers bas	pass on the right and change places. C does
Taille haute	likewise with B

Taille haute	A delivers these three cuts at B, then both
Revers bas	pass and change places. C and D do
Taille haute	likewise

Taille haute	A delivers these three cuts at D, then both
Revers bas	pass and change places. C does like-
Taille haute	wise to B

Taille haute	A delivers these three cuts at B, then both
Revers bas	pass and change places. C and D do
Taille haute	likewise and thus the four dancers find them-
	selves disposed as at the beginning

The above passage is repeated four times and then the round is made.

THE FIFTEEN CUTS PASSAGE

Tune   Gestures of the third passage

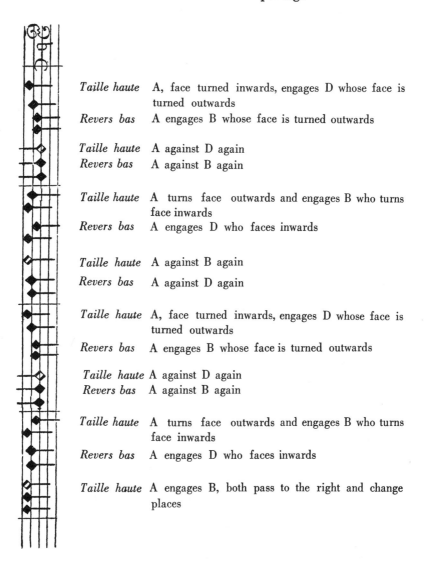

Taille haute   A, face turned inwards, engages D whose face is turned outwards

Revers bas   A engages B whose face is turned outwards

Taille haute   A against D again

Revers bas   A against B again

Taille haute   A turns face outwards and engages B who turns face inwards

Revers bas   A engages D who faces inwards

Taille haute   A against B again

Revers bas   A against D again

Taille haute   A, face turned inwards, engages D whose face is turned outwards

Revers bas   A engages B whose face is turned outwards

Taille haute A against D again

Revers bas   A against B again

Taille haute   A turns face outwards and engages B who turns face inwards

Revers bas   A engages D who faces inwards

Taille haute   A engages B, both pass to the right and change places

This done, A, face turned outwards, engages D whose face is turned inwards; and the passage is repeated throughout four times.

THE THRUST PASSAGE

Tune

Gestures for the fourth passage
Imagine the round made and the four dancers placed as they were at the beginning

Taille haute　　A engages D and C engages B

Revers haut　　A engages D again and C engages B

Taille basse　　A engages D again, and C engages B

Coude retiré ⎤

　　　　　　 ⎢ All four, A, B, C and D draw back their elbows and exchange thrusts at each other's shields

Estocade ⎦

Taille haute　　A against D and C against B

Revers haut　　A against D again, and C against B

Taille basse　　A against D and C against B

Coude retiré ⎤

　　　　　　 ⎢ All four, A, B, C and D, draw back their elbows and exchanging thrusts at each other's shields, they pass to the right and change places

Estocade ⎦

A now engages B and D engages C in the second turn. Then they repeat as before and when the passage has been executed four times they will find themselves placed as they were at the beginning.

THE BASTION PASSAGE

Gestures of the fifth passage

Imagine the four dancers disposed as at the beginning. D and B will place themselves back to back

Tune

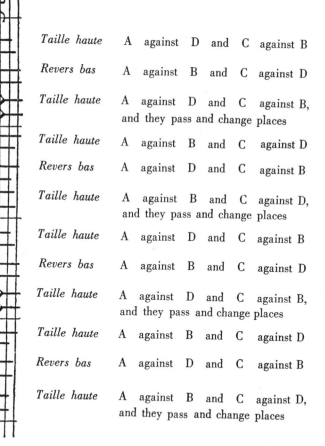

Taille haute	A against D and C against B
Revers bas	A against B and C against D
Taille haute	A against D and C against B, and they pass and change places
Taille haute	A against B and C against D
Revers bas	A against D and C against B
Taille haute	A against B and C against D, and they pass and change places
Taille haute	A against D and C against B
Revers bas	A against B and C against D
Taille haute	A against D and C against B, and they pass and change places
Taille haute	A against B and C against D
Revers bas	A against D and C against B
Taille haute	A against B and C against D, and they pass and change places

After this passage has been repeated four times, the four dancers will be disposed as they were at the beginning. Then, without pause, they will make their rounds, as described before, in preparation for the sixth passage.

THE HAY PASSAGE

Tune   Gestures of the sixth passage

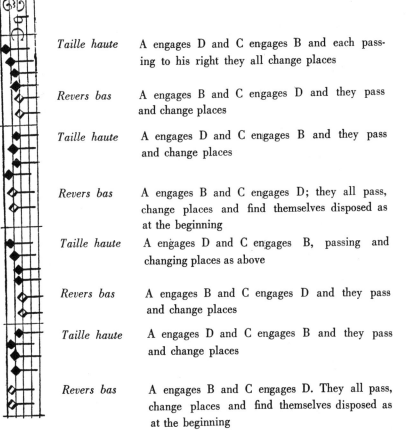

Taille haute   A engages D and C engages B and each passing to his right they all change places

Revers bas   A engages B and C engages D and they pass and change places

Taille haute   A engages D and C engages B and they pass and change places

Revers bas   A engages B and C engages D; they all pass, change places and find themselves disposed as at the beginning

Taille haute   A engages D and C engages B, passing and changing places as above

Revers bas   A engages B and C engages D and they pass and change places

Taille haute   A engages D and C engages B and they pass and change places

Revers bas   A engages B and C engages D. They all pass, change places and find themselves disposed as at the beginning

The hay must now be reversed, which will leave A against B and C against D to commence the repetition. They will then repeat both hay and reverse and when this is all completed the dancers will find themselves disposed as they were at the beginning. They will then withdraw.

CAPRIOL

I thank you, Monsieur Arbeau, for the pains you have taken to teach me dancing.

ARBEAU

I should like to have been able to match the performance to my warm affection for you and may you receive it in this spirit. I look forward to giving you the melodies and movements of a number of ballets and masquerades produced in this town, which shall be dealt with in a second treatise at our earliest leisure. Meanwhile, practise these dances thoroughly and make yourself a worthy companion to the planets who are natural dancers. Or, to those nymphs whom Marcus Varro[123] said he had seen in Lydia rise out of a pool at the sound of the flute, dance and then return to their pool again. And when you have danced with your mistress return to the great pool of your studies to be enriched thereby, as I pray God may grant you the grace.

CERTIFICATE OF COPYRIGHT

Permission is hereby granted to Jehan de Preys, Printer, residing at Langres, to print or have printed a book entitled The Orchesography appearing under the name of Thoinot Arbeau, for six years, with interdiction to all other printers or booksellers to print or have printed the said book during the said six years, under penalty of confiscation of the said books, a discretionary fine and all costs, damages and interest, as more fully set out in his letters of Copyright given at Blois the 22nd of November, 1588, and signed on behalf of the King by his counsel Buyer, sealed in yellow wax with His Majesty's great seal.

TRANSLATOR'S NOTES

[1] Given under the patronage of Catherine de Medici at Versailles in 1581 to celebrate the wedding of Marguerite de Lorraine to the Duc de Joyeuse. Balthasar Beaujoyeux was responsible for its production and it is generally regarded as the progenitor of classical ballet.[a]

[2] The correct heraldic description of the Tabourot coat of arms is, Azure a chevron or between three drums proper, on a chief argent a lion passant sable.

[3] Love grips the man, a mistress claims his mind;
Fires him the more for fight. . . .

[4] The Salii (dancers) were an ancient priesthood at Rome instituted in honour of Mars. They were all of patrician birth and were known as the dancing warrior priests of Mars.

[5] The Corybants were the priests of Cybele. They were Asiatic in origin and a prominent feature of their ritual was a wild dance which was claimed to have power to heal mental disorders.

[6] A masquerade in the 16th century often meant a procession of sumptuously decorated platforms on wheels each bearing a group of actors representing some heroic or erotic scene, usually borrowed from mythology. These floats would stop before the exalted personages present and the actors would declaim in their honour.[b]

[7] Some beat the earth with joyous feet while others chant the tune.

[8] Traffic not with dancing girls.

[9] As the foot was never a standard measurement in the metric system it merely means about the length of the human foot, and appears to be almost as variable.

[10] Whom none excelled with brazen blast to kindle men to war.

[11] Nobly he led the fight by trumpet and his spear.

[12] Two beats to the bar, i.e. 2/4 or common time.

[13] Three beats to the bar, i.e. 3/4 time.

[14] A minim is equivalent to a half note. The late Peter Warlock, in his preface to C. W. Beaumont's translation of the Orchesography, points out that in the sixteenth century the minim was a relatively quick beat and used much as the crotchet (quarter note) would be today.

[15] The Latin passus was equal to 4′ 10″ in English measurement.

[16] A crotchet is equivalent to a quarter note.

[17] A quaver is equivalent to an eighth note.

[18] Aelianus Tacticus, a Greek military writer of the second century A. D. who lived in Rome. The treatise referred to, and much valued in 16th century military circles, was in fact probably dedicated to Trajan as the date 106 A. D. is assigned to it.

[19] A small pipe.[a]

[20] Throughout this translation the musical examples are exact reproductions of the originals. Therefore it should be borne in mind that the beat of a minim in the 16th Century corresponded roughly to that of a crotchet in modern musical notation. No difficulty will be experienced in reading or playing the melodies if the following points are noted. The original staff consisted of eleven lines, which for convenience were split up into various groups of five. There are three clefs[b] which indicate the key note viz. the treble

or G the Bass or F and the C, shown either as or

which latter is movable. Arbeau uses the bar lines to mark the

pattern of a dance quite as much as the value of the bars. Bar lines were by no means in universal use in the 16th century.

[21] "Praise the Lord on the cymbals and pipe."

[22] An instrument with double reed and conical bore, ancestor of the oboe.

[23] The old name for trombone.

[24] Psaltery was an ancient instrument like the dulcimer but played by plucking the strings with the fingers or plectrum.

[25] Forerunner of the tambourine.

[26] A pipe, not brass bound as now, yet brazen as a trumpet.

[27] "The violin family emerges in the early part of the 16th century. The resemblance of its members to those of the viol family is only superficial. . . if they had a common ancestor (which some authorities now doubt) it must have been remote. The violins lived side by side with the viols in rivalry until the latter were ousted at the end of the 17th century." See The Oxford Companion to Music (1942 edition).[a]

[28] Literally low dance. The basse dance was a very early dance type which became extinct before the seventeenth century, but it is interesting today as the ancestor of other dances that survived it. It was performed with the feet kept close to the ground and undoubtedly had its origin in the round choral dances of the 13th century.[b]

[29] A low bow, or in the case of the lady a curtsey.

[30] The literal translation of *branle* is oscillation or shaking movement.

[31] Singles.

[32] The literal translation is resumption.

[33] The literal translation is the return of the basse dance.

[34] Leave.

[35] So far the dispute as to with which leg it were best done remains undecided. In Italy the *révérence* was made to the left, and the hat removed with the left hand which was held to be more gallant as it was nearer the heart.

[36] In other words, one foot following the other without pausing between the steps to bring the heels together.[c]

[37] The pavan was of Italian origin, occasionally written *padovana* suggesting Padua as its birthplace. Because of its great popularity in Spain it was long assumed to have originated there, while others associate the name with the French words *se pavaner*, to move like a peacock. The pavan and the galliard form an example of the musical association of two contrasting dance types, much used by composers in the late 16th century and the forerunner of the instrumental suite and eventually the sonata.[d]

[38] Wheel round.

[39] A variety of pavan popular in the 16th century. Laure Fonta tells us it was performed to singing in the Italian manner, the dancers traversing the length of the ballroom. Hence *passamezzo*, meaning to pass in the centre.[a]

[40] Series of steps linked together as in an *enchainement* in present day ballet parlance.

[41] *Jouyssance vous donneray.*

[42] *Confortez-moy.*

[43] *Toute-frelore.*

[44] *"Trop en ha qui deux en meine."*

[45] The galliard (*gagliardo*) was of Italian origin, the literal meaning is lively or merry. It was the only dance of the period in which the man danced bareheaded, holding his hat in his hand.[b]

[46] *Cinq pas* in French, from which was derived sink-a-pace, a name frequently used for the galliard in England. When referring to a sequence of *five steps* in the galliard, these will appear in italics here to avoid confusion and in conformity with the rest of the dance terminology.

[47] Feet together. The literal translation is feet joined.

[48] Feet apart.

[49] A cubit was 1' 5", supposed to be the length of the forearm.

[50] Passing *revérénce* right.

[51] Passing *révérence* left.

[52] Foot crossed.

[53] The literal translation is mark foot.

[54] The literal translation is mark right heel.

[55] The literal translation is mark toe.

[56] A finger would represent about an inch.

[57] The literal translation is kick.

[58] In Godefroy's *Lexique d'ancien Français*, *grève* is defined as the calf and this movement would entail the use of these muscles. It is also defined as an instrument of torture, known as the boot, and either of these may have suggested it as a suitable name for this pugnacious gesture.[a]

[59] From the Italian *volta*, to turn. In English the définite article became merged in the noun.

[60] In archaic French *entretaille* meant opening, which meaning applied to this movement is borne out by C. d'Albert's definition of the word in his Encyclopaedia of Dancing as the jump preceding any step.

[61] Kick of a horse.

[62] Kick of a cow.

[63] Leap.

[64] Big leap.

[65] Little leap.

[66] Or cabriole, meaning caper.

[67] Cold cabbage warmed up, hence in Juvenal, "stale repetitions".

[68] The note one enjoys oft repeated annoys.

[69] *Rompre l'andouille au genoil* appears to have a similar connotation to taking a sledgehammer to crack a nut.

[70] What could be worthy so pompous a prelude.

[71] God Save the King, or My Country 'Tis of Thee, seems in fact to be a typical galliard tune in rhythm and style.

[72] A moderate leap.

[73] To facilitate reading the music see note 20. Technical difficulties in printing make it impossible to place the corresponding steps and notes exactly opposite one another as Arbeau was able to do in his manuscript.[b] The steps in the tabulations have, therefore, been grouped to follow the pattern of the dance and if read in conjunction with the directions preceding each tabulation will be found to combine naturally with the correct notes.

[74] *La Traditore my fa morire.*

[75] Musical announcement of dawn, originating in the dawn song of the troubadours of Provence.

[76] The cither was an old form of guitar.[a]

[77] *Baisons nous belle, etc.*

[78] *Si j'ayme ou non, etc.*

[79] *La fatigue.*

[80] *La Milannoise.*

[81] *J'aymerois mieulx dormir seulette, etc.*

[82] *L'ennuy qui me tourmente, etc.*

[83] The lavolta was particularly popular in England and James I and Queen Elizabeth both took great pleasure in it. It was banned from the French Court during Louis XIII's reign on account of its indecorum. See note 59.

[84] Of Italian source, the coranto was originally danced off the ground in duple time and later to a rapid gliding step in triple time. The *courante* was Louis XIV's favourite dance and it also enjoyed great popularity with the aristocracy in England. Shakespeare, in Henry V, speaks of "Lavoltas high and swift corantos".[b]

[85] The alman, or *allemande*, seems to have developed from an old German dance in four, or two long beats, to a bar time. A ballroom association grew up between the alman, which was of moderate tempo, and the livelier coranto. This was soon reflected in the classical instrumental suite, where the alman is used by Purcell, Bach and others as the opening movement sometimes preceded by a prelude.[c]

[86] The branle (spelled variously bransle, brawl and braul) is a dance type of French origin. Descended from the basse dance, it was originally a rustic dance but later found favour in the fashionable world. It had a great vogue in England; in Love's Labour's Lost, Armado's page says, "Master, will you win your love with a French Brawl."[d]

[87] The qualifying double or single as applied to the branle appears in English

throughout this translation, but those movements known as *doubles* and *simples* fall under the heading of dance terminology and therefore appear in French.

[88] Bring right foot near to left.

[89] Bring left foot near to right.

[90] Whole notes.

[91] Barrois, or the Duchy of Bar, was an ancient district of France, between Lorraine and Champagne. Bar-le-duc was the principal town.

[92] Montier-en-Der, which is probably the same place, is near Chaumont in the Haute Marne.

[93] *Branles coupés.*

[94] An ancient province of France the capital of which was Poitiers. The minuet sprang from the branle of Poitou.

[95] A corruption of pass-foot which is the literal translation of the French *passe-pied*. Especially popular in Brittany, it was one of the many dance-types that found its way into instrumental music becoming an optional item in a suite and sometimes used in this way by Bach.[a]

[96] Raised heels to the right.

[97] Left foot forward.

[98] Dionysius of Halicarnassus, Greek historian and teacher of rhetoric, who flourished in the reign of Augustus.

[99] A very large Grecian lyre.

[100] This was a weaving back and forth between a line of other dancers.

[101] Spelled variously, hay, haye, and hey, this is a very old country dance, usually a round one, and Dr. Johnson, in his dictionary, suggests that it may have been so called because it was originally danced round a haycock. In Love's Labour's Lost, Dull, the constable says,"I will play on the tabor to the worthies and let them dance the Hay."

[102] This dance came originally from the *Pays de Gap* in France, where the

inhabitants are known as *Gavots*. It became an optional part of the classic instrumental suite and Bach uses it in some of his keyboard suites.

[103] Traditionally an old English folk dance, possibly evolved from the sword dance and believed by some to have been imported by John of Gaunt from Moorish Spain. The blacked face may equally have been responsible for the name morris, i.e. Moorish. From Arbeau's description of this *morisque* it would seem to be a French version of the morris. The leggings worn were known as ruggles.

[104] A kind of castanet or rattle.

[105] A tambourine.

[106] A mediaeval forerunner of the viol.

[107] Deftly to sway a vibrant hip under the castanets.

[108] Gout in the feet.

[109] These are not the traditional Morris steps.

[110] Strike (or tap vigorously) the right heel.

[111] Spelled variously canary, canaries, or canarie, this was a dance in 3/4 or 6/4 time, something like a jig. In England it was thought to be of Spanish origin, where it was believed to have been danced with castanets. This supports the Canary Isles theory. Apparently it was danced to practically the same music as the hay and some Elizabethan pieces are marked for use with either dance. In All's Well That Ends Well, Lafeu says "make you dance Canary with sprightly fire and motion."

[112] In this case, *pied en l'air droit* obviously means right foot sideways in the air, thus constituting a *ru de vache*.

[113] See page 107.

[114] In French the *bouffons*, an ancient sword dance.

[115] The second legendary King of Rome, elected by the Roman people to succeed Romulus. Among other religious innovations he installed the Vestal Virgins to keep the sacred fire burning on the hearth of the city and the Salii to guard the shield that fell from heaven.

[116] Other legends have it that a dance was invented by the Curetes, legendary inhabitants of Crete, in which the harsh sound of their shields and cymbals were employed deliberately to drown the infant's cries and prevent his father from discovering his whereabouts.

[117] Feint.

[118] Thrust.

[119] High cut.

[120] Reverse high cut.

[121] Low cut.

[122] Reverse high cut.

[123] A Roman antiquarian and man of letters. (116-27 B.C.)

EDITOR'S NOTES TO DOVER EDITION

p. 5

a. The facts of Arbeau's life are given by André Mary, " 'L'Orchésographie' de Thoinot Arbeau," in *Les Trésors des Bibliothèques de France*, ed. E. Dacier (Paris, 1935), V, 85–99; they are based upon Pierre Perrenet's *Etienne Tabourot, sa famille et son temps* (Dijon, 1926). Arbeau's birth date is given as March 17, 1520, his death date as July 29, 1595.

b. While this statement is true with regard to sixteenth-century dance, it is not true of fifteenth-century dance. A number of treatises, both manuscript and printed, from the fifteenth century, and extensive modern studies, have yielded considerably more information than is to be found here (see note *b* to p. 51).

p. 10

a. According to Perrenet, quoted in Mary, *op. cit.*, this dedication is to Arbeau's grandnephew, then a lad of fifteen; he may well have been the prototype for Capriol.

b. Des Preyz's reference to "discarded . . . papers which I gathered up long since" emerges as one of those "humble" fictions which abound in the printed books of the period. Arbeau specifically refers to his age at the time of writing as 69 (p. 18); if his birth year was 1520, the year of writing must have been 1589, the same as the year of publication.

p. 11

a. Langres is in eastern France; its cathedral of St. Mammès was the center of a bishopric. Arbeau studied in Paris and Poitiers, receiving his Licentiate of Laws. He then became treasurer of the Chapter of Langres in 1542, then *official* (ecclesiastical judge), and finally vicar-general of his diocese.

b. The University of Orleans, founded in 1305 by Pope Clement V, was an important academic center until the French Revolution.

p. 12

a. On this and on succeeding pages Arbeau reveals himself as a man of the Renaissance, a humanist steeped in the literature of antiquity, as well as a churchman who knows his Bible. His attempts to justify the dance on the basis of Greek views are typical of his period, just as his eagerness to draw unhistorical parallels between the dances of ancient Greece and those of sixteenth-century France reflects the desire of all educated men of the period to emulate antiquity.

p. 13

a. Here Arbeau contradicts a common view that dancing was not permitted by the Catholic Church. It is true that a series of edicts may be traced through-out the Middle Ages, prohibiting dances in churches, churchyards, and public processions (cf. Louis E. Backman, *Religious Dances in the Christian Church and in Popular Medicine,* transl. E. Classen [London, 1952]). Obviously, these edicts are negative proofs that such dancing did exist, but considerable positive evidence may also be cited. That Arbeau was among those who ap-proved of it indicates considerable freedom in these matters in the Renais-sance.

b. Epaminondas (d. 362) was a Theban statesman and soldier of the fourth century B.C.

c. The reference is probably to the *Anabasis* by Xenophon (*ca.* 430 to *ca.* 354 B.C.).

d. Two reformers to whom Arbeau may be referring are G. Paradin, author of *Le Blason des danses* (Beaujeu, 1566), and Lambert Daneau, who wrote the *Traité des danses* (1580). Both discuss the bad effects of dancing and obviously deserve the dreadful recipe Arbeau prescribes.

p. 14

a. Athenaeus (170–230 A.D.) published an extensive work, the *Deipnosophis-tae,* about 200 A.D.

b. "Celius" is probably M. Caelius Rufus (d. 48 B.C.), a friend and corre-spondent of Cicero.

c. This reference is either to Julius Caesar Scaliger (1484–1558), whose fa-mous *Poetics* (1561) gave form to the Renaissance rules for literary genres and who also wrote on the Greek and Roman theater in *De comoedia et tra-*

goedia, or to his son, Joseph Justus Scaliger (1540–1609), who had already begun to publish scholarly works by the 1570's.

d. Lucian (*ca.* 120–190 A.D.), a prolific writer and satirist, was considered in the sixteenth century as the author of the *De Saltatione*, a work on the dance translated from the Greek in 1582 by Filbert Bretin. Doubt has recently been cast on this attribution (cf. Margaret McGowan, *L'Art du ballet de cour en France, 1581–1643* [Editions du Centre National de la Recherche Scientifique, Paris, 1963], p. 14, note 19).

e. Julius Pollux of Naucratis, lexicographer, wrote a thesaurus of Attic words and phrases, the *Onomasticon*, for the Emperor Commodus (reigned 180–192 A.D.). Book IV included material on music, dance, and theater.

f. The *emmeleia* was the characteristic dance of tragedy. According to L. Lawler, who consolidates all primary sources in her numerous articles and summarizes her findings in *The Dance in Ancient Greece* (Wesleyan University Press, Middletown, 1965): "It was noble, and was always carefully adjusted to the mood of the play. Very important in it was *cheironomia*, the code of symbolical gestures . . ." (*op. cit.*, pp. 82–85). It is evident that the *emmeleia*, with its varied miming gestures and choreographies, and its performance by a male chorus (not by couples) resembled the pavan and basse dance (as claimed by Arbeau on p. 15) only in its "noble" character.

g. The *kordax* was the characteristic dance of Old Comedy (flourished *ca.* 480–300 B.C.). Lawler, *ibid.*, p. 87, says, "Unlike the *emmeleia* of tragedy, the *kordax* is described as one specific dance. We are told that it was lascivious, ignoble, obscene, and that its distinguishing feature was a lewd rotation of the abdomen and buttocks, often with the feet held close together." It was performed to the music of the double aulos. The *kordax* continued as a lewd solo dance into the period of the Roman Empire. Arbeau's parallels on p. 15 are totally unfounded.

h. Lawler, *ibid.*, p. 90, tells us that the *sikinnis* was the characteristic dance of the satyr play and, like the *kordax*, a particular dance. "It was lively, vigorous, and lewd, with horseplay and acrobatics, and, at times, an affected, mincing gait, together with exaggerated movements of the hips and shaking of the whole body. We read also of 'swift leaps and kicks', stamping, and whirling turns, the whole accompanied by loud shouts." Its character is in no way similar to that of the double or single branles of the sixteenth century (p. 15).

i. The *Pyrrhic* dance was a sword dance popular throughout Greece; in Sparta it was used as part of the rigorous training of the young men, while in Athens more emphasis seems to have been placed on physical grace than on strength. Arbeau's parallel (p. 15), the *bouffons* or *mattachins*, when performed simply as a mock battle as part of a mascarade, may in fact have been similar to the Pyrrhic. Normally, however, the *bouffons* reveals vestiges of sacrificial agricultural rites (see note *a* to p. 182).

j. The term *trichoria*, meaning triple chorus, is found in Julius Pollux (*op. cit.*).

k. The reference is to Anthoine Arena's *Ad suos compagnones* (Avignon, 1519?), an enormously successful work that went through at least 32 editions between 1529 and 1758. It is a major source of information on the basse dance of the sixteenth century, and Arbeau's indebtedness to Arena on this subject is considerable. Cf. Daniel Heartz, "The basse dance," *Annales Musicologiques* (1958–1963), VI, 287–340, for a survey of the basse dance treatises of the fifteenth and sixteenth centuries.

p. 15

a. For further information on humanistic theories of the dance, theories which strongly influenced the *ballet de cour*, see Margaret McGowan, *op. cit.*, Chapter I.

p. 16

a. Roscius Gallus (d. *ca.* 62 B.C.) was the most celebrated actor at Rome in the first century B.C., and enjoyed the friendship of Cicero and the dictator Sulla. The reference here is to the art of the pantomimist, rather than to the verbal art of the comic actor.

p. 18

a. Claudius Galenus (*ca.* 131 to *ca.* 199 A.D.) was a celebrated Greek physician; he attended Marcus Aurelius, and was a prolific writer. The work Arbeau refers to may be the *Hygieina*, a six-book study on hygiene.

b. The translation is partly incorrect. Bugles and clarinets did not exist as such in the sixteenth century. The original reads, "Les instruments seruants à la marche guerrière, sont les *buccines* & trompettes, *litues* & *clerons* [,] cors et *cornets, tibies, fifres, arigots*, tambours, & aultres semblables, mesmement lesdicts tambours" (italics mine). The history and terminology of musical instruments in the Renaissance are problematical. Sources for this footnote may be found in the bibliography under Apel, Bate, Boyden, Harrison and Rimmer, Reese, and Sachs.

Buccines were either straight trumpets or trombones.

Litues were at this time either crumhorns or cornetts. "Crumhorns" is probably the meaning here, since later Arbeau refers specifically to cornets. The crumhorn (cromorne, etc.) was a double-reed instrument with a slightly curved shape; the reed was enclosed.

Clerons, or clairons or clarions, refers to the folded trumpet of the sixteenth century, in contradistinction to the straight trumpet. In Arbeau's time clairon had already come to mean, as well, playing in the high, or clarino, register.

Cornet at this time was an instrument made of a straight or slightly bent tube of wood, octagonal in cross-section, with six finger-holes and a cup-shaped mouthpiece. Its compass equalled the violin's (g—a^2 or higher), and it was extremely popular from the fifteenth century on, its sound apparently blending remarkably well with the voice. In order to distinguish it from the cornet of today, which it hardly resembles, its name is most commonly spelled *cornett*.

Tibies: it is clear in the text (pp. 47, 49) that Arbeau considered *tibia* to mean flute. Here he was following a standard misconception which has persisted in most writings up to the present day. The Latin *tibia* was equivalent to the Greek *aulos*, a double-reed instrument with a cylindrical bore. It had two pipes.

Fifres: it is clear (p. 39) that Arbeau meant a transverse fife, a type of piccolo.

Arigots: a Provençal term for flageolet, or pipe. Arbeau means a vertical whistle-flute (end-blown) with six holes, four in front and two behind, which traditionally went with the tabor (p. 39).

p. 21

a. This discussion implies a metronome marking of ♦ ♦ ♦ ♦ = 𝅗𝅥 = 80, or a comfortable walking tempo for a long march. Lady Evans throughout uses the English terms for musical note values:

	French	*British Usage*	*American Usage*
♪ = ♩	minime blanche	minim	half note
♩ = ♪	minime noire	crotchet	quarter note
♪ = ♪	crochue	quaver	eighth note

While the modern form of the minim would be a half note, it is, as Arbeau says, the basic unit of beat; today this is usually the quarter note. In the transcriptions accompanying the Labanotation this procedure is followed: ♩ = ♩

p. 22

a. Arbeau's syllabification is based upon the trilled *r*, as in *Fre*, which gives the impression of a drumroll.

p. 36

a. By duple and triple time (French: *mesure binaire, mesure ternaire*) Arbeau merely means the grouping of minims into twos or threes (or, imperfect or perfect semibreves); this may be seen very clearly in the tabulations. Arbeau's time signatures: ₵ and 3, indicate this grouping (see, for example, pp. 154, 156, or 162 for ₵; pp. 122, 147 for 3). The time signatures do not, in most cases, indicate the placement of the bar lines (see Note 20), but actually the subdivision of the *tactus*, " a unit of time-measurement comparable to a slow to moderate beat," which formed the basic concept of tempo in the sixteenth century (W. Apel, *The Notation of Polyphonic Music, 900–1600* [Cambridge, 1945], p. 191). The term "bar lines" is applied here to Arbeau's original lines of division in order to coincide with Lady Evans's usage. Arbeau normally employs the lines to separate the step patterns, and they are not to be confused with modern bar lines.

p. 39

a. The art of improvisation was highly developed during this period. Arbeau's casual references to it on this and on succeeding pages (e.g., p. 43) simply indicate how much it was taken for granted as part of the musician's skill.

b. The "third mode" here refers to one of the church modes or scalar structures which formed the tonal basis of music in general during the Middle Ages and Renaissance. Greek modes and church modes are not the same, but Arbeau, like many of his contemporaries, equates their psychological attributes. The Phrygian, or third church mode, and its plagal version, the Hypophrygian, both with a *finalis* ("tonic") on *e*, have as their most distinctive feature the characteristic minor second, or half-step, between the "tonic" and the second degree. Contemporary theory did not admit of modes on *b*, but classified melodies in *b* as "transposed Phrygian," thus Arbeau's usage on p. 40.

It is suggested that the rules of *musica ficta* could be applied throughout the book in such passages as this; i.e., the *f–b* tritone would be avoided by flatting the *b*, and the seventh degree would be raised a half-step at cadences. Arbeau's practices in this matter are inconsistent; on the whole, however, he avoids such indications. No doubt it was left to the performer to apply *musica ficta*.

p. 44

a. Despite many similarities, including the mode, this is not a simple adaptation of the previous duple-meter tune to triple meter (see note *a* to p. 36 on Arbeau's "meter"). The similarities lie in the melodic figurations, which one may assume reflect the general style of flageolet playing at this time.

p. 46

a. This is no doubt a reference to Isidore, bishop of Seville (602–636 A.D.), who in his *Originum seu Etymologiarum Libri XX* (3, 21, 14) describes the *symphonia* as "lignum cavum ex utraque parte pelle extenta quam virgulis hinc et inde musici feriunt. Fitque in ea ex concordia gravis et acuti suavissimus cantus" ("a hollow piece of wood covered at both ends with skins, which the musician hits on either side with sticks. The combined sounds of the bass and treble produce a most lovely sound").

b. Arbeau is describing snares.

p. 47

a. Diapason: upper octave.

b. The name *chorus* was frequently given to members of the bagpipe family. Bagpipes were quite commonly used as outdoor or military instruments from Greek and Roman times on (C. Sachs, *The History of Musical Instruments* [New York, 1940], p. 281).

c. The exact translation of Hebrew and Aramaic terms for musical instruments is often problematic; Arbeau's simple solutions depend on the Latin (cf. Sachs, *op. cit.*, p. 125).

d. See note *b* to page 18, for an explanation of the *tibia*.

p. 48

a. Arbeau describes the technique of overblowing, which obtains the harmonics above fundamental tones.

p. 49

a. Andria was the first comedy (produced 166 B.C.) by Terence, the Roman playwright (*ca.* 195–159).

p. 50

a. Valerius Maximus, a Roman historian of the first century A.D., wrote *Factorum et dictorum memorabilium libri IX*, a collection of material based mostly on Livy and Cicero.

b. Here Arbeau gets somewhat closer to the truth than he does on p. 49, where he confuses *tibia* with flute.

p. 51

a. The reference to hautboys and sackbuts (French: *haulbois* and *saqueboutes*) calls to mind the many medieval and Renaissance illustrations showing dancers accompanied by a standardized ensemble of two shawms (double-reed instruments) and a sackbut (early trombone). See also p. 59.

b. For recent studies on the much-investigated basse dance, see Heartz, "The basse dance" (note *k* to p. 14), and Ingrid Brainard, *Die Choreographie der Hoftänze in Burgund, Frankreich, und Italien im 15. Jahrhundert* (unpublished doctoral dissertation, Göttingen, 1956). The former summarizes previous studies of the basse dance, and provides a clear chronology of its 150-year history, in particular the musical changes which took place. The latter gives detailed choreographies of fifteenth-century basse dances and *bassadanze* (the Italian type) and correlates them with the music. For an extensive bibliography on the subject see Manfred Bukofzer, "A Polyphonic Basse Dance of the Renaissance," *Studies in Medieval and Renaissance Music* (New York, 1950), pp. 212–216.

c. According to Heartz, *op. cit.*, p. 315, Arbeau's explanation of the differences between common and uncommon basse dances is his own (see also p. 75 of this volume).

p. 52

a. Arbeau's basse dance is in triple meter (i.e., a triple subdivision of the *tactus*), which is typical of the dance in its latest and declining phase. On p. 75 he specifies that any basse dance music in duple meter found in the printed collections of Attaingnant and Nicolas du Chemin must be changed to triple meter, again reflecting the change which took place *ca.* 1525 or later.

Lady Evans here translates *mesure* as "bar," though they are not always identical (see note *a* to p. 36).

p. 54

a. Note that the *révérence* is "accompanied by four bars of the tune on the flute." The *révérence* does not precede the melody, as is frequently supposed.

b. It is especially interesting to note that Poitiers was the childhood home of Rabelais, whose *Gargantua* and *Pantagruel* contain many references to dances also found in Arbeau. Nan Cooke Carpenter, in her *Rabelais and Music* (University of North Carolina Press, 1954), Chapter IV, "The Dance," discusses these references, and also the way in which Rabelais reflects humanistic studies and attitudes on dance.

The sixteenth-century dances mentioned by Rabelais that also appear in Arbeau include the basse dance (danced by Pantagruel as a student at Orléans, the alma mater of our Capriol), the *moresca*, the Trihory de Bretagne, chanson-dances (including the basse dances *Jouissance vous donnerai* and *Patience*), a galliard, an allemande, hayes, and branles of various types; the mock-battle of the *bouffons* appears in his *Sciomachie*. Rabelais's attitude towards the dance as a joyous activity is the same as Arbeau's, and he too makes very little distinction between courtly and peasant dances of the period. His allegorical use of the dance, dance terms, and steps, goes far beyond Arbeau, and adds to our picture of the rich life of the time.

Arbeau makes no direct reference to Rabelais, yet his delightful passage defining dance has a Rabelaisian flavor (see p. 14 for the translation):

> Danser c'est à dire saulter, saulteloter, caroler, baler, treper, trepiner, mouuoir & remuer les piedz, mains, & corps de certaines cadances, mesures & mouuementz, consistans en saultez, pliement de corps, diuarications, claudications, ingeniculations, eleuations, iactations de piedz, permutations & aultres contenances.

In similar catalogue style, Rabelais describes the end of a chess ballet (the only figured ballet in *Gargantua* or *Pantagruel*):

> . . . en cinq cens diversitez si soudain se mouvoir, desmarcher, sauter, voltiger, gambader, tournoyer. . . .

c. This is the version shown in the Labanotation section.

p. 56

a. The difficulty of deciphering this step led Mabel Dolmetsch to suggest that Arbeau had never even seen a basse dance (*Dances of England and France, 1450–1600* [London, 1949], p. 14). If he did see one, it must have been when he was very young, and the memory of a septuagenarian may be hazy.

p. 57

a. Arbeau's frequent linking of pavans with basse dances adds further proof to the obvious choreographic connections between the sixteenth- and fifteenth-century solemn couple dances (i.e., of the six basic steps of the basse dance, the pavan retained at least three). But whereas each basse dance had its own choreography to be memorized by the dancers, the pavans apparently did not, and could therefore serve as purely processional dances. See pp. 58f. and 65ff. for further pavan directions.

That the pavan was "usually danced before the basse dance" is very much to be doubted. There are many confusing passages in this section. On p. 66 Arbeau refers to the "customary practice of following it by a galliard." On p. 57 it is clear that the tordion, "a kind of galliard," followed the basse dance. The more likely combination of dances, then, would be:

EARLY 16TH CENTURY: Basse dance–tordion

MID AND LATE 16TH CENTURY: Pavan–galliard

Pavan–galliard combinations are indeed frequent in the dance collections of the period, and often the tune is identical for a pair. The slow-quick tempo pattern for paired dances is age-old.

It is clear in the text that the pavan was not just the simple dance described on p. 57. Most likely the steps were preceded and followed at least by a *révérence* and *congé.* The *double* was probably divided up in *ad libitum* variations drawn from the galliard, as described on pp. 66–67, when the dance was not a solemn processional of the court, but at other times when skilled dancers were pleased to show their abilities.

See Heartz, ed., *Preludes, Chansons and Dances for Lute Published by Pierre Attaingnant, Paris (1529–1530)* (Neuilly-sur-Seine, Société de Musique d'Autrefois, 1964), Chapter Three, xlviii, for further discussion of the relationships between the pavan and the basse dance, and also the question of tempo. Heartz points out a likely connection between the pavan *simple* step and the so-called "wedding step" of today (p. 1).

The earliest source of the pavan, musically, is Dalza's *Intabulatura de lauto* of 1508. For another, more complicated, choreography, see Fabritio

Caroso's *Pavaniglia* in *Il Ballarino* (Venice, 1581). Caroso's tune is the same as Arbeau's *Spanish pavan*. Arbeau and Caroso are our only instructional choreographic sources for this extremely important dance of the sixteenth century, although Dolmetsch, *op. cit.*, pp 94f., 97, cites two step-sequences for the pavan found in a Bodleian Library manuscript: Rawlinson Poet. 1570.

The pavan had a long and important musical history which continued into the seventeenth century, even after it was no longer danced.

p. 59

a. The length of the pavan must have been optional, but obviously, to circle the hall two or three times requires more than one playing of a melody of the standard type given by Arbeau.

p. 60

a. The tune, "Belle qui tiens ma vie," belongs to type A of the two standard melody-types of the pavan, which were well-established by about 1580 (both are related to the famous *folia* and *passamezzo* discants; the bass here shows a more distant relation to those basses). A short list of concordances is given by Walter Kob, *The Pavan* (unpublished master's thesis, Eastman School of Music, 1943), p. 73. See also O. Gombosi, "Italia: Patria del basso ostinato," *Rassegna Musicale*, VII (1934), 14–25.

Further concordances with this particular melody may be found in the *Fitzwilliam Virginal Book*, eds. J. A. Fuller Maitland and W. Barclay Squire (1899; Dover Publications reprint, 1963), II: a *Coranto* by William Byrd (p. 305), and an anonymous *Corrãto* (p. 311).

p. 63

a. In the Contra-tenor part, third measure, the sharp sign indicates that the *b*, normally flatted because of the key signature, is to be raised to *b*-natural.

p. 65

a. All spellings have been modernized.

p. 66

a. The suggestion here is that the basse dance (sixteenth-century style) was somewhat faster than the pavan.

p. 67

a. For a summary of information on *Jouissance vous donnerai*, see Heartz,

"The basse dance," pp. 313–315. For a bibliography of *Jouissance* see Jean Rollin, *Les Chansons de Clément Marot* (Paris, 1951), pp. 190–193. The music was written originally by Claudin de Sermisy, and first printed by Attaingnant in *Chansons nouvelles à quatre parties* (1527).

p. 75

a. Pierre Attaingnant (d. 1552) was the most important Parisian music publisher of the first half of the sixteenth century. His valuable and numerous publications appeared from 1528 to 1549, and included both sacred and secular, vocal and instrumental music. Many dances, including basse dances, are to be found among his instrumental works. Arbeau gives the correct address.

b. Nicolas du Chemin (*ca.* 1510–1576) published in Paris from 1540 to the year of his death.

c. Arbeau quotes Arena directly for the three irregular *(incommune)* basse dances (Heartz, *op. cit.*, pp. 315, 335f.).

p. 77

a. Arbeau's description of the choreographic pattern of the galliard indicates a dance that calls for considerable endurance. To follow this sequence would require a number of repetitions of any given galliard tune of the time.

To dance it "in a manner known as the Lyonnaise" calls for less endurance and turns the dance into a kind of mixer; as such, however, its length would certainly be increased.

The passages on this page give many hints to the dancer. The miming qualities are clearly indicated, the "going and comings," and the turnings. While the first description may be a somewhat nostalgic recollection of former customs, it may also indicate mid-century practices quite precisely.

p. 78

a. This statement is a mistranslation. The original reads, "Mais ledit tourdion se dance plus *doulcement* [gently], & auec les actions & gestes moings violents" (italics mine). Lady Evans corrects her error on p. 94, where it is clear that, because it is danced closer to the ground, the tordion is more rapid than the galliard.

p. 82

a. Here Arbeau uses the plural form, *pieds largis*; in the dance tabulations, however, only the singular is used: *pied largi gauche, pied largi droit.* The only distinction may be that the plural indicates a position already taken, while the singular indicates which foot takes the position, and therefore the direction in which one is moving. The plural is never used in the tabulations, so that the distinction is quite academic.

p. 85

a. The French for this passage reads, ". . . l'vn des pieds *estant getté* & posé pour soustenir le corps" (italics mine). This indicates a leap or hop *onto* the supporting foot, a fact that is not made clear in the translation.

b. As above. The French reads, "Quand au contraire on marche du tallon du l'vn des pieds, l'aultre pied *estant getté*, pour demeurant ferme soustenir le corps de celuy qui dance. . . ."

p. 87

a. See notes *a* and *b* to p. 85. Again the French indicates that this is not stepped, but leaped, in this case as in a *coupé*, "Ledit mouuement de greue est faict & causé aulcunes fois quand le danceur gette & met l'vn de ses pieds en la place de l'aultre pied, & cependant ledit autre pied est esleué en l'air deuant: Et telle mouuement s'appelle entretaille. . . ." The verb *getter*, "to throw," is not well served by "to place" or "to transfer."

p. 89

a. The French reads, "Quand les deux pieds sont gettez & posez à terre. . . ." The translation given here is not necessarily the only one. "When both feet have been thrown and landed on the ground," is a more literal translation. The significance of the ambiguity in this passage becomes apparent when one is interpreting the basic *five steps* of the galliard (pp. 95, 100), for the instructions preceding the *posture* on the cadence there do not indicate leaping off *both* feet, but off one. Some over careful interpreters have been misled by the translation into adding a *plié* on both feet immediately preceding the *saut*; this procedure turns the *five steps* into six, slows down the dance, and makes it considerably less graceful (Mabel Dolmetsch, *Dances of England and France*, p. 109, makes this error).

b. The "soft landing" described here is clearly reflected in the pattern, ♩ ♩ ♩ ♩. ♪ ♩, the typical rhythm of the galliard. The dotted note should be performed double-dotted where possible, so that the short note coincides with the landing on the back foot.

p. 91

a. Clausula is the term usually applied to the cadential formula of sixteenth-century polyphonic music. Here Arbeau employs the word simply to mean the final steps and beats of the basic galliard pattern.

b. French: "ils remuent les pieds en l'air"—literally, "they shake (or wag) their feet in the air." This is similar to the *entrechat*, in ballet terms.

p. 92

a. The references on this page and the next to the onlookers and concern for their pleasure and critical opinion make it evident that this is a show-off dance, in contradistinction to the branles, in which, as Arbeau says, many people can participate.

p. 94

a. The tune given here is also found in Jacques Moderne's *Musique de Joye* (*ca.* 1550) (reprint: Nagel's Verlag, ed. Giesbert [Kassel, 1934]). Arbeau omits the dotted rhythm for purposes of clarity.

b. The fact that the repeat signs are omitted here and in the tabulations for this tune is probably of no significance.

p. 96

a. French: "Air du tourdion reduict en minimes blanches *qui font la mesure du temps.*" The words italicized here were omitted by Lady Evans, but are important, since they clarify Arbeau's conception of the minim as the unit of beat.

p. 99

a. This melody appears in Pierre Phalèse, *Liber primus* (1571), and *Chorearum molliorum Collectanea* (1583) (cf. Friedrich Blume, *Studien zur Vorgeschichte der Orchestersuite im 15. und 16. Jahrhundert* [Leipzig, 1925], pp. 135–151).

b. The sixteenth-century Romanesca was one of the most widely known of the double grounds (both melody and bass form the basis for a series of variations). Compositions on the Romanesque (or Romanesca) were of all types, for all performance media, and in the sixteenth and seventeenth centuries they number in the hundreds. In its early history the Romanesca was closely allied with the *folia* and *passamezzo antico*, which were similar grounds. It is no wonder that Capriol finds the tune trite.

Possibly this is the passage that led to the misunderstanding, still prevalent today, that the Romanesca and the galliard were identical. Praetorius says of the galliard that "as it is believed to be of Roman origin, it is therefore called the Romanesca," and *Grove's Dictionary of Music and Musicians* (5th ed., 1954), VII, 215 simply identifies the Romanesca with the galliard. For further information, see E. H. Meyer, "Galliarde," *Musik in Geschichte und Gegenwart* (Kassel and Basel, 1955), IV, cols. 1285–86.

c. This is the only mention anywhere in the book of the lute as a possible accompanying instrument for the dance. Yet the suggestion is implicit in the tremendous number of dances in lute collections of the sixteenth and seventeenth centuries that it was a standard accompanying instrument. Paintings of court balls and the bills for court entertainments of the period are further evidence that the lute was employed for dances. No conclusions can be drawn from the contradiction; we might suggest only that the lute was not one of Arbeau's favorite dance instruments.

d. The two melodies on this page show two different ways of repeating the musical phrases (a repetition sign has obviously been omitted at the end of *Antoinette*). When *Antoinette* appears on the following pages, however, the repetitions of the music are omitted, even though Arbeau advises repetition for the dance steps. The casualness with which these signs are treated simply reflects the degree to which they were taken for granted.

p. 104

a. That is, turn right shoulder towards partner with *grève droite*, and left shoulder towards partner with *grève gauche*. This turning is quite difficult to execute at a fair tempo, if performed on every *grève*; considerable skill is required to do it gracefully. An alternate solution to this passage, though less accurate, is to turn the right shoulder once towards partner for the entire *five-step* pattern which begins with a *grève droite*, and so on.

b. This galliard probably continues through to the bottom of p. 106.

p. 105

a. The *five-step* pattern in three movements on this page and the next literally involves a change of accent for the dancer, from $\overline{1}$ 2 3 $\overline{4}$ 5 6 to $\overline{1}$ 2 $\overline{3}$ 4 $\overline{5}$ 6. In musical terms this is known as the hemiola. Musical hemiolas were very frequent in the galliard, and later in the courante. It could be assumed that a musical *hemiola* was meant to be matched by a danced *hemiola,* and when performed this way the effect is excellent. There is nothing in Arbeau, however, to indicate that this should be done. Arbeau's tune retains its accents on 1 and 4 despite the change for the dancer. The last measures of pp. 111 and 112, however, show the *hemiola* in the music as well as in the dance steps.

p. 107

a. There may be an error in the music here, for both measures contain seven minims. Correlation with the text above suggests that the removal of the rests will solve the problem. Another solution would be to remove the minim preceding each rest (see Labanotation, p. 251).

p. 108

a. The French reads: "Tornez le corps à main gaulche à la partie opposite, & faictes greue droicte." The absence of a comma after "gaulche" suggests quite a different translation from Lady Evans's (which is Beaumont's also). The following is suggested as better suiting the tempo and style of the dance: "Turn the body towards the left (i.e., in the opposite direction), and make a right *grève.*"

b. French: *mignardé.* The coordination of steps here is probably:

1	and	2	and	3	and	4	and
leap	step	leap	step	leap	step	leap	step

This is a graceful step when done with a very low leap *(petit saut).*

p. 109

a. French:

> . . . car ymaginant la derniere minime blanche estre coupee en deux noires [,] des deux premiers pas, vous en feriez trois. . . .

This should be translated:

> . . . because imagining that the second minim [of the two white minims] is divided into two black notes, of the first two steps you will now make three. . . .

p. 111

a. By superimposing two-beat patterns on music organized into three-beat musical groupings, the fleurets create interesting cross accents. The tune is the same as *The seconde Milanoise* in Le Roy, *Fantaisies et Danses* from *A briefe and Easye Instruction to Learne the Tableture to Conducte and Dispose*

Thy Hande unto the Lute (1568), ed. Pierre Jansen (Centre National de la Recherche Scientifique, Paris, 1962).

p. 113

a. I.e., turning around; see p. 114.

b. This melody continues to the middle of p. 115. It is also found as *J'aymerey mieux dormir* in Le Roy, *Fantaisies et Danses*, ed. P. Jansen, no. 18.

p. 115

a. The first note is an *f*-natural.

b. According to Heartz, "Etude des concordances," in Adrian Le Roy, *Premier Livre de tabulature de luth (1551)*, eds. André Souris and Richard de Morcourt (Paris, Editions du Centre National de la Recherche Scientifique, 1960), p. xviii, this galliard is to be found in Attaingnant's *Troisième Livre de danceries* (1550). In Le Roy it appears as the galliard to the pavan, *Sy je m'en vois*. Other concordances for this melody are also given in the same edition. The tune continues through p. 118.

p. 117

a. The complicated steps given on these pages suggest considerably restricted tempi, even when performed by a skilled dancer.

p. 121

a. The hand-hold by the man is difficult to decipher. The French reads:

> . . . gettés vostre bras gaulche sur son dos, en la prenant & serràt de vostre main gaulche par le faulx du corps au dessus de sa hanche droicte, & en mesme instant getterez vostre main droicte au dessoubz de son busq pour l'aider à sauter quand la pousserez deuant vous auec vostre cuisse gaulche.

"Faulx du corps" means "narrow part of the body above the hips," which is not necessarily the waist. Dolmetsch, *Dances of England and France*, p. 130, suggests that it is the *arm* which is placed above the right hip, and that the hand is actually closer to the left hip. This arm placement contradicts Arbeau, and furthermore, would be difficult to execute with the wide, stiff costume of the lady of that time. Placing the hand as shown in the Labanotation reflects Arbeau's text as faithfully as possible, and does justice to the iconographic evidence as well. The key point, however, is that the lady stands at a right angle to the gentleman.

p. 122

a. The alignment of steps with music for the volta shows the *saut* on beat 4, and the final *pieds joints* on beat 6. This contradicts the description on p. 119 (the translation is accurate), which gives the *saut* on beat 3 and the *pieds joints* on beat 4! Either Arbeau contradicts himself, or his printer was mistaken in the tabulation. If one follows the tabulation, however, the dance takes on a grace and excitement, a swirling movement, which well accords with its literary descriptions. Of the two patterns given, then, the editors have shown the second in the Labanotation.

b. The directions have definitely been for turning to the *right*; the reverse directions in the next sentence are for turning to the *left*. Arbeau was either confused here, or meant that, in turning to the right, the left arm and left leg are in active motion, directing the woman.

p. 123

a. Both Lady Evans and Beaumont give "spring off" as their translation. Arbeau's term is "sauterez *sur* le pied droict," or "spring *on* the right foot." The distinction is an important one. In the directions for the branle of Haut Barrois (p. 135) Arbeau gives "sauterez *des* deux pieds," or "spring *off* both feet." The difference in steps would be that the first term indicates a hop *on* one foot prior to the next step, while the second is a leap *from* a stationary position to a new one.

p. 126

a. This is the same as the *Allemande Savoye* in Pierre Phalèse, *Liber primus* (1571) (cf. Blume, *Studien . . .* , pp. 135–151).

p. 127

a. The original simply says, ". . . comme la courante, auec les mouuements." Lady Evans has added the last phrase.

p. 130

a. Arbeau's references to *reprise* and *branle* are to steps in the basse dance.

p. 131

a. The description of the customs connected with branles makes it quite clear that, though done in a line or a circle, they were arranged in couples.

p. 133

a. French: *par deux mesures ternaires.* See note *a* to p. 36 for the explanation

of Arbeau's "mesure." Heartz, *Preludes, Chansons and Dances*, xlii, analyzes
Arbeau's differences here from Praetorius, de Lauze, and Mersenne, and suggests that the tempo for this branle must have been "rather slow, because
steps were made to the minim." Such a conclusion is unfounded. The dance
can be done quite rapidly with small steps (as shown in the Labanotation), or
it can be performed more slowly. We have chosen the faster tempo to suit the
description on p. 129, but there is of course no absolute proof for any tempo.

p. 135

a. The same tune is found in Pierre Phalèse, *Liber primus* (1571) and
Chorearum molliorum Collectanea (1583), as the *Branle d'Escosse* (cf.
Blume, *Studien, loc. cit.*).

b. The branle of Haut Barrois is the "rarest of all branles in the musical
sources" (Heartz, *Preludes, Chansons and Dances*, p. xliv), and was sup-
posedly first introduced to courtly circles in 1556.

p. 137

a. Arbeau gives a number of branles with mixed meter, e.g., *branle simple*,
branle Charlotte, *branle appellée Pinagay*. The bar lines are placed to coincide with the changes in step patterns.

p. 139

a. The sharp sign is probably an error, a flat being intended instead.

p. 143

a. There is no doubt that the description here is only the bare skeleton of
what must have been a miming dance. Such mock-battle dances were common
in the entertainments of the sixteenth century (see note *a* to p. 182 on the
bouffons and note *a* to p. 177 on the *morisque*). The footwork in this is so dull
that it is difficult to understand why the dance was included without any further commentary.

p. 147

a. Arbeau notated this tune with nine minims (or three perfect semibreves)
to a measure, the equivalent of our $\frac{9}{4}$. Heartz, *ibid.*, p. xliv, finds a concordance
between this tune and d'Estrée's seventeenth *branle de Poitou* in his *Second
livre de Danseries* (1559). The same collection contains eighteen other
branles de Poitou in the same meter. Another in the same meter appears in Le
Roy, *Fantaisies et Dances*, ed. Jansen. Other *branles de Poitou*, however, have

only two perfect semibreves to a measure (e.g., Gervaise, reprinted in H.
Expert, ed., *Maîtres Musiciens de la Renaissance française*, Vol. 23 [1908]).
It is entirely possible that there were several types of branles from this area.

The problem is compounded by Arbeau himself, however, in his later reference to the "second and third bars" of triple time. If we apply his normal
definition of *mesure* (transl. "bar") here, the foot-stampings would occur in
the first measure of p. 148 on the fourth through ninth minims. Actually, they
are shown in the tabulation on the first through sixth minims of the second
measure. Arbeau's definition of *mesure* seems to have changed at this point to
match the bar lines (see note *a* to p. 36 for an explanation of his normal
usage); it may now refer to *tempus perfectum* (Apel, *Notation of Polyphonic
Music*, p. 96).

The passage translated at the bottom of this page clearly contains an
error:

> . . . les deuxieme & troisieme mesures ternaires, qui contiennent six minimes
> blāches, *sur chacune desquelles*, elles font six pieds en l'air, à rechange, ainsi
> que voyez icy dessoubz (italics mine).

Literally, he says that on *each* minim "they make six pieds en l'air." At any
feasible tempo this is not possible, nor is it shown thus in the tabulation. The
translator has corrected this error. The confusion with regard to *mesure*
remains.

p. 153
a. The order of the Knights of Malta was actively and prominently engaged
against the Turks throughout the sixteenth century. This mimed branle is
obviously designed to imitate the Turks, not the Knights, and is only one
example of the sixteenth-century interest in the exotic to be found in Arbeau.
Daniel Heartz, "Etude des Concordances," in Adrian Le Roy, *Fantaisies et
Danses* (Paris, 1962), p. xii, finds Arbeau's tune identical with Le Roy's second *branle de Malte*. Le Roy, however, gives the music for the entire ballet.

p. 156
a. Paul Nettl, "Die Tänze Jean d'Estrées," *Die Musikforschung* (1955), VII,
442f., gives a concordance for this tune with d'Estrée, *Premier livre de danceries* (1559). It also appears in Phalèse, *Liber primus* (1571), under the
same title (Blume, *Studien*, pp. 135–151). It is noteworthy that the d'Estrée
version shows all but one of the *f*'s as *f*-sharps.

p. 158

a. This branle may have been designed to imitate peas popping out of their pods. At any rate, it is a charming dance (French: *branle des Pois*).

p. 159

a. Arbeau's supposition about the origin of this dance is no doubt correct. The dance is not only comical, but silly; his objections, however, seem to be purely a matter of form. There is no indication in the tabulation on p. 161 as to how many times the dancers bow their heads. We suggest once with each *marque pied*.

p. 161

a. This dance makes a very attractive mixer.

p. 162

a. Nettl, *op. cit.*, p. 441, finds concordances for this melody in d'Estrée, *Troisième livre* . . . (1559), and Praetorius, *Terpsichore* (1612).

p. 163

a. Johann Rosinus (1551–1626) was a sixteenth-century antiquarian. He published his *Romanarvm antiqvitatvm libri decem ex variis scriptoribvs svmma fide singvlarique diligentia collecti* in Basle in 1583. Note how up-to-date Arbeau is in his reading.

b. French: *branle des sabots*, which would more properly be translated as "Branle of the Wooden Shoes."

p. 164

a. This melody has been found in Pierre Phalèse, *Liber primus* (1571) and *Chorearum molliorum Collectanea* (1583) (Blume, *Studien, loc. cit.*); it is also in d'Estrée, *Second livre* (Nettl, *op. cit.*, pp. 443f.).

p. 168

a. Nettl, *op. cit.*, p. 441, finds a distant relationship between this tune and the *branle Montirandé* of d'Estrée, *Troisième livre*.

p. 169

a. Arbeau describes the hay exactly as it is still done in English country dancing today, as well as elsewhere in Europe. His "passing to their left" is usually taught as "passing right shoulders"—the movement is identical.

The term may be pictorially derived from "la haye," French for an artificial hedge, "formed of upright wooden stakes interlaced with transverse strands consisting of thin supple stems" (Dolmetsch, *op. cit.*, p. 64).

p. 172
a. French: *branle de l'Official.* The title probably refers to the *office* (that is, household servants). The description of the dance, with its springs as in the Haut Barrois (which Arbeau says is danced by "lackeys and serving wenches, and sometimes by young men and damsels of gentle birth in a masquerade, disguised as peasants and shepherds . . .") would bear out such an interpretation.

It should be noted, however, that an *official* of the Church was an ecclesiastical judge, and that Arbeau held this position at one time. Thus it is also possible that he originated or named this dance for himself; on the other hand, its peasant-like character makes the first solution more likely.

p. 174
a. The four steps given here seem to contradict the statement on p. 172 that the men remain firmly on the ground while lifting the women. It is also possible, however, that they are supposed to make two *pieds en l'air* without *saut* during the time their partners are in the air (i.e., to make two small steps). The exact timing of the lift is not given.

p. 175
a. Although this is Arbeau's only mention of a kissing dance, literary and iconographic evidences indicate that kissing was a part of many dances, a courtesy that, in England at least, was expected of a gentleman towards a lady (e.g., Shakespeare, *Henry VIII*, i, 4, 47, "I were unmannerly to take you out [to dance] and not to kiss you").

From Praetorius's *Terpsichore* to the present, the gavotte has been considered to have come from the "gavots," the inhabitants of the *pays du Gap* in Dauphiné. Doubt is cast on this theory by the fact that, although the dance does not appear in that area now, it is still to be found in Brittany, danced in a style similar to Arbeau's description; it also occurs in Provence and the Basque country. Whatever its origins, Arbeau's statement that it is a new dance is borne out by musical sources and other commentaries. In the first quarter of the seventeenth century it became a regular part of the court ball (according to Mersenne, 1636), and was usually the light and rapid conclusion to a group of branles (cf. Claudie Marcel-Dubois, "Gavotte," *Musik in Geschichte und Gegenwart*, IV, cols. 1510–14).

p. 176

a. The steps given by Arbeau are not clear. For example, *marque pied droit croisé* could mean (1) touching the toe of the right foot to the left of the left foot, (2) touching the toe of the right foot to the right of the left foot, but with the right heel crossing over the left foot, (3) touching the toe of the right foot quickly in its usual way, then going into a normal *pied croisé*. This writer inclines towards the first interpretation.

There was obviously a great deal more to the dance than Arbeau provides (he states that he gives only "the first branle in the suite of gavottes").

p. 177

a. Cf. Paul Nettl, "Die Moresca," *Archiv für Musikwissenschaft*, XIV (1957), pp. 165–174; Curt Sachs, *World History of the Dance* (New York, 1952), pp. 335–341; Carl Engel, "Moresca, Moriskentänze," *Musik in Geschichte und Gegenwart*, IX, cols. 575–580; Cecil Sharp and Herbert MacIlwaine, *The Morris Book* (2nd ed., London, 1912–1919), I–V. The best discussion of the early morris/moresca in England is to be found in Barbara Lowe, "Early Records of the Morris in England," *Journal of the English Folk Dance and Song Society*, VIII, No. 2 (1957), pp. 61–82.

The exact relationship between the English morris dance (Lady Evans's term) and the *morisque*, as Arbeau calls it, is not yet entirely clear. Fifteenth-century English sources indicate that a relationship of some sort is certain, but complicated by the admixture of old English customs with the acrobatic dance imported from the continent. After the fifteenth century the English morris followed its own line of development to the present day—hence Lady Evans's statement that the steps are not the same as Arbeau's; today's Morris steps seem, in fact, to be closely allied to the steps of the galliard.

There were, furthermore, various types of *moresca*, for the name was applied in the fifteenth to seventeenth centuries throughout Europe (1) to miming dances on allegorical, humanistic subjects which frequently contained swordplay and mock battles (often the word was used merely as a synonym for "mascarade"); (2) to highly exotic, acrobatic, "savage," dances by a ring of men, each dancing alone, for a prize from a lady (this was the usual form in central Europe, and was illustrated frequently by such fifteenth-century artists as Israhel van Meckenem); (3) to dance-battles imitating the wars between the Saracens and Christians, or the Moors and the Spaniards; (4) and in Italy, particularly Naples, to obscene skits for which the dialect and manners of the Negro descendants of slaves provided the basis (as in Lassus' *Moresche* of 1555 and 1581). Blackening of the face was common, and has been variously explained.

What Arbeau describes here is obviously a pale reflection of the central-European dance around the lady. Apparently in the Langres area it had already lost much of its popularity, although in other places and guises it continued through the eighteenth century. Nettl and Rowe also relate the *moresca* to the *bouffons*, or *mattachins* (see note *a* to page 182).

b. Macrobius was a Platonic philosopher and Latin grammarian (*fl.* 400 A.D.) who was reprinted frequently in the Renaissance.

c. Jodocus Badius (1462–1535) was an eminent scholar who became an important printer at Paris; at his printing-house, known as *Prelum Ascensianum*, he published classics with his own commentaries, among other works.

p. 178
a. This tune is found in T. Susato's *Het derde Muziekboexken* (1551), as *La mourisque* (Blume, *Studien*, pp. 135–151). For further concordances of the melody see Nettl, *op. cit.* Sachs, *op. cit.*, states that Arbeau's tune was printed as a Morris melody as early as 1550 in England, but indicates no source.

p. 180
a. Throughout the seventeenth century the dance appeared in triple time, with the first note of each measure dotted, and usually it was over a short, traditional ground bass, such as the *passamezzo moderno* (I IV V I). Such a bass would fit Arbeau's tune easily. Arbeau's duple meter coincides with that of the earliest Canary known to this writer, a *Canario* in a Spanish vihuela collection by Diego Pisador (1552). There is some question, however, as to whether Pisador's *endechas de Canario*, a funeral dance, and the exotic Canary, were in fact related. Whether the dance did indeed originate in the Canary Islands, or was merely intended, as Arbeau supposes, to suggest the savage and exotic, is an open question.

Praetorius gives the same tune in $\frac{6}{4}$ in *Terpischore*, no. XXXI.

P. 181

a. For many concordances and discussions of this tune see Kob, *The Pavan*, pp. 74–80, and Diana Poulton, "Notes on the Spanish Pavan," *The Lute Society Journal* (1961), II, 5–16. Both writers agree that the version by Cabezón, in his *Obras de Musica para tecla, arpa y vihuela* (1578), under the title "Pauana Italiana," is the first yet traced. Kob points out that the subject is closely allied to the *passamezzo* and *folia* melodies, and calls it a derivative of type B of the pavan discants.

b. The initial steps are identical to the first two steps of the pavan. It seems clear that the dance consists of a series of variations on the basic pavan steps (note the forward and backward movements). Arbeau may link it with the Canary (p. 66) because that dance too is performed with forward and backward movements and with many variations.

p. 182

a. Lady Evans has used *Buffens* for her title; this does appear in some English dance collections of the sixteenth century, although *Buffons* was just as frequent and far more accurate. Arbeau's claim that it is directly descended from the Pyrrhic dance would be difficult to support.

The *bouffons*, or *mattachins*, was related to the Morris and Fastnachtspiel sword dances, and to the English Mummers' Play. It may also have included a "rose" figure (crossed swords) and a symbolic beheading, both age-old customs of agricultural fertility rituals (cf. Enid Welsford, *The Fool* [New York, 1935?], p. 70, and Barbara Lowe, *op. cit.*, pp. 77–78).

There is also a possible connection between the *mattachins* and the *moresca* of the mimed-battle type, for they are both lively sword dances. In addition, however, the *mattachins* may also be a dance of death (as in parts of Italy).

According to Nettl, "Die Moresca," p. 170, the Castilian *matachín* is a comical figure, similar to Harlequin, who dances with grotesque leaps.

Arbeau's dance is nothing more than a mock sword-fight; all other elements, with the exception of the bells on the legs, are missing. Perhaps it would have been staged as part of a ballet, for mock battles were stereotyped parts of many entertainments of the period (cf. McGowan, *L'Art du ballet de cour en France, 1581–1643*, p. 39 and elsewhere).

p. 186

a. For some concordances and a discussion of this tune, see Nettl, "Die Moresca," p. 170, and "Die Tänze Jean d'Estrées," p. 440.

p. 197

a. See Margaret McGowan, *op. cit.*, for an excellent study of the many mascarades and ballets which preceded this, and a discussion of the tremendous contribution of the humanists to the development of the ballet. Poets, painters, composers, and choreographers joined forces to produce a highly allegorical art which would perfectly reflect the full gamut of man's experience and emotions. It was the mimed dance, they felt, that could best serve as the vehicle for their ideas. The *Balet comique de la Royne* is the first known example of a conscious effort to realize in one spectacle the union of the arts so desired by the theorists (McGowan, p. 42). It should be noted that Arbeau most frequently employs the word *ballet*, rather than *mascarade*, in describing mimed dances.

b. See editor's note just above. Dialogue, music, and dance, often with mock battles, were also extremely important parts of this allegorical amalgam of the arts. Rich and exotic costumes and fabulous machinery (e.g., clouds from which the gods descended, dragons from whose mouths strange creatures poured) fed the eye as well as the ear.

p. 198

a. That is, a vertical whistle-pipe.

b. The description of the clefs is incorrect. *All* the clefs are movable. There is no *F* clef in the collection resembling our modern bass clef. It is represented instead by ⣿⣿⣿⣿⣿ (see pp. 20–38), or else as in the Bassus of the pavan (pp. 60 and 61): ⣿⣿⣿⣿⣿ ; this clef is also movable (see pp. 27, 78, and elsewhere). There is only one *C* clef: ⣿⣿⣿⣿⣿ .

p. 199

a. Here and on p. 129 Arbeau uses the word *violon*, a term which by this time in the sixteenth century was consistently applied to members of the violin family, and was distinct from *viole*, or viol. While the violin had not yet achieved final form, its distinctive characteristics—four strings tuned in fifths, curved peg-box, bow held overhand—were well established. The sloping shoulders of the instrument in the drawing may be indicative of the evolutionary stage of the violin at the time. From its earliest days, the instrument was associated with the dance, and was known as the instrument of professional musicians and dancing masters (D. Boyden, *The History of Violin Playing from Its Origins to 1761* [London, Oxford University Press, 1965]).

b. See note *b* to page 51, for more information.

c. This explanation is incorrect. The French reads:

> Arena et aultres, de sa sequelle fōt le simple d'vn mesme pied, marquant pour le premiere mesure du pied gauche a cousté du droit, puis aduanceant ledit gauche. Et aultant du pied droit.

The term *marque pied*, which is implied here *(marquant . . . du pied)*, is explained by Arbeau later as a placing of the toe next to the standing foot (p. 85). Dolmetsch's translation *(Dances of England and France*, p. 9) is more accurate:

> . . . make the single with one and the same foot, marking the first beat with the left foot beside the right, and then advancing the said left.

d. For further information, see note *a* to p. 57; note *a* to p. 59; note *a* to p. 60.

ꞏp. 200

a. French: *passe meze.* The explanation given in Note 39 is only one of several which may be equally valid. The most commonly accepted meaning today is "step-and-a-half," a literal translation of *pass'e mezzo*; the choreographic meaning remains unclear. There is considerably more musical significance to the passamezzo than indicated in the text, for although it was indeed a type of pavan, the melody was usually played over one of two well-known sixteen-measure bass lines: the *passamezzo antico* (English: "passing measures pavan"), and the *passamezzo moderno* (English: "Quadran pavan"). Thus, the passamezzo belongs to that extremely important body of music of the sixteenth and seventeenth centuries that consisted of variations over a harmonic ground. (See note *b* to page 99 for a discussion of the Romanesca, a similar ground.) Directions for the dance may be found in Caroso, *Il Ballarino* (1581), fol. 49. Since it was first known outside Italy as early as 1536, it is obvious that these are directions for a late stage in the development of the dance (cf. Moe, "Pavane," *Musik in Geschichte und Gegenwart*, X, cols. 976–977; John Ward, "Passamezzo," *MGG*, X, cols. 877–890; Robert Donington, "Passamezzo," *Grove* [1954], VI, pp. 576–577).

b. This statement is incorrect. Arbeau distinctly shows the hat on the head in all pictures of the galliard steps. Other iconographic evidence also bears this out; for example, a woodcut by Jost Amman (1570) (Dolmetsch, *op. cit.*, face p. 96) shows a galliard being performed at court with hats on. Arbeau describes the *révérence* preceding the dance, and then specifies that the hat should be replaced firmly on the head (see also p. 93). Dolmetsch, p. 107, quotes Cesare Negri, *Nuove Inventioni*, 1604, who says, apropos of the galliard, "The Cavalier then going to dance with the Lady: after he has made the reverence, and a passeggio round the room, replaced his hat upon his head and arranged his cloak and sword. . . ." Arbeau's drawings omit the sword.

The galliard was certainly the most popular and customary rapid dance of the sixteenth-century couple dances. Both instrumental and vocal galliards are known. Frequently the tune was the same as for the pavan or passamezzo that normally preceded it, but varied to suit the new meter (this type of pairing led to the variation suite). Separate galliards are also commonly found in the numerous dance collections of the period. Queen Elizabeth is supposed to have danced six or seven galliards before breakfast daily; Sir Toby's "sink-apace" (Shakespeare, *Twelfth Night*, i, 3) is of course a galliard.

In the seventeenth century the musical character and tempo of the galliard changed, and it gradually died out as a dance; nevertheless, it continued to be popular as a musical type into the last quarter of the century (cf. E. H. Meyer, "Galliarde," *Musik in Geschichte und Gegenwart*, IV, cols. 1285–93).

p. 201

a. French: *greue.* In older French the word refers to the shank of the leg, and to shin armor (English: *greaves*).

There seems to be little question that *grève* is the correct word in modern French. Beaumont, however, uses *grue*, which means "crane." In all fairness to Beaumont, the terms *faire la jambe de grue* and *faire le pied de grue* were known in the sixteenth century, and meant "to dance attendance."

b. So far as can be determined, the manuscript is no longer in existence; the reference here is to the original printing of 1589. (See Editor's Introduction for further discussion.)

p. 202

a. French: *guiterne.* It had an oval belly and back, as did the lute, and wire strings.

b. The courante described by Arbeau is definitely in duple meter; musical examples of this type are rare, and the question arises of adapting these steps to the usual $\frac{6}{4}$ or $\frac{6}{8}$ pattern. Mabel Dolmetsch, *op. cit.*, p. 133, assumes that Arbeau's "mesure binaire legière" somehow means "the accented beat to be twice the length of the other," i.e., ♩ ♪ ♩ ♪ , thus deriving a compound duple time. Arbeau, however, is always crystal-clear as to whether the grouping of minims is *binaire* (duple) or *ternaire* (triple). His step-pattern can easily be adapted to the triple grouping, but we cannot be certain that the results are authentic.

Most scholars today agree that the courante was of French origin. Its development and popularity were most marked in the seventeenth century.

c. While the allemande may have arisen in Germany (similar music exists in German sources of the fifteenth to seventeenth centuries, frequently under the title *Deutscher Tanz*), its popularity under the name *allemande* was widest elsewhere, especially in the sixteenth century in France and the Low Countries. By the time it became part of the baroque instrumental suite it was linked with the courante in typical slow-fast pairing. Even in Arbeau the allemande and courante appear as adjacent dances, though in reverse order.

d. Branle is a generic term for the circle or broken-circle dances of the sixteenth and seventeenth centuries in France; as can be seen here, some were slow and sedate, others lively, some mimetic (extracted from ballets of the time), others flirtatious. Arbeau gives twenty-five, but there were many more. The suite of branles to which he frequently refers undoubtedly foreshadowed the baroque instrumental suite.

While the original meaning of the verb *branler* is, "to totter, shake, or wag," a definition of 1606 quoted by Heartz, *Preludes, Chansons and Dances*, p. xxxix, suggests the graceful motion illustrated in many paintings of the time:

> Bransle, m. C'est balancement d'un costé a l'autre, *Mutatio Vacillatio*. Il se prent aussi pour une manière de danse, ou plusieurs hommes et femmes s'entretenans par les mains ores en cerne, ores en long vont dansant de flanc à l'autre : et non de droit fil de derrière en avant, comme on fait es basses danses, pavanes et gaillardes. A cause duquel danser a costé à autre, ceste dite manière de danser est appellée bransle, de bransler, qui signifie proprement balancer d'un costé à autre : et moins proprement vaciller en quelque manière que ce soit (Jean Nicot, *Thresor de la langue françoyse*, Paris, 1606).

Heartz goes on to suggest (p. xl) that since Arena and Arbeau contradict one another, Arena prescribing a forward and backward motion for the branle, and Arbeau a side step, the solution might be found in an oblique or diagonal position of the dancers in the circle. This is the solution proposed by Sachs (*World History*, p. 385). Attractive as this proposal is, and as much as some iconography of the period seems to bear it out, the specific directions by Arbeau do not contain any of the oblique positions he carefully describes on pp. 81 and 82. While this might quite possibly be an oversight, the editors have chosen to adhere strictly to Arbeau's instructions as given on p. 128, and the Labanotation shows the movement directly to the side. (For the musical and social history of the branle, see F. Lesure's masterly article "Branle," in *Musik in Geschichte und Gegenwart*, II, cols. 219–223.)

p. 203

a. The passepied definitely originated in Brittany. This origin is referred to in the sixteenth century not only by Arbeau, but by Noel de Fail (1549), and also in connection with the celebrations arranged by Catherine de Médicis in Bayonne in 1565. It is still danced today in Brittany, either as a couple dance, or as a dance for men. It involves strenuous leaps for the men, cross-steps, back-steps, and other steps calling for considerable skill. If the passepied of Arbeau's time was similar, then he has given us only a hint of it (cf. Claudie Marcel-Dubois, "Passepied," *Musik in Geschichte und Gegenwart*, X, cols. 885–886).

BIBLIOGRAPHY

(ADDITIONS TO LISTINGS ON P. 8)

Apel, Willi, ed. *Harvard Dictionary of Music.* Cambridge, Harvard University Press, 1944; 15th printing, 1964.

_____*The Notation of Polyphonic Music, 900–1600.* Cambridge, Harvard University Press, 1945.

Arena, Antoine. *Ad suos compagnones.* Avignon [1519?].

Backman, Louis E. *Religious Dances in the Christian Church and in Popular Medicine.* Transl. E. Classen. London, Allen and Unwin, 1952.

Barker, E. Phillips. "Master Thoinot's Fancy," *Music and Letters* XI (1930), 383–393.

_____"Some notes on Arbeau," *The Journal of the English Folk Dance Society,* Series Two, No. 3 (1930), 2–12.

Bate, Phillip. *The Trumpet and Trombone.* New York, W. W. Norton, 1966.

Beaumont, Cyril, transl. *Orchesography by Thoinot Arbeau.* 1925. Reprint, New York, Dance Horizons, 1965.

Blume, Friedrich. *Studien zur Vorgeschichte der Orchestersuite im 15. und 16. Jahrhundert.* Leipzig, F. Kistner and C. F. W. Siegel, 1925.

Boyden, David D. *The History of Violin Playing from Its Origins to 1761.* London, Oxford University Press, 1965.

Brainard, Ingrid. *Die Choreographie der Hoftänze in Burgund, Frankreich, und Italien im 15. Jahrhundert.* Unpublished doctoral dissertation, Göttingen, 1956.

Bukofzer, Manfred. *Music in the Baroque Era.* New York, W. W. Norton, 1947.

_____*Studies in Medieval and Renaissance Music.* New York, W. W. Norton, 1950.

Caroso, Marco Fabrizio. *Il Ballarino.* Venice, F. Ziletti, 1581.

Carpenter, Nan Cooke. *Rabelais and Music.* Chapel Hill, University of North Carolina Press, 1954.

de Lauze, F. *Apologie de la Danse.* 1623. Modern edition, with a translation, introduction, and notes by Joan Wildeblood. London, Frederick Muller Ltd., 1952.

237

Dolmetsch, Mabel. *Dances of England and France, 1450–1600*. London, Routledge and Paul, 1949.

_____*Dances of Spain and Italy, 1400–1600*. London, Routledge and Paul, 1954.

Donington, Robert. "Passamezzo," *Grove's Dictionary of Music and Musicians*, 5th ed., ed. Eric Blom. New York, St. Martin's Press, 1954. Vol. VI, pp. 576—577.

Engel, Carl. "Moresca, Moriskentänze, *MGG*,* IX (1961), cols. 575—580.

Fuller-Maitland, J. A., and W. Barclay Squire, eds. *The Fitzwilliam Virginal Book*. Reprint of 1899 Breitkopf & Härtel edition. New York, Dover Publications, 1963.

Gervaise, Claude. *Danseries* (H. Expert, ed.), in *Les Maîtres Musiciens de la Renaissance française*, Vol. 23. Paris, A. Leduc, 1908.

Gombosi, Otto. "Italia: Patria del basso ostinato," *Rassegna Musicale* VII (1934), 14–25.

Harrison, Frank Ll., and Joan Rimmer. *European Musical Instruments*. London, Studio Vista Limited, 1964.

_____Introduction and captions to Filippo Bonanni, *The Showcase of Musical Instruments* (1723). Reprint by Dover Publications, New York, 1964.

Heartz, Daniel. "The basse dance," *Annales Musicologiques* VI (1958–1963), 287–340.

_____"Etude des concordances," in Adrian Le Roy, *Fantaisies et Danses* from *A briefe and Easye Instruction to Learne the Tableture to Conducte and Dispose Thy Hande unto the Lute* (1568), ed. Pierre Jansen. Paris, Centre National de la Recherche Scientifique, 1962.

_____"Etude des concordances," in Adrian Le Roy, *Premier Livre de tabulature de luth* (1551), eds. André Souris and Richard de Morcourt. Paris, Editions du Centre National de la Recherche Scientifique, 1960.

_____ed., *Preludes, Chansons and Dances for Lute Published by Pierre Attaingnant, Paris (1529–1530)*. Neuilly-sur-Seine, Société de Musique d'Autrefois, 1964.

_____*Sources and Forms of the French Instrumental Dance in the Sixteenth Century*. Unpublished doctoral dissertation, Harvard University, 1956.

* In this bibliography, *MGG* stands for *Musik in Geschichte und Gegenwart*, ed. Friedrich Blume, Kassel and Basel, Bärenreiter Verlag, 1949–

Jacquot, Jean, ed. *Les Fêtes de la Renaissance*, Vols. I and II. Paris, Centre National de la Recherche Scientifique, 1960.

Kob, Walter. *The Pavan*. Unpublished master's thesis, Eastman School of Music, 1943.

Lawler, Lillian. *The Dance in Ancient Greece*. Middletown, Wesleyan University Press, 1965.

Lesure, François. "Branle," *MGG*, II, cols. 219–223.

Lowe, Barbara. "Early Records of the Morris in England," *Journal of the English Folk Dance and Song Society* VIII, No. 2 (1957), 61–82.

Marcel-Dubois, Claudie. "Gavotte," *MGG*, IV, cols. 1510–14.

_____"Passepied," *MGG*, X, cols. 885–886.

Marcuse, Sybil. *Musical Instruments*. New York, Doubleday, 1964.

Mary, André. " 'L'Orchésographie' de Thoinot Arbeau," in *Les trésors des Bibliothèques de France*, ed. E. Dacier. Paris, Les Editions d'Art et d'Histoire, 1935. Vol. V, pp. 85–99.

McGowan, Margaret, *L'Art du ballet de cour en France, 1581–1643*. Paris, Centre National de la Recherche Scientifique, 1963.

Meyer, Ernst Hermann. "Galliarde," *MGG*, IV, cols. 1285–86.

Moderne, Jacques. *Musique de Joye* (*ca.* 1550), ed. Giesbert. Kassel, Nagel's Verlag, 1934.

Moe, Lawrence. "Pavane," *MGG*, X, cols. 976–977.

Negri, Cesare. *Nuove Inventioni di Balli*. Milan, Bordone, 1604.

Nettl, Paul. "Die Moresca," *Archiv für Musikwissenschaft*, Jg. 14 (1957), 165–174.

_____*The Story of Dance Music*. New York, Philosophical Library, 1947.

_____"Die Tänze Jean d'Estrées," *Die Musikforschung* VII (1955), 437–444.

Poulton, Diana. "Notes on the Spanish Pavan," *The Lute Society Journal* II (1961), 5–16.

Praetorius, Michael. *Terpsichore*. Wolfenbüttel, 1612. Facsimile reprint in the *Gesamtausgabe der musikalischen Werke*, eds. F. Blume, A. Mendelssohn, W. Gurlitt. Wolfenbüttel, G. Kallmeyer, 1928–1960.

Rollin, Jean. *Les Chansons de Clément Marot*. Paris, Fischbacher, 1951.

Reese, Gustave. *Music in the Renaissance*. New York, W. W. Norton, 1954, 1959.

Sachs, Curt. *The History of Musical Instruments*. New York, W. W. Norton, 1940.

——*Real-Lexikon der Musikinstrumente*. New York, Dover Publications, 1964.

——*World History of the Dance*, trans. Bessie Schönberg. New York, W. W. Norton, 1937.

Sharp, Cecil, and Herbert MacIlwaine. *The Morris Book*. 2nd ed., London, Novello, 1912–1919, Parts 1–5.

Ward, John. "Passamezzo," *MGG*, X, cols. 877–890.

Welsford, Enid. *The Fool*. New York, Farrar and Rinehart [1935].

Wood, Melusine. *Historical Dances*. London, The Imperial Society of Teachers of Dancing, 1952.

——*More Historical Dances*. London, The Imperial Society of Teachers of Dancing, 1956.

INTRODUCTION TO THE LABANOTATION

In this section basic steps and representative dance patterns have been provided in Labanotation; they are correlated with the music Arbeau provides for them, which has been transcribed into modern notation with metronomic suggestions.

The authors are fully cognizant of the problems of interpretation that arise when working with a text in which many points of styling are taken for granted. The complexity of the problems may easily be seen by studying Arbeau's instructions as translated by Lady Evans and Cyril Beaumont, further expounded and stylized for performance by Mabel Dolmetsch (*op. cit.*) and Melusine Wood (*Historical Dances* [London, 1952]; *More Historical Dances* [London, 1956]), and by *then* going back to the original French text. One discovers, for example, that Arbeau's ubiquitous *saut* has been variously translated as "hop," "skip," "jump," or "leap." It is not always possible to tell by the context which meaning Arbeau has in mind, and varying interpretations result. Some authorities believe that the lacunae in a book such as this may be filled by referring to other texts of the period. It is our feeling, however, that none of the other sixteenth-century texts (e.g., those by Arena, Caroso, or Negri) are exactly of the same period or geographical location. One must recognize the fact that court dance styles changed in the sixteenth century, although not perhaps so quickly as styles today, as courts vied with each other to obtain the best and most up-to-date dancing masters; one must also realize that national stylistic differences in all the arts were recognized, despite the general internationalism of Renaissance culture. This text, then, is our primary source.

The steps and patterns chosen for Labanotation represent the dances most popular at the time Arbeau wrote: pavan, galliard, branles of various types, and the volta. The allemande, Spanish Pavan, and Canary are given because of particular historical interest, even though Arbeau supplies only limited information on the latter two (see notes). The tune of the Spanish Pavan (and perhaps the steps) migrated all over Europe, while the Canary is representative of an exoticism which went hand in hand with the geographical explorations and discoveries of the time.

Of those dances omitted in this section, the most important is perhaps the basse dance. Arbeau may have forgotten a dance he says had been defunct for forty or fifty years when he wrote; it is even possible, as Mabel Dolmetsch suggests, that he had never seen one of the steps he describes (the *reprise,* as he explains it, is very different from the same step in fifteenth-century manuals, and so far has remained a mystery). Thus we felt that nothing was to be gained by notating Arbeau's version. Of other important dances left out, the *moresca* is said by Arbeau himself to be almost obsolete, and the instructions he provides for it are very limited; the courante as described here is in duple meter rather than triple, and seems to have little relation to the later dance; the gavotte, despite its later importance, has been omitted here because Arbeau refers to it as a new dance with which he is unfamiliar.

Arbeau's instructions are usually for the man; it is implied that his partner will perform the same or complementary movements, but in a more gentle, subdued manner. Arbeau says the woman's feet are to be more turned out than the man's, and her leg gestures closer to the ground. Both points reflect the differences between male and female costumes and manners of the period.

For performance, the dancer may wish to elaborate a little, adding some body and arm movements (with restraint), and a little rising and falling in the slow steps. These movements are not indicated in the Labanotation unless specifically given by Arbeau; omitted also are the repetitions, which are assumed by Arbeau to be done *ad libitum.* It is strongly recommended that the dancer study the key carefully and refer to the text for further elucidation of subtle matters of style (e.g., the damsel's glances). Arbeau, it should be noted, consistently emphasizes grace and poise in his instructions, but just as consistently warns against exaggeration. The sharply pointed toes and stretched leg movements of modern ballet technique are noticeably absent from the drawings, and would seem to be inconsistent with a pre-ballet style. While skill in dancing was highly valued by the humanistic courts, there was as yet no corps of professional dancers; the skill was rather that of the trained dilettante, accustomed to gallant, yet manly gestures.

For the musical performance of the dances, modern transcriptions of appropriate dance music found in the original volumes of Attaingnant,

Le Roy, and their contemporaries are recommended (provided the rhythmic patterns and barring are correlated with Arbeau). The most common instrumental combination, and the one preferred by Arbeau, is the pipe and tabor; a violin is also shown; today a recorder, flute, or violin, with drum, will suffice (see p. 51 for further suggestions). It was probably customary for the musicians to improvise rather freely around the basic melody in the repetitions; some clues to this may be found in the fife tabulations on pp. 40–46. A further discussion of musical performance is beyond the scope of this book.

All steps and dances have been carefully tried; many possible interpretations have been explored. The authors are indebted to the members of the Renaissance Dancers of New York for their patience during rehearsals, to Allan Miles and the Dance Notation Bureau for checking the notation, and to Odette Blum and Raymond Cook for sight-reading the notation. The Labanotation conforms to current usage as approved by the Dance Notation Bureau in 1966.

MIREILLE BACKER
JULIA SUTTON

New York City
June, 1966

Labanotation is the trademark of the Dance Notation Bureau, Inc. The notation contained in the following section has been approved as conforming to the Laban method of dance notation. The dance notation symbols as printed herein may not be reproduced without permission.

BASIC MOVEMENTS, GLOSSARY AND KEYS

pp. 54-56, 79, 83

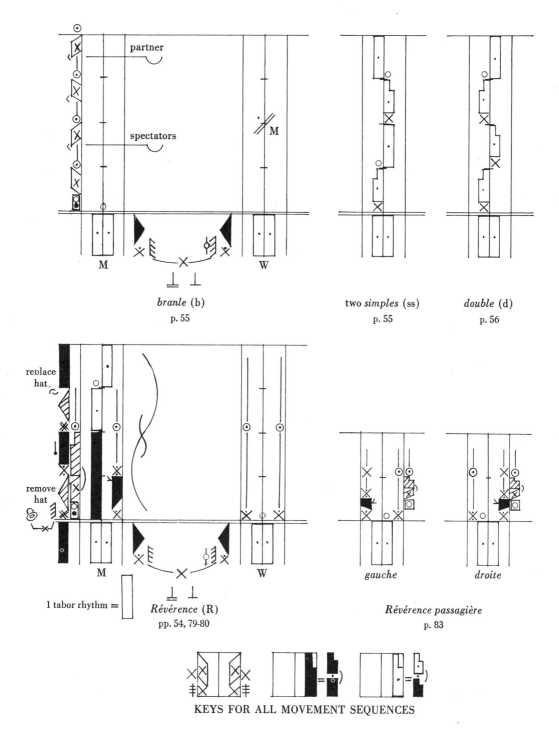

partner

spectators

M

branle (b)
p. 55

two simples (ss)
p. 55

double (d)
p. 56

replace
hat

remove
hat

M

W

1 tabor rhythm =

Révérence (R)
pp. 54, 79-80

gauche

droite

Révérence passagière
p. 83

KEYS FOR ALL MOVEMENT SEQUENCES

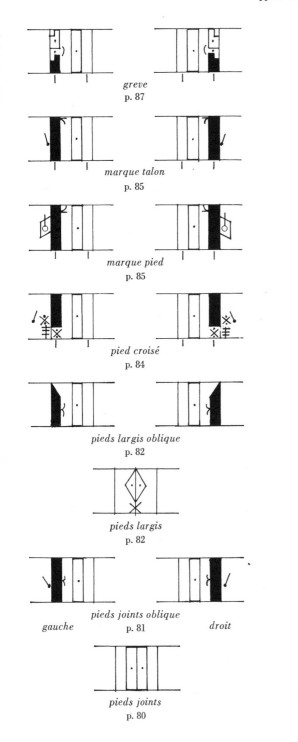

greve
p. 87

marque talon
p. 85

marque pied
p. 85

pied croisé
p. 84

pieds largis oblique
p. 82

pieds largis
p. 82

pieds joints oblique

gauche　　　p. 81　　　*droit*

pieds joints
p. 80

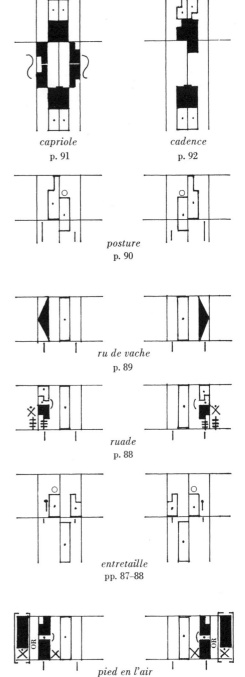

capriole　　　*cadence*
p. 91　　　p. 92

posture
p. 90

ru de vache
p. 89

ruade
p. 88

entretaille
pp. 87–88

pied en l'air

gauche　　　　　　*droit*

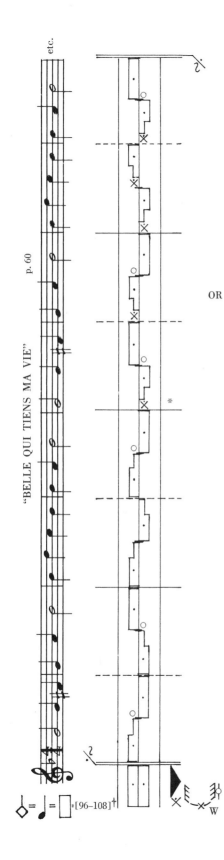

OR

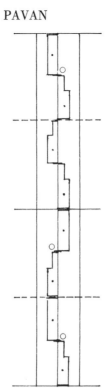

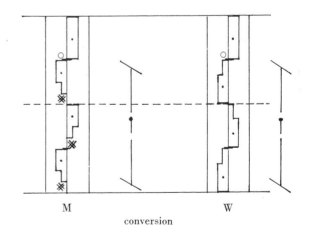

Basic step pattern
ss d ss d, etc.
pp. 57–67

M   W

conversion

* Smaller steps conjectural.

†All numbers in square brackets on these pages are suggested metronome markings.

TORDION

pp. 96–97

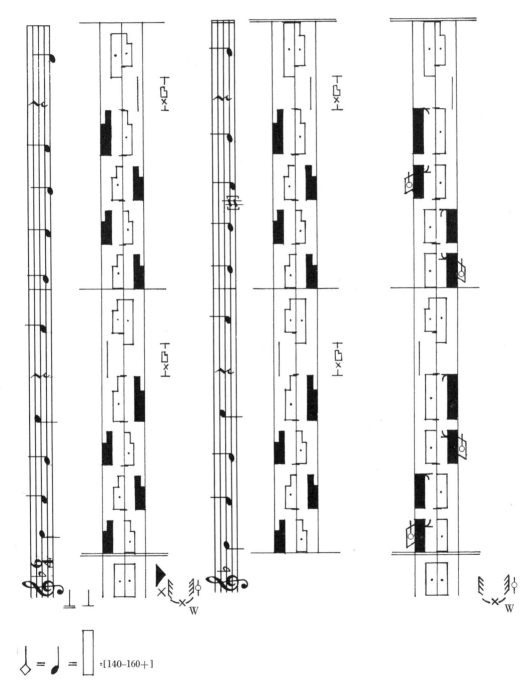

GALLIARD
pp. 100–102

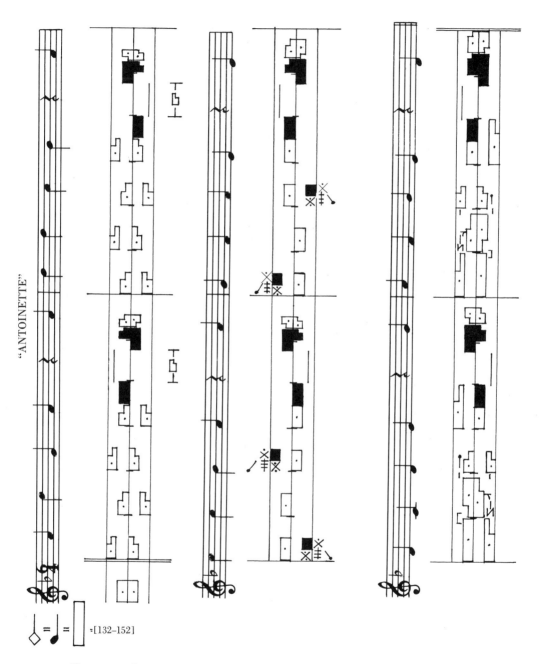

The patterns shown are not necessarily intended to be performed in this order. Arbeau gives them as possible variations, and shows them with a continuous tune. Sequences may be combined or repeated *ad libitum*, and may be performed progressing or in place. The order of patterns chosen will determine whether to begin the next pattern with an open or closed position. See pp. 103–104 for further discussion.

250

GALLIARD VARIATIONS
pp. 105–106

"WHETHER I LOVE OR NO" (*Si j'ayme ou non*)

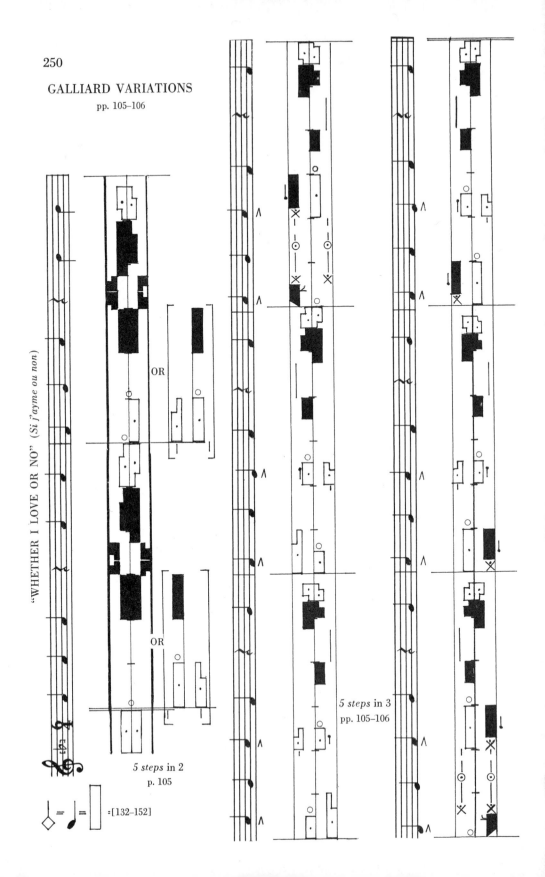

OR

OR

5 steps in 2
p. 105

5 steps in 3
pp. 105–106

♢ = ♪ = ▯ = [132–152]

GALLIARD VARIATIONS

pp. 107, 113–114

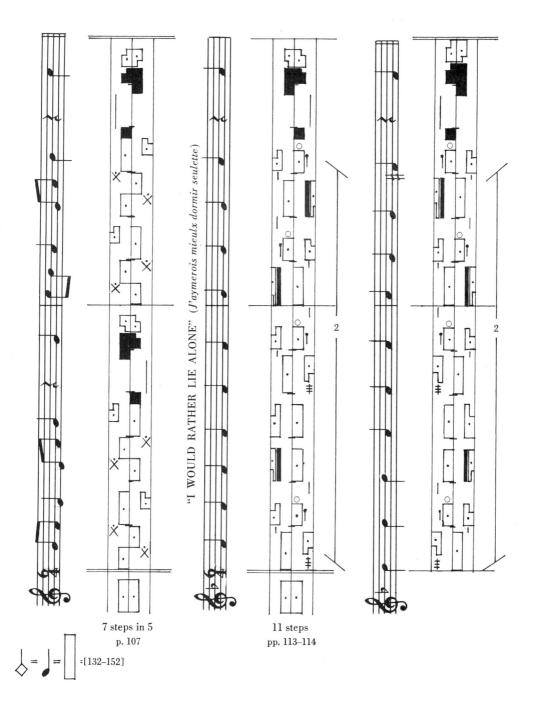

"I WOULD RATHER LIE ALONE" (*J'aymerois mieulx dormir seulette*)

7 steps in 5
p. 107

11 steps
pp. 113–114

LAVOLTA

Arbeau gives two contradictory
explanations for the volta: one in
the text and another in the tabulation. The second is followed here.

Preparatory exercise

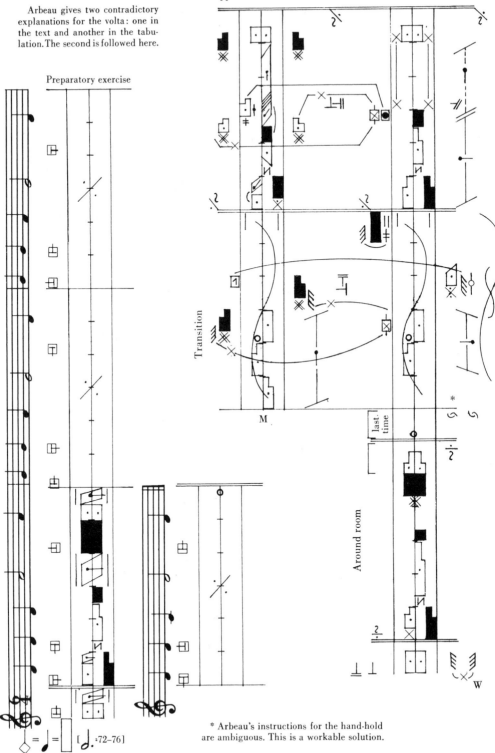

* Arbeau's instructions for the hand-hold
are ambiguous. This is a workable solution.

ALMAN

pp. 126–127

ctc.

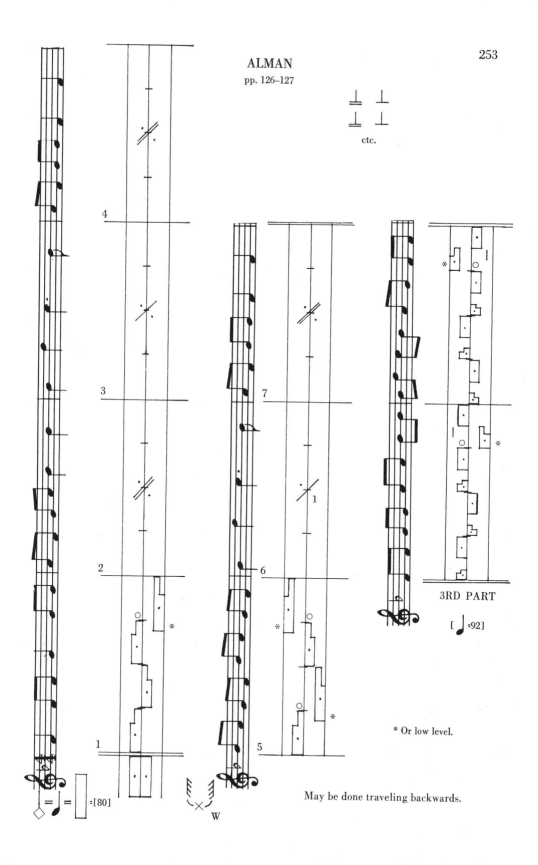

4

3

2

1

≒[80]

7

6

5

W

1

3RD PART

[♩ =92]

* Or low level.

May be done traveling backwards.

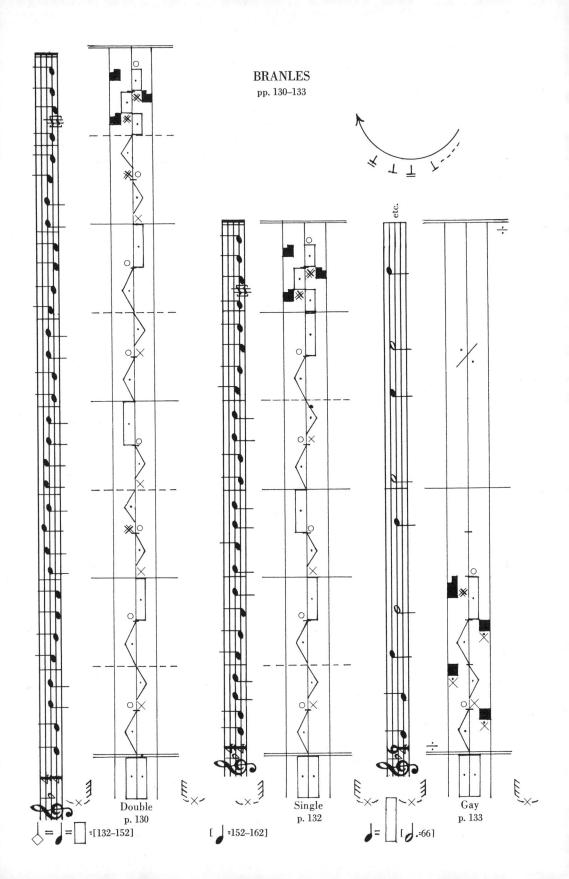

BRANLES
pp. 130–133

Double
p. 130

Single
p. 132

Gay
p. 133

BRANLES
pp. 135–136

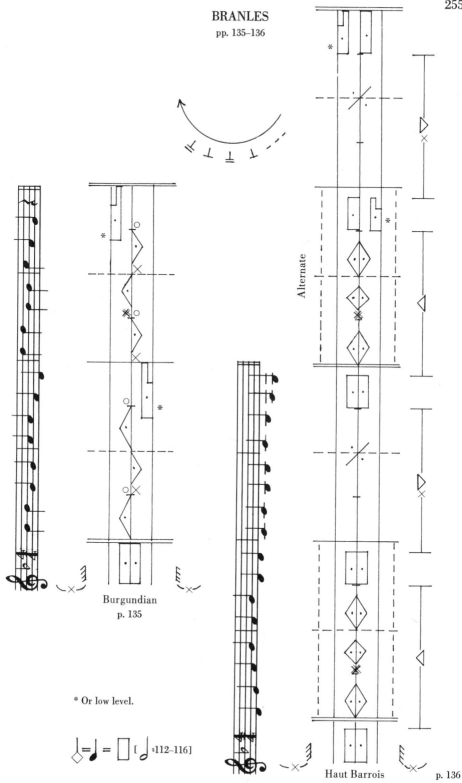

Burgundian
p. 135

Alternate

Haut Barrois

p. 136

* Or low level.

BRANLE
CALLED PINAGAY
p. 139

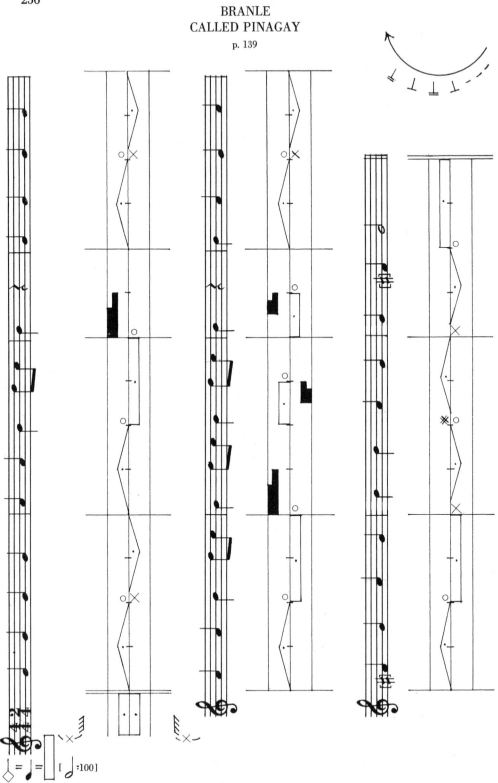

BRANLE OF POITOU

pp. 147–148

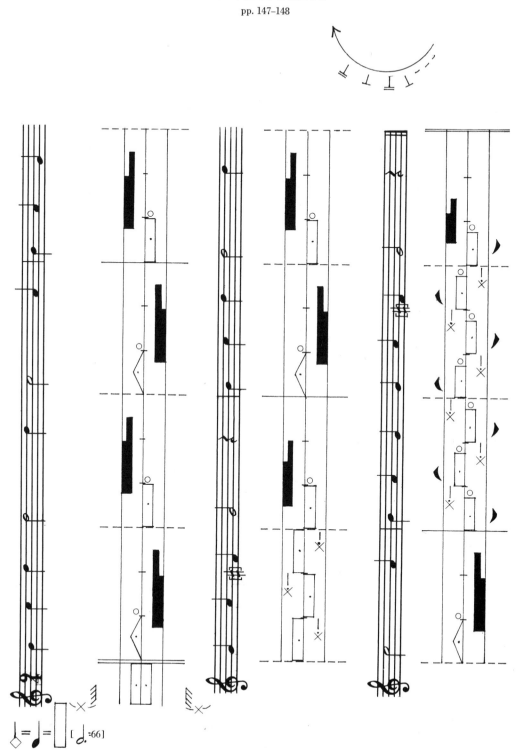

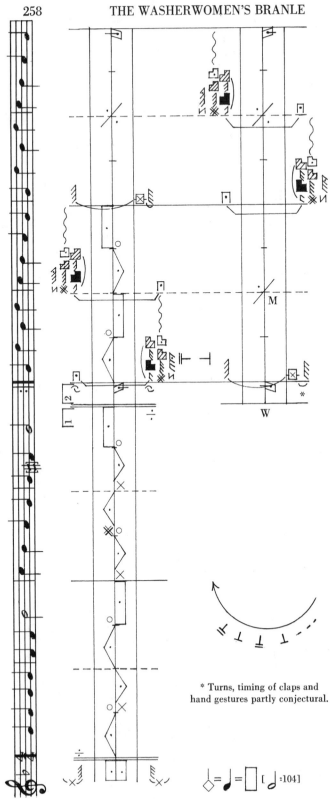

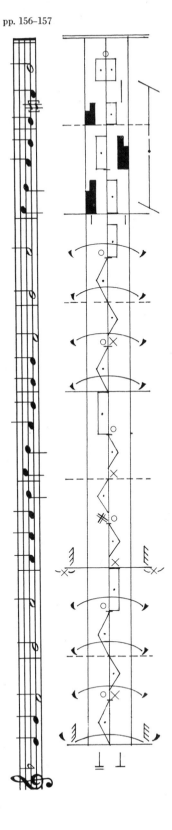

M

W

* Turns, timing of claps and
hand gestures partly conjectural.

THE CANARY

p. 180

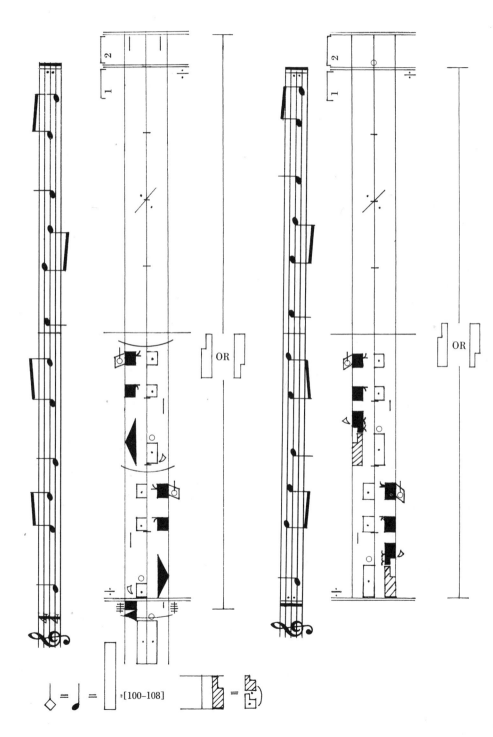

THE SPANISH PAVAN
pp. 181–182

* Travel backward on repeat.
The gestures would probably remain
forward, thus:

INDEX

Aaron, 19
Achilles, 13
Aelian, 37
Aeneas, 19
Aeneid, 13, 19
Alexander the Great, 39
Allemande   N. 85
All's Well That Ends Well   N. 111
Alman, 125
  see Tabulations
Alphonse, King of Aragon, 12
Amazons, 185
Andria, 49
Appius Claudius, 13
Arena, Anthony of, 14, 55, 56, 75
Aridan (branle), 145
  see Tabulations
Arigot, 39, etc.
  see Tabulations
Arquebus, 37
Aspasia, 13
Athenaeus, 14
Attaignant, 75
Aubades   N. 75
Augustus   N. 98
Avignon (branle), 137

Bacchus, 39
Bach   Ns. 85, 95, 102
Badius, 177
Ballet Comique de la Reine, 6
Barbiton, 163
Bar-le-duc   N. 91
Basques, 47
Basse Dance, 15   N. 28
  see Tabulations
Béarnais, 47
Beaujoyeux, Balthasar de   N. 1
Beaumont, C. W.   N. 14
Bouffons   N. 114

Branle (movement), 53, etc.
  see Basse Dance Tabulation
Branles, 15, etc.
  see Tabulations
Branles (mimed), 153
  see Tabulations
Branles (mixed)
  see Tabulations
Buffens, 115, 182, 186   N. 114
  see Tabulations
Bugles, 18
Burgundy (branle), 15
  see Tabulations

Cadence, 66, 91
Camp (branle), 137
Canary, 66, 179
  see Tabulations
Candlestick (branle)
  see Tabulations
Capriole, 91
Carians, 13
Cassandra (branle)
  see Tabulations
Castanet   N. 104
Castor, 13
Catherine de Medici   N. 1
Celius, 14
Champagne (branle), 15, 129
Charlotte (branle)
  see Tabulations
Chares, 81
Chorus, 47
Cicero, 12, 13, 16, 17
Cithers, 99
Claudin, 140
Claudius, 49
Clausula, 91

261

SONG TITLES

A CATALOGUE OF SELECTED DOVER BOOKS
IN ALL FIELDS OF INTEREST

A CATALOGUE OF SELECTED DOVER
BOOKS IN ALL FIELDS OF INTEREST

CELESTIAL OBJECTS FOR COMMON TELESCOPES, T. W. Webb. The most used book in amateur astronomy: inestimable aid for locating and identifying nearly 4,000 celestial objects. Edited, updated by Margaret W. Mayall. 77 illustrations. Total of 645pp. 5⅜ x 8½.
20917-2, 20918-0 Pa., Two-vol. set $9.00

HISTORICAL STUDIES IN THE LANGUAGE OF CHEMISTRY, M. P. Crosland. The important part language has played in the development of chemistry from the symbolism of alchemy to the adoption of systematic nomenclature in 1892. ". . . wholeheartedly recommended,"—Science. 15 illustrations. 416pp. of text. 5⅝ x 8¼.   63702-6 Pa. $6.00

BURNHAM'S CELESTIAL HANDBOOK, Robert Burnham, Jr. Thorough, readable guide to the stars beyond our solar system. Exhaustive treatment, fully illustrated. Breakdown is alphabetical by constellation: Andromeda to Cetus in Vol. 1; Chamaeleon to Orion in Vol. 2; and Pavo to Vulpecula in Vol. 3. Hundreds of illustrations. Total of about 2000pp. 6⅛ x 9¼.
23567-X, 23568-8, 23673-0 Pa., Three-vol. set $26.85

THEORY OF WING SECTIONS: INCLUDING A SUMMARY OF AIR-FOIL DATA, Ira H. Abbott and A. E. von Doenhoff. Concise compilation of subatomic aerodynamic characteristics of modern NASA wing sections, plus description of theory. 350pp. of tables. 693pp. 5⅜ x 8½.
60586-8 Pa. $7.00

DE RE METALLICA, Georgius Agricola. Translated by Herbert C. Hoover and Lou H. Hoover. The famous Hoover translation of greatest treatise on technological chemistry, engineering, geology, mining of early modern times (1556). All 289 original woodcuts. 638pp. 6¾ x 11.
60006-8 Clothbd. $17.95

THE ORIGIN OF CONTINENTS AND OCEANS, Alfred Wegener. One of the most influential, most controversial books in science, the classic statement for continental drift. Full 1966 translation of Wegener's final (1929) version. 64 illustrations. 246pp. 5⅜ x 8½.   61708-4 Pa. $4.50

THE PRINCIPLES OF PSYCHOLOGY, William James. Famous long course complete, unabridged. Stream of thought, time perception, memory, experimental methods; great work decades ahead of its time. Still valid, useful; read in many classes. 94 figures. Total of 1391pp. 5⅜ x 8½.
20381-6, 20382-4 Pa., Two-vol. set $13.00

A MAYA GRAMMAR, Alfred M. Tozzer. Practical, useful English-language grammar by the Harvard anthropologist who was one of the three greatest American scholars in the area of Maya culture. Phonetics, grammatical processes, syntax, more. 301pp. 5⅜ x 8½. 23465-7 Pa. $4.00

THE JOURNAL OF HENRY D. THOREAU, edited by Bradford Torrey, F. H. Allen. Complete reprinting of 14 volumes, 1837-61, over two million words; the sourcebooks for *Walden,* etc. Definitive. All original sketches, plus 75 photographs. Introduction by Walter Harding. Total of 1804pp. 8½ x 12¼. 20312-3, 20313-1 Clothbd., Two-vol. set $50.00

CLASSIC GHOST STORIES, Charles Dickens and others. 18 wonderful stories you've wanted to reread: "The Monkey's Paw," "The House and the Brain," "The Upper Berth," "The Signalman," "Dracula's Guest," "The Tapestried Chamber," etc. Dickens, Scott, Mary Shelley, Stoker, etc. 330pp. 5⅜ x 8½. 20735-8 Pa. $3.50

SEVEN SCIENCE FICTION NOVELS, H. G. Wells. Full novels. *First Men in the Moon, Island of Dr. Moreau, War of the Worlds, Food of the Gods, Invisible Man, Time Machine, In the Days of the Comet.* A basic science-fiction library. 1015pp. 5⅜ x 8½. (Available in U.S. only) 20264-X Clothbd. $8.95

ARMADALE, Wilkie Collins. Third great mystery novel by the author of *The Woman in White* and *The Moonstone.* Ingeniously plotted narrative shows an exceptional command of character, incident and mood. Original magazine version with 40 illustrations. 597pp. 5⅜ x 8½. 23429-0 Pa. $5.00

MASTERS OF MYSTERY, H. Douglas Thomson. The first book in English (1931) devoted to history and aesthetics of detective story. Poe, Doyle, LeFanu, Dickens, many others, up to 1930. New introduction and notes by E. F. Bleiler. 288pp. 5⅜ x 8½. (Available in U.S. only) 23606-4 Pa. $4.00

FLATLAND, E. A. Abbott. Science-fiction classic explores life of 2-D being in 3-D world. Read also as introduction to thought about hyperspace. Introduction by Banesh Hoffmann. 16 illustrations. 103pp. 5⅜ x 8½. 20001-9 Pa. $1.75

THREE SUPERNATURAL NOVELS OF THE VICTORIAN PERIOD, edited, with an introduction, by E. F. Bleiler. Reprinted complete and unabridged, three great classics of the supernatural: *The Haunted Hotel* by Wilkie Collins, *The Haunted House at Latchford* by Mrs. J. H. Riddell, and *The Lost Stradivarius* by J. Meade Falkner. 325pp. 5⅜ x 8½. 22571-2 Pa. $4.00

AYESHA: THE RETURN OF "SHE," H. Rider Haggard. Virtuoso sequel featuring the great mythic creation, Ayesha, in an adventure that is fully as good as the first book, *She.* Original magazine version, with 47 original illustrations by Maurice Greiffenhagen. 189pp. 6½ x 9¼. 23649-8 Pa. $3.50

CATALOGUE OF DOVER BOOKS

AMERICAN BIRD ENGRAVINGS, Alexander Wilson et al. All 76 plates. from Wilson's *American Ornithology* (1808-14), most important ornithological work before Audubon, plus 27 plates from the supplement (1825-33) by Charles Bonaparte. Over 250 birds portrayed. 8 plates also reproduced in full color. 111pp. 9⅜ x 12½. 23195-X Pa. $6.00

CRUICKSHANK'S PHOTOGRAPHS OF BIRDS OF AMERICA, Allan D. Cruickshank. Great ornithologist, photographer presents 177 closeups, groupings, panoramas, flightings, etc., of about 150 different birds. Expanded *Wings in the Wilderness*. Introduction by Helen G. Cruickshank. 191pp. 8¼ x 11. 23497-5 Pa. $6.00

AMERICAN WILDLIFE AND PLANTS, A. C. Martin, et al. Describes food habits of more than 1000 species of mammals, birds, fish. Special treatment of important food plants. Over 300 illustrations. 500pp. 5⅜ x 8½. 20793-5 Pa. $4.95

THE PEOPLE CALLED SHAKERS, Edward D. Andrews. Lifetime of research, definitive study of Shakers: origins, beliefs, practices, dances, social organization, furniture and crafts, impact on 19th-century USA, present heritage. Indispensable to student of American history, collector. 33 illustrations. 351pp. 5⅜ x 8½. 21081-2 Pa. $4.00

OLD NEW YORK IN EARLY PHOTOGRAPHS, Mary Black. New York City as it was in 1853-1901, through 196 wonderful photographs from N.-Y. Historical Society. Great Blizzard, Lincoln's funeral procession, great buildings. 228pp. 9 x 12. 22907-6 Pa. $7.95

MR. LINCOLN'S CAMERA MAN: MATHEW BRADY, Roy Meredith. Over 300 Brady photos reproduced directly from original negatives, photos. Jackson, Webster, Grant, Lee, Carnegie, Barnum; Lincoln; Battle Smoke, Death of Rebel Sniper, Atlanta Just After Capture. Lively commentary. 368pp. 8⅜ x 11¼. 23021-X Pa. $8.95

TRAVELS OF WILLIAM BARTRAM, William Bartram. From 1773-8, Bartram explored Northern Florida, Georgia, Carolinas, and reported on wild life, plants, Indians, early settlers. Basic account for period, entertaining reading. Edited by Mark Van Doren. 13 illustrations. 141pp. 5⅜ x 8½. 20013-2 Pa. $4.50

THE GENTLEMAN AND CABINET MAKER'S DIRECTOR, Thomas Chippendale. Full reprint, 1762 style book, most influential of all time; chairs, tables, sofas, mirrors, cabinets, etc. 200 plates, plus 24 photographs of surviving pieces. 249pp. 9⅞ x 12¾. 21601-2 Pa. $6.50

AMERICAN CARRIAGES, SLEIGHS, SULKIES AND CARTS, edited by Don H. Berkebile. 168 Victorian illustrations from catalogues, trade journals, fully captioned. Useful for artists. Author is Assoc. Curator, Div. of Transportation of Smithsonian Institution. 168pp. 8½ x 9½. 23328-6 Pa. $5.00

AN AUTOBIOGRAPHY, Margaret Sanger. Exciting personal account of hard-fought battle for woman's right to birth control, against prejudice, church, law. Foremost feminist document. 504pp. 5⅜ x 8½.
20470-7 Pa. $5.50

MY BONDAGE AND MY FREEDOM, Frederick Douglass. Born as a slave, Douglass became outspoken force in antislavery movement. The best of Douglass's autobiographies. Graphic description of slave life. Introduction by P. Foner. 464pp. 5⅜ x 8½.
22457-0 Pa. $5.50

LIVING MY LIFE, Emma Goldman. Candid, no holds barred account by foremost American anarchist: her own life, anarchist movement, famous contemporaries, ideas and their impact. Struggles and confrontations in America, plus deportation to U.S.S.R. Shocking inside account of persecution of anarchists under Lenin. 13 plates. Total of 944pp. 5⅜ x 8½.
22543-7, 22544-5 Pa., Two-vol. set $11.00

LETTERS AND NOTES ON THE MANNERS, CUSTOMS AND CONDITIONS OF THE NORTH AMERICAN INDIANS, George Catlin. Classic account of life among Plains Indians: ceremonies, hunt, warfare, etc. Dover edition reproduces for first time all original paintings. 312 plates. 572pp. of text. 6⅛ x 9¼.
22118-0, 22119-9 Pa.. Two-vol. set $11.50

THE MAYA AND THEIR NEIGHBORS, edited by Clarence L. Hay, others. Synoptic view of Maya civilization in broadest sense, together with Northern, Southern neighbors. Integrates much background, valuable detail not elsewhere. Prepared by greatest scholars: Kroeber, Morley, Thompson, Spinden, Vaillant, many others. Sometimes called Tozzer Memorial Volume. 60 illustrations, linguistic map. 634pp. 5⅜ x 8½.
23510-6 Pa. $7.50

HANDBOOK OF THE INDIANS OF CALIFORNIA, A. L. Kroeber. Foremost American anthropologist offers complete ethnographic study of each group. Monumental classic. 459 illustrations, maps. 995pp. 5⅜ x 8½.
23368-5 Pa. $10.00

SHAKTI AND SHAKTA, Arthur Avalon. First book to give clear, cohesive analysis of Shakta doctrine, Shakta ritual and Kundalini Shakti (yoga). Important work by one of world's foremost students of Shaktic and Tantric thought. 732pp. 5⅜ x 8½. (Available in U.S. only)
23645-5 Pa. $7.95

AN INTRODUCTION TO THE STUDY OF THE MAYA HIEROGLYPHS, Syvanus Griswold Morley. Classic study by one of the truly great figures in hieroglyph research. Still the best introduction for the student for reading Maya hieroglyphs. New introduction by J. Eric S. Thompson. 117 illustrations. 284pp. 5⅜ x 8½.
23108-9 Pa. $4.00

A STUDY OF MAYA ART, Herbert J. Spinden. Landmark classic interprets Maya symbolism, estimates styles, covers ceramics, architecture, murals, stone carvings as artforms. Still a basic book in area. New introduction by J. Eric Thompson. Over 750 illustrations. 341pp. 8⅜ x 11¼.
21235-1 Pa. $6.95

HOUSEHOLD STORIES BY THE BROTHERS GRIMM. All the great Grimm stories: "Rumpelstiltskin," "Snow White," "Hansel and Gretel," etc., with 114 illustrations by Walter Crane. 269pp. 5⅜ x 8½.
21080-4 Pa. $3.00

SLEEPING BEAUTY, illustrated by Arthur Rackham. Perhaps the fullest, most delightful version ever, told by C. S. Evans. Rackham's best work. 49 illustrations. 110pp. 7⅞ x 10¾.
22756-1 Pa. $2.50

AMERICAN FAIRY TALES, L. Frank Baum. Young cowboy lassoes Father Time; dummy in Mr. Floman's department store window comes to life; and 10 other fairy tales. 41 illustrations by N. P. Hall, Harry Kennedy, Ike Morgan, and Ralph Gardner. 209pp. 5⅜ x 8½.
23643-9 Pa. $3.00

THE WONDERFUL WIZARD OF OZ, L. Frank Baum. Facsimile in full color of America's finest children's classic. Introduction by Martin Gardner. 143 illustrations by W. W. Denslow. 267pp. 5⅜ x 8½.
20691-2 Pa. $3.50

THE TALE OF PETER RABBIT, Beatrix Potter. The inimitable Peter's terrifying adventure in Mr. McGregor's garden, with all 27 wonderful, full-color Potter illustrations. 55pp. 4¼ x 5½. (Available in U.S. only)
22827-4 Pa. $1.25

THE STORY OF KING ARTHUR AND HIS KNIGHTS, Howard Pyle. Finest children's version of life of King Arthur. 48 illustrations by Pyle. 131pp. 6⅛ x 9¼.
21445-1 Pa. $4.95

CARUSO'S CARICATURES, Enrico Caruso. Great tenor's remarkable caricatures of self, fellow musicians, composers, others. Toscanini, Puccini, Farrar, etc. Impish, cutting, insightful. 473 illustrations. Preface by M. Sisca. 217pp. 8⅜ x 11¼.
23528-9 Pa. $6.95

PERSONAL NARRATIVE OF A PILGRIMAGE TO ALMADINAH AND MECCAH, Richard Burton. Great travel classic by remarkably colorful personality. Burton, disguised as a Moroccan, visited sacred shrines of Islam, narrowly escaping death. Wonderful observations of Islamic life, customs, personalities. 47 illustrations. Total of 959pp. 5⅜ x 8½.
21217-3, 21218-1 Pa., Two-vol. set $12.00

INCIDENTS OF TRAVEL IN YUCATAN, John L. Stephens. Classic (1843) exploration of jungles of Yucatan, looking for evidences of Maya civilization. Travel adventures, Mexican and Indian culture, etc. Total of 669pp. 5⅜ x 8½.
20926-1, 20927-X Pa., Two-vol. set $7.90

AMERICAN LITERARY AUTOGRAPHS FROM WASHINGTON IRVING TO HENRY JAMES, Herbert Cahoon, et al. Letters, poems, manuscripts of Hawthorne, Thoreau, Twain, Alcott, Whitman, 67 other prominent American authors. Reproductions, full transcripts and commentary. Plus checklist of all American Literary Autographs in The Pierpont Morgan Library. Printed on exceptionally high-quality paper. 136 illustrations. 212pp. 9⅛ x 12¼.
23548-3 Pa. $7.95

PRINCIPLES OF ORCHESTRATION, Nikolay Rimsky-Korsakov. Great classical orchestrator provides fundamentals of tonal resonance, progression of parts, voice and orchestra, tutti effects, much else in major document. 330pp. of musical excerpts. 489pp. 6½ x 9¼. 21266-1 Pa. $6.00

TRISTAN UND ISOLDE, Richard Wagner. Full orchestral score with complete instrumentation. Do not confuse with piano reduction. Commentary by Felix Mottl, great Wagnerian conductor and scholar. Study score. 655pp. 8⅛ x 11. 22915-7 Pa. $12.50

REQUIEM IN FULL SCORE, Giuseppe Verdi. Immensely popular with choral groups and music lovers. Republication of edition published by C. F. Peters, Leipzig, n. d. German frontmaker in English translation. Glossary. Text in Latin. Study score. 204pp. 9⅜ x 12¼.
23682-X Pa. $6.00

COMPLETE CHAMBER MUSIC FOR STRINGS, Felix Mendelssohn. All of Mendelssohn's chamber music: Octet, 2 Quintets, 6 Quartets, and Four Pieces for String Quartet. (Nothing with piano is included). Complete works edition (1874-7). Study score. 283 pp. 9⅜ x 12¼.
23679-X Pa. $6.95

POPULAR SONGS OF NINETEENTH-CENTURY AMERICA, edited by Richard Jackson. 64 most important songs: "Old Oaken Bucket," "Arkansas Traveler," "Yellow Rose of Texas," etc. Authentic original sheet music, full introduction and commentaries. 290pp. 9 x 12. 23270-0 Pa. $6.00

COLLECTED PIANO WORKS, Scott Joplin. Edited by Vera Brodsky Lawrence. Practically all of Joplin's piano works—rags, two-steps, marches, waltzes, etc., 51 works in all. Extensive introduction by Rudi Blesh. Total of 345pp. 9 x 12. 23106-2 Pa. $14.95

BASIC PRINCIPLES OF CLASSICAL BALLET, Agrippina Vaganova. Great Russian theoretician, teacher explains methods for teaching classical ballet; incorporates best from French, Italian, Russian schools. 118 illustrations. 175pp. 5⅜ x 8½. 22036-2 Pa. $2.50

CHINESE CHARACTERS, L. Wieger. Rich analysis of 2300 characters according to traditional systems into primitives. Historical-semantic analysis to phonetics (Classical Mandarin) and radicals. 820pp. 6⅛ x 9¼.
21321-8 Pa. $10.00

EGYPTIAN LANGUAGE: EASY LESSONS IN EGYPTIAN HIERO-GLYPHICS, E. A. Wallis Budge. Foremost Egyptologist offers Egyptian grammar, explanation of hieroglyphics, many reading texts, dictionary of symbols. 246pp. 5 x 7½. (Available in U.S. only)
21394-3 Clothbd. $7.50

AN ETYMOLOGICAL DICTIONARY OF MODERN ENGLISH, Ernest Weekley. Richest, fullest work, by foremost British lexicographer. Detailed word histories. Inexhaustible. Do not confuse this with Concise Etymological Dictionary, which is abridged. Total of 856pp. 6½ x 9¼.
21873-2, 21874-0 Pa., Two-vol. set $12.00

SECOND PIATIGORSKY CUP, edited by Isaac Kashdan. One of the greatest tournament books ever produced in the English language. All 90 games of the 1966 tournament, annotated by players, most annotated by both players. Features Petrosian, Spassky, Fischer, Larsen, six others. 228pp. 5⅜ x 8½. 23572-6 Pa. $3.50

ENCYCLOPEDIA OF CARD TRICKS, revised and edited by Jean Hugard. How to perform over 600 card tricks, devised by the world's greatest magicians: impromptus, spelling tricks, key cards, using special packs, much, much more. Additional chapter on card technique. 66 illustrations. 402pp. 5⅜ x 8½. (Available in U.S. only) 21252-1 Pa. $3.95

MAGIC: STAGE ILLUSIONS, SPECIAL EFFECTS AND TRICK PHOTOGRAPHY, Albert A. Hopkins, Henry R. Evans. One of the great classics; fullest, most authorative explanation of vanishing lady, levitations, scores of other great stage effects. Also small magic, automata, stunts. 446 illustrations. 556pp. 5⅜ x 8½. 23344-8 Pa. $6.95

THE SECRETS OF HOUDINI, J. C. Cannell. Classic study of Houdini's incredible magic, exposing closely-kept professional secrets and revealing, in general terms, the whole art of stage magic. 67 illustrations. 279pp. 5⅜ x 8½. 22913-0 Pa. $3.00

HOFFMANN'S MODERN MAGIC, Professor Hoffmann. One of the best, and best-known, magicians' manuals of the past century. Hundreds of tricks from card tricks and simple sleight of hand to elaborate illusions involving construction of complicated machinery. 332 illustrations. 563pp. 5⅜ x 8½. 23623-4 Pa. $6.00

MADAME PRUNIER'S FISH COOKERY BOOK, Mme. S. B. Prunier. More than 1000 recipes from world famous Prunier's of Paris and London, specially adapted here for American kitchen. Grilled tournedos with anchovy butter, Lobster a la Bordelaise, Prunier's prized desserts, more. Glossary. 340pp. 5⅜ x 8½. (Available in U.S. only) 22679-4 Pa. $3.00

FRENCH COUNTRY COOKING FOR AMERICANS, Louis Diat. 500 easy-to-make, authentic provincial recipes compiled by former head chef at New York's Fitz-Carlton Hotel: onion soup, lamb stew, potato pie, more. 309pp. 5⅜ x 8½. 23665-X Pa. $3.95

SAUCES, FRENCH AND FAMOUS, Louis Diat. Complete book gives over 200 specific recipes: bechamel, Bordelaise, hollandaise, Cumberland, apricot, etc. Author was one of this century's finest chefs, originator of vichyssoise and many other dishes. Index. 156pp. 5⅜ x 8. 23663-3 Pa. $2.50

TOLL HOUSE TRIED AND TRUE RECIPES, Ruth Graves Wakefield. Authentic recipes from the famous Mass. restaurant: popovers, veal and ham loaf, Toll House baked beans, chocolate cake crumb pudding, much more. Many helpful hints. Nearly 700 recipes. Index. 376pp. 5⅜ x 8½. 23560-2 Pa. $4.50

THE AMERICAN SENATOR, Anthony Trollope. Little known, long unavailable Trollope novel on a grand scale. Here are humorous comment on American vs. English culture, and stunning portrayal of a heroine/villainess. Superb evocation of Victorian village life. 561pp. 5⅜ x 8½.
23801-6 Pa. $6.00

WAS IT MURDER? James Hilton. The author of *Lost Horizon* and *Goodbye, Mr. Chips* wrote one detective novel (under a pen-name) which was quickly forgotten and virtually lost, even at the height of Hilton's fame. This edition brings it back—a finely crafted public school puzzle resplendent with Hilton's stylish atmosphere. A thoroughly English thriller by the creator of Shangri-la. 252pp. 5⅜ x 8. (Available in U.S. only)
23774-5 Pa. $3.00

CENTRAL PARK: A PHOTOGRAPHIC GUIDE, Victor Laredo and Henry Hope Reed. 121 superb photographs show dramatic views of Central Park: Bethesda Fountain, Cleopatra's Needle, Sheep Meadow, the Blockhouse, plus people engaged in many park activities: ice skating, bike riding, etc. Captions by former Curator of Central Park, Henry Hope Reed, provide historical view, changes, etc. Also photos of N.Y. landmarks on park's periphery. 96pp. 8½ x 11. 23750-8 Pa. $4.50

NANTUCKET IN THE NINETEENTH CENTURY, Clay Lancaster. 180 rare photographs, stereographs, maps, drawings and floor plans recreate unique American island society. Authentic scenes of shipwreck, lighthouses, streets, homes are arranged in geographic sequence to provide walking-tour guide to old Nantucket existing today. Introduction, captions. 160pp. 8⅞ x 11¾. 23747-8 Pa. $6.95

STONE AND MAN: A PHOTOGRAPHIC EXPLORATION, Andreas Feininger. 106 photographs by *Life* photographer Feininger portray man's deep passion for stone through the ages. Stonehenge-like megaliths, fortified towns, sculpted marble and crumbling tenements show textures, beauties, fascination. 128pp. 9¼ x 10¾. 23756-7 Pa. $5.95

CIRCLES, A MATHEMATICAL VIEW, D. Pedoe. Fundamental aspects of college geometry, non-Euclidean geometry, and other branches of mathematics: representing circle by point. Poincare model, isoperimetric property, etc. Stimulating recreational reading. 66 figures. 96pp. 5⅝ x 8¼.
63698-4 Pa. $2.75

THE DISCOVERY OF NEPTUNE, Morton Grosser. Dramatic scientific history of the investigations leading up to the actual discovery of the eighth planet of our solar system. Lucid, well-researched book by well-known historian of science. 172pp. 5⅜ x 8½. 23726-5 Pa. $3.00

THE DEVIL'S DICTIONARY. Ambrose Bierce. Barbed, bitter, brilliant witticisms in the form of a dictionary. Best, most ferocious satire America has produced. 145pp. 5⅜ x 8½. 20487-1 Pa. $2.00

YUCATAN BEFORE AND AFTER THE CONQUEST, Diego de Landa. First English translation of basic book in Maya studies, the only significant account of Yucatan written in the early post-Conquest era. Translated by distinguished Maya scholar William Gates. Appendices, introduction, 4 maps and over 120 illustrations added by translator. 162pp. 5⅜ x 8½.

23622-6 Pa. $3.00

THE MALAY ARCHIPELAGO, Alfred R. Wallace. Spirited travel account by one of founders of modern biology. Touches on zoology, botany, ethnography, geography, and geology. 62 illustrations, maps. 515pp. 5⅜ x 8½.

20187-2 Pa. $6.95

THE DISCOVERY OF THE TOMB OF TUTANKHAMEN, Howard Carter, A. C. Mace. Accompany Carter in the thrill of discovery, as ruined passage suddenly reveals unique, untouched, fabulously rich tomb. Fascinating account, with 106 illustrations. New introduction by J. M. White. Total of 382pp. 5⅜ x 8½. (Available in U.S. only) 23500-9 Pa. $4.00

THE WORLD'S GREATEST SPEECHES, edited by Lewis Copeland and Lawrence W. Lamm. Vast collection of 278 speeches from Greeks up to present. Powerful and effective models; unique look at history. Revised to 1970. Indices. 842pp. 5⅜ x 8½. 20468-5 Pa. $8.95

THE 100 GREATEST ADVERTISEMENTS, Julian Watkins. The priceless ingredient; His master's voice; 99 44/100% pure; over 100 others. How they were written, their impact, etc. Remarkable record. 130 illustrations. 233pp. 7⅞ x 10 3/5. 20540-1 Pa. $5.00

CRUICKSHANK PRINTS FOR HAND COLORING, George Cruickshank. 18 illustrations, one side of a page, on fine-quality paper suitable for watercolors. Caricatures of people in society (c. 1820) full of trenchant wit. Very large format. 32pp. 11 x 16. 23684-6 Pa. $5.00

THIRTY-TWO COLOR POSTCARDS OF TWENTIETH-CENTURY AMERICAN ART, Whitney Museum of American Art. Reproduced in full color in postcard form are 31 art works and one shot of the museum. Calder, Hopper, Rauschenberg, others. Detachable. 16pp. 8¼ x 11.

23629-3 Pa. $2.50

MUSIC OF THE SPHERES: THE MATERIAL UNIVERSE FROM ATOM TO QUASAR SIMPLY EXPLAINED, Guy Murchie. Planets, stars, geology, atoms, radiation, relativity, quantum theory, light, antimatter, similar topics. 319 figures. 664pp. 5⅜ x 8½.

21809-0, 21810-4 Pa., Two-vol. set $10.00

EINSTEIN'S THEORY OF RELATIVITY, Max Born. Finest semi-technical account; covers Einstein, Lorentz, Minkowski, and others, with much detail, much explanation of ideas and math not readily available elsewhere on this level. For student, non-specialist. 376pp. 5⅜ x 8½.

60769-0 Pa. $4.50

GEOMETRY, RELATIVITY AND THE FOURTH DIMENSION, Rudolf Rucker. Exposition of fourth dimension, means of visualization, concepts of relativity as Flatland characters continue adventures. Popular, easily followed yet accurate, profound. 141 illustrations. 133pp. 5⅜ x 8½.
23400-2 Pa. $2.75

THE ORIGIN OF LIFE, A. I. Oparin. Modern classic in biochemistry, the first rigorous examination of possible evolution of life from nitrocarbon compounds. Non-technical, easily followed. Total of 295pp. 5⅜ x 8½.
60213-3 Pa. $4.00

PLANETS, STARS AND GALAXIES, A. E. Fanning. Comprehensive introductory survey: the sun, solar system, stars, galaxies, universe, cosmology; quasars, radio stars, etc. 24pp. of photographs. 189pp. 5⅜ x 8½. (Available in U.S. only)
21680-2 Pa. $3.00

THE THIRTEEN BOOKS OF EUCLID'S ELEMENTS, translated with introduction and commentary by Sir Thomas L. Heath. Definitive edition. Textual and linguistic notes, mathematical analysis, 2500 years of critical commentary. Do not confuse with abridged school editions. Total of 1414pp. 5⅜ x 8½.
60088-2, 60089-0, 60090-4 Pa., Three-vol. set $18.50

DIALOGUES CONCERNING TWO NEW SCIENCES, Galileo Galilei. Encompassing 30 years of experiment and thought, these dialogues deal with geometric demonstrations of fracture of solid bodies, cohesion, leverage, speed of light and sound, pendulums, falling bodies, accelerated motion, etc. 300pp. 5⅜ x 8½.
60099-8 Pa. $4.00

Prices subject to change without notice.

Available at your book dealer or write for free catalogue to Dept. GI, Dover Publications, Inc., 180 Varick St., N.Y., N.Y. 10014. Dover publishes more than 175 books each year on science, elementary and advanced mathematics, biology, music, art, literary history, social sciences and other areas.